Sociology for AQA Revision Guide 2

Sociology for AQA Revision Guide 2

2nd-Year A Level

KEN BROWNE

polity

First published in 2017 by Polity Press

Polity Press
65 Bridge Street
Cambridge CB2 1UR, UK

Polity Press
350 Main Street
Malden, MA 02148, USA

ISBN-13: 978-1-5095-1625-4
ISBN-13: 978-1-5095-1626-1 (pb)

A catalogue record for this book is available from the British Library.

Typeset in 11/14pt Frutiger LT Std by
Servis Filmsetting Ltd, Stockport, Cheshire
Printed and bound in Italy by Rotolito Lombarda

For further information on Polity, visit our website:
politybooks.com

CONTENTS

About this Guide   *page* vi

1   Preparing for the Exam and Answering Questions   1
2   Beliefs in Society   13
3   Global Development   41
4   The Media   76
5   Stratification and Differentiation   105
6   Theory and Methods   134
7   Crime and Deviance   160

Index   195

ABOUT THIS GUIDE

This revision guide, based on examiners' advice and Browne, Blundell and Law's *Sociology for AQA Volume 2: 2nd-Year A Level* (Polity 2016), covers the second year of A level. It provides a quick overall summary for final revision, and assumes you already know and can apply much of the material in the accompanying textbook – page references in the textbook are included to help you find the relevant sections.

The subject content of the first year of the AQA A level specification is identical to the AS. This is covered in Ken Browne's *Sociology for AQA Volume 1: AS and 1st-Year A Level* (Polity 2015), and in the accompanying revision guide, Ken Browne's *Sociology for AQA Revision Guide 1: AS and 1st-Year A Level* (Polity 2017). For comprehensive and complete coverage at A level, you will need both textbooks and the first-year revision guide, as well as this one.

Although the subject content for the first year is the same as for AS, the A level exam papers have some different types of questions from those in the AS exam papers, and contain an additional Theory and Methods question on paper 1 which may draw on material from the second year of the course. The A level also includes more Topics in Sociology options, which are covered in this guide and the accompanying textbook.

1
PREPARING FOR THE EXAM AND ANSWERING QUESTIONS

Three exam papers. Each worth 80 marks and each 2 hours.
All questions are compulsory – no choice

Paper 1: Education with Theory and Methods	Paper 2: Topics in Sociology	Paper 3: Crime and Deviance with Theory and Methods
Education: 50 marks One 4-mark question: *Outline two . . .* (ways/factors/reasons, etc.) (4 marks) One 6-mark question: *Outline three . . .* (6 marks) One 10-mark question, linked to an Item: *Applying material from Item [A], analyse two . . .* (10 marks) One 30-mark extended essay, linked to an Item: *Applying material from Item [B] and your knowledge, evaluate . . .* (the view/usefulness of/explanations, etc.) (30 marks) **Methods in Context: 20 marks** One 20-mark essay, linked to an Item, on applying a particular research method to a particular educational context/situation: *Applying material from Item [C] and your knowledge of research methods, evaluate the strengths and limitations of using (a research method) to investigate (an issue in education)* (20 marks) **Theory and Methods: 10 marks** One 10-mark question: *Outline and explain two . . .* (reasons/ways, etc.) (10 marks)	**Section A: 40 marks** Choose ONE from Culture and Identity; Families and Households; Health; Work, Poverty and Welfare. One 10-mark question: *Outline and explain two . . .* (reasons/explanations, etc.) (10 marks) One 10-mark question, linked to an Item: *Applying material from Item [A], analyse two . . .* (10 marks) One 20-mark question, linked to an Item: *Applying material from Item [B] and your knowledge, evaluate . . .* (the view/usefulness of/explanations, etc.) (20 marks) **Section B: 40 marks** Choose ONE from Beliefs in Society; Global Development; The Media; Stratification and Differentiation. The questions follow the same format as those in Section A	**Crime and Deviance: 50 marks** One 4-mark question: *Outline two . . .* (ways/factors/reasons, etc.) (4 marks) One 6-mark question: *Outline three . . .* (6 marks) One 10-mark question, linked to an Item: *Applying material from Item [A], analyse two . . .* (10 marks) One 30-mark extended essay, linked to an Item: *Applying material from Item [B] and your knowledge, evaluate . . .* (the view/usefulness of/explanations, etc.) (30 marks) **Theory and Methods: 30 marks** One 10-mark question: *Outline and explain two . . .* (reasons/explanations etc.) (10 marks) One 20-mark question, linked to an Item: *Applying material from Item [C] and your knowledge, evaluate . . .* (the view/usefulness of/explanations, etc.) (20 marks)

What will you be examined on?

At A level Sociology, you are assessed on three main objectives:

AO1: Knowledge and understanding (44% of the marks)

This involves demonstrating what you actually know – your knowledge and understanding of sociological theories, concepts, key terms and evidence, and of the range of research methods and sources of information used by sociologists, and the practical, ethical and theoretical issues arising in sociological research.

AO2: Application (31% of the marks)

This involves applying sociological theories, concepts, evidence and research methods to the issues raised in the exam question. You must show how the material – the sociologists, theories, research, methods and examples you use – are relevant (applied) to the question being asked.

AO3: Analysis and evaluation (25% of the marks)

Analysis means being able to explain the issue or point that is being raised in the question, such as being able to recognise sociologically significant information. Evaluation involves making critical points, such as the strengths and weaknesses of sociological theories and evidence, presenting arguments, making judgements and reaching conclusions based on the arguments and evidence for and against a view or statement presented in the question.

EXAM TIPS:

➤ Always focus on the wording of the question and apply what you know to the specific issue being asked about – don't generalise.
➤ Where the question involves an Item, you must refer to that Item: e.g. 'As shown by Item [A] . . .'

See pages viii–ix in the accompanying textbook to find out more about how to address these three objectives in your exam answers.

How to answer 4- and 6-mark questions

These questions appear in the Education section of Paper 1, and in the Crime and Deviance section of Paper 3, and take the form:

Outline two/three . . . (ways/factors/reasons/advantages/differences, etc.).

Outline means you identify a reason/factor/idea/concept, etc., say what it means, and briefly expand on its relevance to that question, perhaps using an example. Make the two/three points clear to the examiner by using *firstly.* . ., *secondly.* . ., etc.. . .

Example of a top-mark answer

Q. Outline **three** reasons why the media may exaggerate the extent of crime in society. (6 marks)

A. Firstly, journalists report crime using values and assumptions about what they think will appeal to media audiences. These are called news values. [1 mark for identifying news values] This means the media are more likely to report dramatic crimes like serious violence or robbery which are more newsworthy and attract audiences, and ignore more routine everyday offences like shoplifting. This can exaggerate the extent of crime by giving the impression that most crime is very serious when in reality most offences are, in comparison, relatively trivial. [+1 mark for explaining link to question – exaggeration of crime]
(2 marks awarded)

Secondly, the media often see themselves as playing the role of moral entrepreneurs and protecting what they see as society's main values. [1 mark for media as moral entrepreneurs] They do this by labelling and stereotyping of individuals and groups who commit offences they see as a serious threat to these values. They might exaggerate such crimes e.g. child abuse or violence by young people, to cause a moral panic and public outcry to encourage action to be taken against them. [+1 mark for explaining link to exaggeration of crime]
(2 marks awarded)

Thirdly, the media may exaggerate crime by presenting it as infotainment, packaged to entertain and thrill audiences with dramatic reconstructions of high profile individual offences e.g. Crimewatch. [1 mark for infotainment] This means the media focus on particular rare dramatic incidents, like murder, rather than less dramatic more common offences, and so give an exaggerated impression of the extent of these crimes to entertain audiences. [+1 mark for linking infotainment to exaggeration of crime]
(2 marks awarded)

How to answer 10-mark questions

These questions take two forms:

Question style 1

Outline and explain two . . . (ways/factors/reasons/advantages/differences, etc.)
➤ These questions appear in the Theory and Methods sections of Paper 1 and Paper 3, and in both sections A and B of Paper 2.
➤ You should spend about 15 minutes on these questions, writing about 1–1½ pages/400 words. There is no need for an introduction or conclusion.

> **Outline and explain** means you first identify a reason/factor/idea/concept, etc. – say what it means – and then expand on how it explains the issue in the question (e.g. 'This means that . . .'). Then expand on these reasons, etc., and show how they are relevant to the question, perhaps using examples. Make the two points clear to the examiner by using, e.g., *the first reason . . ., the second reason . . . .*

Answer these questions using this **PEL** formula:

Point – what are the issues the question raises? State your first reason.

Explain in more detail how your reason links to the question, and explains it. Give *evidence* from research studies or examples to back up/illustrate your explanation.

Link your point back to the question . . . e.g. *This shows* . . . A useful device is to refer back to the wording of the question.

DO THIS TWICE – ONCE FOR EACH REASON.

> **EXAM TIP:**
>
> To get high application marks, you need to refer to some wider issues from your course, e.g. explaining rising divorce due to secularisation; explaining people's fear of crime due to media exaggeration; explaining the weaknesses of participant observation because positivists don't see it as scientific.

Example of a top-band 'outline and explain' answer

Q. Outline and explain **two** ways in which the emergence of religious fundamentalism may be a consequence of globalisation. (10 marks)

A. Religious fundamentalism means people base their religious beliefs on the literal meaning of religious texts, and promote norms and values that they think conform with the meanings of those texts e.g. ideas about the values of traditional family life and the division of labour between men and women into instrumental and expressive roles. In almost every major religion in the world there has been a growth of fundamentalism in the last 25–30 years e.g. Christian and Islamic fundamentalism. Bruce suggests this growth is due to globalisation, as countries around the world become more interconnected, and the cultures of different countries become more alike.

[Examiner comment: Good identification of the meaning of religious fundamentalism and globalisation, and good example of family values]

The first way the emergence of fundamentalism may be a consequence of globalisation is shown by cultural imperialism. This means that the world's culture is increasingly becoming dominated by Western cultural values and a secular culture spread by a globalised but mainly Western-based media, including the internet. Bruce suggests this has threatened traditional religious beliefs in many countries, and religious fundamentalism, like Islamic and Christian fundamentalism, has emerged as a form of cultural defence to re-establish and enforce traditional religious values e.g. on the family, appropriate dress and gender roles, and to resist the threats to them posed by this secular Western culture.

[Examiner comment: Well-developed and explained first consequence (cultural imperialism and secular culture) linked clearly to globalisation via media, and explanation using cultural defence, with good examples]

A second way fundamentalism might be a result of globalisation is shown by what's been called deter-ritorialisation. This means that religions are less tied to particular countries or areas of the world e.g.

Muslims and Christians are now found in most countries. This has happened because of the big growth in migration as the world becomes more interconnected, and also because the globalised media, cheaper and faster air travel, and mass tourism have brought different cultures and religions into closer contact than ever before. Huntington suggests that this can lead to a clash of civilisations between the life-styles, beliefs and cultures linked to different religions e.g. Western Christianity's growing acceptance of divorce, homosexuality, and changing gender roles, which some Christians and Muslims reject. Kurtz says this aspect of globalisation has created a culture war leading to a strengthening of traditional religious traditions as shown by the growth of Islamic fundamentalism, and Christian fundamentalism especially in the US, as a way of strengthening traditional beliefs and avoiding contamination of traditional beliefs by ideas drawn from other religions or ideas in the same religion, as in Christian fundamentalism.

[Examiner comment: Well-developed and explained second consequence (deterritorialisation) again linked clearly to various relevant features of globalisation (migration, etc.) and culture wars/clash of civilisations. Good use of examples (divorce, gender roles and sexuality)]

Question style 2

Applying material from Item [A], analyse two. . . (ways/factors/reasons/advantages/differences, etc.)
➤ These questions appear in the Education section of Paper 1, sections A and B of Paper 2, and the Crime and Deviance section of Paper 3.
➤ You should spend about 15 minutes on these questions, writing about 1–1½ pages/400 words. There is no need for an introduction or general conclusion.

> **Analyse** means you first identify a reason/factor/idea/concept, etc. – say what it means – and then present and expand on an argument about how it explains the issue in the question, e.g. 'functionalists believe this shows . . .'. Then make a brief judgement on that argument, e.g. 'but Marxists see this as inadequate . . .'. Make the two points clear to the examiner by using, for example, *the first reason . . ., the second reason . . . .*

Answer these questions using this **PEAL** formula:
Point – Identify the issue the question raises, and state your first reason, which must be developed from something in the Item.
Explain and **A**rgue – Describe in more detail how your reason links to the question, and explains it. Give evidence from the Item, related research studies or examples to back up/illustrate your explanation/argument. Make a brief judgement of the strengths/weaknesses/limitations of your argument.
Link – Tie your reason back to the Item and the question and reach a brief conclusion, e.g. *This shows . . . .* A useful device is to refer back to the wording of the question.
DO THIS TWICE – ONCE FOR EACH REASON.

> **EXAM TIP:**
>
> You MUST apply ONLY material in the Item in these questions to get top marks – you will get limited to the bottom mark band if you only use material from elsewhere that is not referenced in the Item in some way. Use words like 'As shown in Item [A] . . .', 'As Item [A] suggests . . .', or quote words from the Item, to show the examiner you're doing this.

Example of a top-band 'Applying material from Item [A], analyse two . . .' answer

Q. Read Item A below and answer the question that follows.

Item A

State crimes are those carried out by the state in pursuit of its policies, and involve violations of human rights as defined by international law. It can be difficult to investigate the extent of state crimes, because governments have the power to adopt strategies to either deny or justify human rights abuses, or to reclassify them as something else that is not criminal.

Applying material from **Item A**, analyse two reasons why it may be difficult for sociologists to investigate the extent of state crimes. (10 marks)

A. As Item A says, state crimes involve violations of human rights which are defined by international law. These include offences like torture, war crimes, genocide, imprisonment without a fair trial and cruel or unjustified punishments.

The first reason it can be difficult to investigate the extent of state crimes is because, as Item A suggests, governments use strategies to deny they are committing such offences. Cohen called these strategies of denial. These are used to deny human rights abuses are occurring, or to reclassify them as something else that is not criminal, or as temporary lapses, or deny state responsibility by scapegoating rogue individuals acting without state approval. Even if there are human rights abuses, Cohen points out states adopt techniques of neutralisation to try to deny they were really abuses, by justifying them by an appeal to higher loyalties e.g. the detention without trial and torture of terrorist suspects, might be denied as real human rights crimes as they are justified by the need to protect the human rights of innocent people. Such strategies of denial and techniques of neutralisation mean it is sometimes difficult to investigate the extent of state crime because it is hard to define or discover what is or isn't a state crime under international law.

[Examiner comment: Well-explained and analysed reason. Good use of examples. Clearly linked to the Item ('strategies to deny, etc.') and to the question]

A second reason is the power of governments referred to in Item A. Government power can control information and cover up state illegal activities. State secrecy means there are no official statistics or victim surveys to show the extent of such crime, and researchers often have to rely on secondary data like media reports or reports by victims, which may not be valid as they could be exaggerated. Tombs and Whyte point out that this power of governments means that researchers often face strong official resistance to hinder them from researching state crimes e.g. threats, refusals to provide funding or access to official documents. It might mean the ethical risks of harm to the researcher, as in less democratic societies sociologists risk imprisonment, torture or death, and even in democracies the state can use the law, like the Official Secrets Act, to control and prosecute researchers who investigate state crimes.

As Item A points out, governments therefore have the power to make it difficult for sociologists to research state crimes, by problems for sociologists in discovering both what to investigate, and practical and ethical barriers to investigating their extent.

[Examiner comment: A second well-explained and analysed reason. Issue of state power is picked up and developed from the Item ('governments have the power . . .'), with a good analysis of why this power can make it a difficult topic to research]

How to get top marks in the 20-mark questions

Note: the 20-mark Methods in Context question on Paper 1 is covered in the first year revision guide (pages 10–12).

These questions appear in both sections A and B of Paper 2, and in the Theory and Methods section of Paper 3, and take the form:

Applying material from Item [A] and your knowledge, evaluate . . . (the problems/the view/the advantages/the disadvantages, etc.) (20 marks).

You should spend about 30 minutes on these questions, writing about 2–3 pages/600–750 words.

Evaluate means you should make criticisms, and weigh up the strengths and weaknesses of sociological theories, views and evidence provided in the Item and from your own knowledge gained during your course, and present arguments and alternative views, make judgements and reach conclusions based on the arguments and evidence you've provided in your answer, and linked backed to the material in the Item.

Write a brief introduction identifying the issues/concepts/ideas/views shown in the Item ('As Item [A] suggests . . .'), then organise your answer using this **PEEL** formula:

Point(s) – Identify the issue/concept/idea/research you're raising (linked to the information in the Item).

Explain – Describe in more detail, referring to evidence from research or examples, and drawing on material in the Item and your own knowledge gained during your course

Evaluate – Consider any strengths/weaknesses/alternative views to that shown in the Item, and to the points you raise from your own knowledge

Link – Tie your points back to the Item, e.g. 'This shows the view in Item [A] is mistaken.' Refer back to the wording of the question.

EXAM TIP:

To get top marks you MUST apply/use material referred to in the Item – ideally use words like 'As shown in Item [A] . . .', 'As Item [A] suggests . . .', or quote words from the Item, as well as using your own knowledge.

Example of a top-band answer

Q. Read **Item A** below and answer the question that follows.

Item A

Some argue that it is possible and desirable for sociologists to study society in a completely value-free, objective way. Others suggest that sociologists cannot avoid the influence of values completely, and it is therefore impossible for them to conduct value-free research. A third position is that sociology should not be value-free, even if it were possible, and research should involve a value commitment to improving the lives of the disadvantaged.

Applying material from **Item A** and your knowledge, evaluate the view that value-freedom is an ideal to strive for in sociology, but is impossible to achieve.   (20 marks)

A. The value-free objective study of society means that the personal opinions, prejudices and values of sociologists should not influence their research. As Item A suggests, there are three main views on whether it is possible or desirable to achieve this.

Positivists argue sociology can be value-free as it involves studying objective social facts 'out there' in society which exist independently of researchers and which can be observed and measured. Value-freedom is achieved if researchers study social facts using the hypothetico-deductive scientific approach like that used in the natural sciences, and remain detached and avoid personal involvement in their studies by using quantitative methods like the use of official statistics, and impersonal structured questionnaires and interviews. This value freedom is reinforced by letting other researchers repeat research, or check findings for any bias arising from the researcher's values. An example of this value-free positivist approach is Durkheim's study of the social causes of suicide. Durkheim argued suicide rates were caused by the social facts of social integration and moral regulation, which were social forces that existed independently of the researchers' values, and could be discovered by using objective suicide statistics.

Positivists are criticised by those who say it is impossible to conduct value-free research, as Item A suggests. This is because any research, including that of positivists, involves some subjective assumptions about how society operates, what's worth studying, and how data is interpreted. Interpretivists don't believe there are objective social facts 'out there' waiting to be discovered. Society is socially constructed by the actions of individuals, who act in the ways they do because of the meanings they give to their behaviour. The only way to understand these meanings is by sociologists using their values to judge the significance of these meanings. This can only be achieved by using qualitative research methods like unstructured interviews or participant observation which enable close involvement with those being researched, not the detachment positivists see as important for value-freedom. Weber called this Verstehen. Positivists criticise this for not being value-free, as the process of interpretation involves the researchers' own values and judgements, and it is hard for others to check whether their interpretations are correct. So value judgements affect the research methods used and the types of data (quantitative or qualitative) that are collected. This is shown by Atkinson's interpretivist approach to suicide. He sees suicide statistics as social constructions, not as the objective social facts positivists claim. They are just a record of the subjective opinions of coroners that result in some sudden deaths being labelled as suicide while others are not.

Value judgements affect what topic to research e.g. feminists choosing to study inequalities between men and women in patriarchal societies, or Marxists studying class divisions and social conflict. Values also influence what questions are asked, and what findings to include in research reports. The values of those funding research can also influence the research topic and the methods used e.g. funders often prefer research topics that are useful to them, and positivist statistical evidence rather than the qualitative data used by interpretivists. For these reasons, it is impossible for sociology to be completely value-free.

Item A identifies a third view that sociology should not strive for value-freedom, even if it was possible to achieve. Gouldner argues that value-freedom is a myth, and just an ideology used by sociologists to build their careers by selling their supposedly value-free objective research to the highest bidders. Sociologists should show value commitment and take responsibility for the uses and consequences of their research. Becker argued all knowledge favours somebody, and values are unavoidable when trying to understand and judge the significance of what you're studying. He argues sociologists should make a clear value commitment and choose whose side they're on when choosing what to research. This is shown by the value commitment of feminist sociologists like Oakley to improving the lives of women by their research on housework and gender inequalities in the family.

As the question suggests, complete value-freedom is impossible to achieve for the reasons given above. However, although values will influence the choice of topic and method, Weber argued sociologists, regardless of whether or not they show value commitment, should strive to keep their values out of the actual research process itself, otherwise they will only produce biased and invalid research findings. Weber suggested sociologists could achieve this by collecting data using carefully planned research methods, drawing conclusions based only on this evidence, and making this evidence available to others to scrutinise for any bias in findings due to the researcher's values.

[Examiner comment: Overall, this is a good and substantial answer, which shows a fairly sophisticated knowledge and understanding of a variety of issues relating to the value-freedom debate. There is good use and application of appropriate concepts, theories and reference to research methods and these are used accurately. The answer is well ordered and uses the Item very effectively to answer the question. It keeps a clear focus on the question throughout, and applies the information in Item A well for ongoing analysis and evaluation to contrast the different positions. Examples and research are appropriate and applied well to the question (suicide/Durkheim/Atkinson, Marxism, feminism, etc.). The conclusion is distinctive and appropriate, and ties everything together linked directly back to the question]

How to answer 30-mark questions

These appear in the Education section of Paper 1, and the Crime and Deviance section of Paper 3, and take the following form:

Applying material from Item [B] and your knowledge, evaluate . . . (the view/usefulness of/explanations, etc.)

You should spend about 45 minutes on these questions, writing about 3–4 pages/900–1,000 words.

Evaluate means you should make criticisms, and weigh up the strengths and weaknesses of sociological theories, views and evidence provided in the Item and from your own knowledge gained during your course, and present arguments and alternative views, make judgements and reach conclusions based on the arguments and evidence you've provided in your answer, and linked backed to the material in the Item.

You can use the **PEEL** formula discussed earlier to organise your essay.

EXAM TIP:

To get top marks you MUST apply/use material referred to in the Item – ideally use words like 'As shown in Item [A] . . .', 'As Item [A] suggests . . .', or quote words from the Item, as well as using your own (relevant) knowledge from anywhere else in your Sociology course.

Example of a top-band answer

Q. Read **Item B** below and answer the question that follows.

Item B

Punishment of criminals may act in various ways: as retribution or revenge; as rehabilitation to prevent reoffending; as deterrence to others; as restoration of the harm caused to victims; as social protection from those who are dangerous; as reinforcement of social values; or as an assertion of the power and authority of a sovereign or of a dominant social class.

Applying material from **Item B** and your knowledge, evaluate sociological explanations of the role of punishment in the prevention and reduction of crime.　　　　　　　　　　　(30 marks)

A. Functionalists see the main aims of punishment identified in item B, except for the final one, as important to prevent and reduce crime and maintain social stability and conformity. Foucault and Marxists view punishment as mainly concerned with asserting the power and control of a sovereign or a dominant social class.

Functionalists like Durkheim argue laws are based on a value consensus, which keeps society stable in everyone's interests. Punishment, as identified in Item B, helps to prevent and reduce threats to social solidarity and stability. Retribution, for example, strengthens social values by highlighting the rules about right and wrong behaviour, and punishing those who don't conform to them. Punishment also acts as deterrence, as Item B suggests, by showing others the consequences of breaking laws e.g. the severe sentences given for offences normally seen as minor after the 2011 riots. Through rehabilitation, punishment aims to integrate offenders back into society, and so reduce their risk of reoffending. Restorative justice aims to make offenders realise the harm they have caused to victims, and to restore some of the damage done to them to encourage them not to offend again and so reduce crime. Punishment, particularly incapacitation through imprisonment, also protects society from the most dangerous criminals who are most likely to reoffend when retribution, rehabilitation and deterrence don't work. Functionalists therefore see punishment acting in various ways to reduce crime and protect society, social values and stability.

Marxists argue that laws are not based on a value consensus as functionalists suggest, but on ruling class ideology. Punishment is part of the repressive state apparatus aimed at social control of the working class in the interests of the ruling class, as Item B suggests. The most severe punishments are usually handed out to the most disadvantaged who have the least power in society e.g. poor people or those from minority ethnic groups, particularly black men. Newburn argues middle class white-collar and corporate criminals rarely face punishment for wrong-doing, and if they do are usually leniently sentenced compared to working class criminals. Punishment therefore doesn't prevent or reduce the crimes of the powerful, like white collar, corporate, state and green crimes, and supports ruling class ideology by suggesting the working class are the main criminals.

Marxist approaches have been criticised because it is hard to see all punishments linked to ruling class interests e.g. penalties for assault and drug abuse, and speeding fines seem to fit more with the functionalist view of punishments concerned with protecting social norms in the interests of everyone.

A criticism of the role of punishments like imprisonment, fines, curfew orders or community punishment in preventing or reducing crime is that they may be dysfunctional, and not help in re-establishing social order as functionalists suggest. Right realists, for example, see punishment as a key way of deterring people from offending by increasing the costs of crime, but some punishments, especially prisons, can actually create more crime rather than preventing or reducing it. Interactionists like Goffman suggest prison subcultures make bad people worse rather than rehabilitating them and only confirm the criminal label. Becker suggests this labelling becomes a master status, and the stigma attached to offenders can make it difficult for them to re-enter conforming mainstream society successfully e.g. jobs are hard to find, and increases the risk of re-offending. For some young offenders, having a criminal record like an ASBO or community payback order can be a status symbol giving street-cred and encouraging more crime. Punishments therefore may encourage more crime not reduce it.

Item B also refers to the role of punishment in asserting the power of a sovereign, with those threatening this power defined as criminals. Foucault sees public brutal punishments like cutting off hands and public hanging as reducing crime by deterring people by public demonstrations of the supreme power of the sovereign – the monarch – over criminals. He referred to this form of punishment as sovereign power.

Foucault argued sovereign power has now been replaced in most countries by disciplinary power. This involves punishment with constant surveillance e.g. in prisons, through probation, curfews and electronic tagging. Foucault thought constant surveillance would reduce crime by encouraging criminals to control their own behaviour. Foucault saw this disciplinary power of surveillance extending into wide areas of life in contemporary society e.g. CCTV, automatic number plate recognition and mobile phone tracking, which have now probably replaced punishment as the main form of deterrence in the prevention and reduction of crime. The main criticism of this is that criminals are now aware of widespread surveillance, so will take steps to avoid it, so it may not be as effective as punishment as a deterrent to crime.

Feminists argue that many crimes by men against women in patriarchal societies e.g. rape, sexual assaults, and domestic violence, don't get reported to the police, because many don't result in conviction and punishment of offenders. Feminists argue more convictions and punishment may deter men from committing such offences once they realise they are less likely to get away with them. Feminists also point out that women often face harsher punishments for similar offences to those committed by men, as socialisation means women are generally expected to be more conformist than men. Punishment may make it harder to reduce further crime by women, as they face double stigmatisation for being both criminal and women, which may make a return to conformity after labelling more difficult.

As suggested above, the various aims of punishment mentioned in Item B are not always successful in reducing and preventing crime. Left realists argue that tackling the risk factors for crime, like poverty, may be more effective than punishment after the event. Right realists see punishment as important, but also emphasise other measures like stricter socialisation in families e.g. parenting orders, and reducing opportunities for crime by situational crime prevention, and zero tolerance policing to prevent the decline of neighbourhoods and increasing social disorder and crime as suggested by Wilson and Kelling's broken windows thesis.

To conclude, some of the aims of punishment in Item B may not be effective. They could increase rather than reduce and prevent crime, and the alternative measures suggested by left and right realists may work better than punishment in reducing crime.

[Examiner commentary: This is a clearly written answer that uses the language of sociology appropriately and shows good knowledge and understanding of a range of ways punishment may operate to prevent and reduce crime. The material is relevant, and links directly to the question and the purposes of punishment referred to in Item B. It keeps a clear focus on the question throughout. There is ongoing analysis, and some explicit evaluation, and the answer compares/contrasts in an evaluative way a range of perspectives on the role of punishment explicitly linked to the question and Item B. There is good use and application of appropriate concepts and theories, and these are used accurately. The conclusion is appropriate, and ties everything back to the Item and the question. There are enough points to make this a top band answer]

2
BELIEFS IN SOCIETY

TOPIC 1
Ideology, science and religion, including both Christian and non-Christian religious traditions (pages 4–15)

Belief systems (pages 4–6)

Beliefs are ideas about things we hold to be true. There are three main types:
- *Religion* – Beliefs in supernatural powers or spiritual forces of some kind.
- *Ideology* – Beliefs that provide a means of interpreting the world and that represent the outlook, and justify the interests, of a social group:
    - *Pluralist ideology* suggests that there are many different types of social group, each with its own ideology. There is no single dominant ideology.
    - *Dominant ideology* is a Marxist view that the dominant ideas in society are those held by the most powerful groups and, in particular, by the ruling class in society. It justifies the disadvantages of those who lack wealth, power and influence and aims to preserve existing patterns of inequality. Althusser suggested the dominant ideology was spread through a series of ideological state apparatuses, e.g. the family, the education system and the media.
    - *Patriarchal ideology* is a set of ideas that supports and tries to justify the power of men in a patriarchal society.
    - *Political ideology* provides interpretation of how society should work, and how power should be used by governments to change society through policy-making and political action.
- *Science* – Beliefs that suggest the scientific method and empirical evidence are the best means of gaining true knowledge about the world. Many scientists do not accept that science is the only means of understanding the world, and their scientific beliefs often exist alongside religious and ideological beliefs.

What is science? (pages 6–8)

Scientific beliefs claim to be true because they rest on scientific methods that formulate hypotheses and explanations that are:
- Based on reason and logic.
- Capable of being tested against empirical evidence through systematic observation and/or experimentation.

➤ Capable of being proven false (Popper's principle of falsification). No hypothesis can ever finally be proven true, as there is always the possibility of some future exception. However, a hypothesis can easily be proven false, as the observation of just one exception can disprove a hypothesis.
➤ Abandoned if found to be untrue.
➤ Objective – free from bias and open to scrutiny by other scientists.
➤ Value-free – research and evidence should not be influenced by the beliefs and prejudices of scientists.
➤ Able to establish cause-and-effect relationships rooted in evidence.
➤ Able to provide precise predictions about what will happen in the same circumstances in future.

(Note: there is more on science and the scientific method on pages 147–150 in this book.)

EXAM TIP:

In any question on objectivity and value-freedom in science, you should make reference to Kuhn's work on paradigms, and the social influences on science on pages 7–8 of the textbook. These suggest scientists are not always as objective, value-free and independent of prejudices and social pressures as scientists might like to claim, and do not always attempt to falsify and question their findings. Science may in these aspects be more like an ideology, justifying the interests of the mainstream scientific community.

What is religion? (pages 8–9)

The functional and inclusivist definition of religion
➤ Includes a wide range of beliefs to which people give a sacred quality.
➤ Does not necessarily include beliefs in a supra-human, supernatural being or power.
➤ Focuses on the function of beliefs in society, and the way in which things that people regard as sacred can contribute to social integration.
➤ Includes both conventional religious beliefs and any beliefs in things to which some people give a sacred quality, e.g. football, the lives of celebrities and royalty.

The substantive and exclusivist definition of religion
This is a narrower definition, adopted by most sociologists. It generally involves:
➤ *Beliefs in spiritual, supernatural and/or extra-worldly powers* – e.g. some sort of belief in God or gods.
➤ *Theology* – a set of teachings and beliefs.
➤ *Practice* – a series of rituals or ceremonies.
➤ *Institutions* – some form of organisation of the worshippers/believers.
➤ *Consequences* – a set of moral or ethical values that are meant to guide or influence the everyday behaviour of believers.

Science and religion (pages 10–12)

How science differs from religion	
Science	**Religion**
Ideas based on empirical (observable) evidence. Can be tested and falsified through observation and experimentation.	Ideas based on faith – a strong sense of trust and conviction – not on empirical, testable or falsifiable evidence.
Based on objectivity, value-freedom and detachment.	Based on subjective feelings and emotional involvement.
An *open belief system* (Popper) – ideas are open to questioning, testing and falsifying by others, and subject to change as more evidence is collected.	A *closed belief system* – a closed, all-embracing and unchanging set of beliefs, claims and assertions that cannot be questioned, tested, disproved or overturned.

Science and the displacement of religious explanations in modernity

Bruce argues the scientific method challenged religious explanations of the world as society moved towards modernity.

➤ The application of reason, science and the scientific method became the basis for understanding nature and the development and organisation of human societies.

➤ Comte argued these displaced explanations based on things occurring due to the actions of spirits, gods or other abstract entities and forces, like the power of Nature.

➤ Modernity brought with it what Weber called a growing 'disenchantment with the world' – rational argument and explanation displaced understandings based on religion, faith, intuition, tradition, magic and superstition.

Evaluative points

Although many people accept most scientific explanations of the world, religious and other supernatural beliefs remain significant features of life in many contemporary societies.

➤ Many millions of people continue to worship and identify themselves with the world's traditional religions.

➤ Many continue to believe in unproven mysterious spiritual or life forces with the capacity to intervene in life for individual or social benefit, e.g. magic, superstitions, ghosts, demonic possession, and extrasensory perception.

➤ There has been a growth of Christian and Islamic fundamentalism.

Ideology and religion (pages 9–10)

➤ Ideology, like religion, provides a framework of ideas for understanding, interpreting and explaining the world.

➤ Ideologies differ from religions as they are not necessarily based on faith in supernatural beliefs, but on the interests of particular social groups.

➤ Religion may become part of an ideology, as a social group may use religion for its own ends – e.g. Marx saw religion as part of the dominant ideology used to justify ruling-class interests.

Postmodernism and ideology, science and religion (pages 12–15)

➤ Postmodernists regard ideology, science and religion as metanarratives (Lyotard) – broad, all-embracing big theories or belief systems that try to provide comprehensive explanations and knowledge of the world and how societies operate. Such metanarratives are all equally valid.

➤ Science can no longer lay claim to the superiority of its scientific method. Science repeatedly fails to rise to the challenges it faces – e.g. antibiotic-resistant superbugs, global warming and climate change are all products of science. Many scientists have shown themselves to be serving the interests of wealthy corporations and governments, rather than pursuing objective and value-free research.

➤ Bauman suggested there is a 'crisis of meaning' in postmodern society, as people reject traditional religious (and ideological) metanarratives they no longer regard as credible.

➤ There's a fragmentation of beliefs, and people are abandoning once taken-for-granted religious and ideological beliefs and the authority of religious ideas and institutions.

➤ Religion has declined as a source of collective identity based on traditions handed down by the socialisation process.

➤ The beliefs people hold are now purely a matter of personal taste; they 'pick 'n' mix' beliefs – or reject them – in accordance with their personal lifestyle choices and the identities they wish to project.

➤ Religion and ideology are just consumer products, and lifestyle and identity choices, among many others in a consumer-driven society.

➤ People are choosing to create their own do-it-yourself personalised cocktails of beliefs – which may not embrace any particular religious, spiritual or ideological ideas at all.

➤ Postmodern societies have become media-saturated and dominated by global media, which enable people to pick 'n' mix beliefs from across the world.

TOPIC 2

The relationship between social change and social stability, and religious beliefs, practices and organisations (pages 16–29)

Theories of religion (page 16)

Theories of religion seek to explain religion's effects for *individuals* and for *society*. There are two main approaches:

1. Religion acting as a conservative force – functionalist, Marxist, interpretivist and feminist approaches:
   - Building and maintaining social solidarity and social stability.
   - Protecting traditional values and the existing state of affairs in society, or changing society to restore traditional values and ways of life that may be at risk of disappearing or have already disappeared.
2. Religion acting as a force for social change – neo-Marxists and Weber.

> **EXAM TIP:**
>
> In any question on religion as a conservative force, good answers will explain that 'conservative' can mean different things – e.g. maintaining present arrangements or changing things to go back to a previous state of affairs.

Religion as a conservative force: the functionalist perspective (pages 16–21)

Functionalists like Durkheim, Malinowski and Parsons argue religion maintains the status quo, because the existing social and moral order is regarded as 'sacred'. Religion acts as a conservative force as it:

- Is a source of socialisation and social control – promoting learning of and conformity to traditional social values and forms of behaviour.
- Provides a sacred/moral underpinning for social norms and values (Parsons) – e.g. rules about killing and stealing.
- Acts as a kind of social glue, promoting social harmony and stability, social integration and social solidarity/cohesion (Durkheim).
- Provides a sense of social identity and security, integrating individuals into social groups and the culture of their society.
- Provides a source of psychological support and comfort during periods of stress, and makes sense of/gives meaning to suffering and disasters (Malinowski, Parsons).
- Builds a moral community, and protects individuals from loss of meaning in life (Durkheim, Parsons).
- Acts as a focal point for the defence of community identity, and for support during the period of transition and adaptation to a new culture.

Civil religions

Durkheim suggested that, even if the supernatural dimensions of religion eventually disappeared, other 'civil religions' might take on the functions of religion. People would give sacred qualities to, and worship, non-supernatural aspects of society in the same way as in traditional religious ideas – e.g. the devotion and rituals people display towards royalty, the lives of celebrities, or football.

Evaluation of the functionalist view

- ✓ Religion can perform positive functions which help keep society together, and provide support for individuals.
- ✗ It downplays the role that religion can sometimes play in social change – e.g. liberation theology in South America.
- ✗ It neglects religion's role as a source of conflict and division, as in religiously based wars, conflicts within and between religions, and community conflicts.
- ✗ It can only fulfil some of the functions that functionalists claim if people actually hold and practise religious beliefs. There is diminishing religiosity and growing secularisation in many Western European countries, so religion may no longer be performing the functions it once did.

EXAM TIPS:

- ➤ When answering questions on the role or functions of religion, you should include functions for individuals as well as society and also include several perspectives, e.g. functionalism, Marxism, neo-Marxism, feminism, interpretivism, postmodernism.
- ➤ For evaluation, draw on a range of perspectives to criticise the particular approach suggested by the question.

Religion as a conservative force: the traditional Marxist perspective (pages 21–23)

Traditional Marxists see religion acting as a conservative force because it:

- ➤ Is an ideology which distorts the true nature of society, suggesting society is controlled by a supernatural power that cannot be challenged.
- ➤ Is an ideological state apparatus (Althusser) that spreads the dominant ruling-class ideology that explains and justifies inequalities in wealth and power.
- ➤ Manufactures hegemony (Gramsci), encouraging consent and acceptance by the working class that their positions are unchangeable and inevitable, maintaining the capitalist system.
- ➤ Is an instrument of social control and oppression that keeps the working class in their place.
- ➤ Presents suffering as God's will, and a challenging test of faith, which means people are less likely to question or change their circumstances.
- ➤ Acts as the 'opium of the people' – an hallucinatory, pain-relieving drug cushioning the pain of oppression and exploitation in unequal societies by promising rewards in the afterlife.

Evaluation of the traditional Marxist view

- ✓ It recognises religion can be divisive and oppressive.
- ✗ It ignores the positive aspects of religion that functionalists identify.
- ✗ It focuses on class oppression, but doesn't consider religious patriarchy and the oppression of women.
- ✗ It ignores the positive roles of religion in minority ethnic communities (cultural defence and transition).
- ✗ It's outdated – religion can only act as an instrument of oppression if people actually hold and practise religious beliefs, and religion has institutional power in society. There is diminishing religiosity and declining power of religious institutions in many Western European countries, so religion may no longer be performing the ideological role Marxists suggest.
- ✗ Neo-Marxists such as Maduro have argued religion is not always a part of the dominant ideology acting as a conservative force serving ruling-class interests. Religion can sometimes promote social change and show alternative ways of organising societies.

Functionalism and traditional Marxism compared (page 23)

- ➤ Both explain the origins and functions of religion in terms of social factors.
- ➤ Both see religion as a human creation, with the supernatural having no reality.
- ➤ Both see religion as a conservative force, integrating society and maintaining the status quo.
- ➤ Functionalists see religion's role as necessary and justified, while Marx saw religion as repressive.

EXAM TIP:

Remember to refer to theorists and researchers when discussing perspectives – e.g. Durkheim, Malinowski and Parsons on functionalism; Marx, Gramsci and Maduro on Marxism/neo-Marxism.

Religion as a conservative force: the interpretivist perspective (pages 23–25)

Interpretivism studies the meanings and interpretations that people give to religion in order to understand people's behaviour. Religion acts as a conservative force by contributing to the maintenance of social stability within existing society, as religion:

- ➤ Provides what Berger calls a 'universe of meaning' – a religious framework of beliefs and values that helps people make sense of the world, and gives life some focus, order and meaning.
- ➤ Provides a theodicy – a religious framework that enables people to make sense of seemingly inexplicable and fundamental questions about human existence, e.g. the meaning of life and death, and the presence of widespread suffering and evil in the world.
- ➤ Acts as a sacred canopy stretching over society, helping people to interpret and make sense of the world. This provides a shield that protects people from the uncertainties and inexplicable events in life, helping them come to terms with their position in society.
- ➤ Acts as a general compensator for the miseries and mysteries of life (Stark and Bainbridge), with the promise of life after death helping people to come to terms with an uncertain world.

Evaluation: does religion still provide a universe of meaning and a sacred canopy?

Berger argues that, in modern and postmodern societies, religion is losing its validity for most people as the provider of a universe of meaning. It may also be losing its role as a compensator. This is because science and the media have largely replaced faith and superstition in people's consciousness, and there is growing secularisation and disenchantment with the world.

Religion as a conservative force: the feminist perspective (p. 25)

Many feminists see religion acting as a conservative force because it reproduces patriarchy, with many religious institutions dominated by and serving the interests of men.

➤ Women are marginalised in many organised religions, e.g. excluded from the priesthood.

➤ Many religious doctrines justify, reinforce and reproduce inequality based on male dominance and control of women by men, e.g. the subordinate roles of women as wives and mothers shown in religious scriptures, sacred texts, and the portrayal of women as morally polluting and corrupting.

➤ Some religious laws and customs give women fewer rights than men, e.g. in divorce and property rights, and women often being expected to act and dress differently to men, e.g. the veil in Islam.

Evaluation

✓ This perspective highlights that patriarchy is found in most religions – men and women are treated differently and unequally.

✗ Not all religions are patriarchal – e.g. female goddesses in ancient Egypt and Greece, and in Hinduism; New Age religions, like Wicca; the Quakers.

✗ Some argue the veiling of women in Islam is not a sign of patriarchy, but a means of resisting patriarchy and freeing women from the male gaze.

Religion and social change (pages 26–29)

Weber and the Protestant Ethic

Weber was a social action theorist, who believed that people's beliefs, like their religious beliefs, affect the way they think and act. He argued that:

➤ The Protestant ethic of Calvinism in seventeenth-century Europe promoted the belief that material success through hard work, austerity, self-denial and self-discipline were religious virtues and signs of God's grace.

➤ The Protestant ethic promoted, as virtues, making money through hard work, and the reinvestment of profits back into the business – rather than spending them on self-indulgence, luxuries and high living.

➤ The Protestant ethic meant making money to reinvest and expand a business was not just good capitalist business practice, but also good religious morality.

➤ This 'spirit of capitalism' in Calvinism, alone of all the religions, provided the religious ideology which encouraged the development of industrial capitalist economies first in the Protestant countries of Europe, rather than elsewhere.

Neo-Marxism

➤ Neo-Marxists, like Gramsci and Maduro, disagree with classical Marxism that religion is simply a part of the dominant ideology and always serves the interests of the ruling class. They suggest religion can have some relative autonomy – some independence – from the interests of the ruling class. It can be a force for social change and does not always act as a conservative force.

➤ Gramsci believed religion could sometimes support the interests of the oppressed class. Religion could sometimes be a focus for a counter-hegemony – a set of ideas challenging the ruling class and its ideology, and showing alternative ways of organising societies.

EXAM TIPS:

➤ In questions on religion as a conservative force or as a force for social change, don't oversimplify different approaches. Functionalists, Marxists, interpretivists and feminists see religion playing a significant role as a conservative force, but there are differences between them in who benefits from this. Weber and neo-Marxists do not agree that religion always acts as a conservative force. Evaluate arguments by comparing and contrasting the different theories to pick up valuable marks for evaluation.

➤ When answering questions on religion and social change, try to illustrate your answer with contemporary examples drawn from recent news events.

Evaluation – is religion a conservative stabilising force, a force for social change or a source of conflict? (pages 29–30)

EXAM TIP:

Remember that top marks are most likely to be awarded to students who can show evaluation skills by giving a range of arguments and counter-arguments, tied to theories and evidence/examples.

There's no simple answer

➤ There is a range of evidence that can be used to support the functionalist, Marxist, interpretivist and feminist views that religion acts as a conservative, stabilising and integrating force, protecting the patriarchal status quo in society.

➤ Religion can act *at the same time* as a conservative force and as an agent of social change – e.g. Islamic and Christian fundamentalism trying to reverse what many might regard as progressive, modernising changes.

➤ Religion can be a destabilising source of social division and conflict in societies with religious pluralism, as different religions and factions within religions clash with one another.

➤ Religion can be a source of conflict between societies – Huntington's 'clash of civilisations'.

➤ Religion can act as a means for radical change, as Weber and the neo-Marxists like Gramsci and Maduro suggest.

Religion is most likely to be influential either as a conservative force or a force for social change in societies

➤ Where most people hold strong religious beliefs.

➤ Where religion is a major part of the culture of everyday life – e.g. Catholicism in many South American countries; Islam in North Africa and the Middle East.

➤ Where religious organisations are closely involved in political and economic life and have strong central authority/political power – e.g. Islam in contemporary Iran or Saudi Arabia; Catholicism and liberation theology in Latin America.

EXAM TIP:

Questions about religious fundamentalism are quite popular with examiners. Fundamentalism can be used in answers to illustrate the idea of religion being, at the same time, both a conservative force and a force for social change, and may be used in answers on the effects of globalisation on religion. Make sure you have a good grasp of what fundamentalism is, and why it has in recent years become so significant (see page 27 of the textbook).

TOPIC 3

Religious organisations and their relationship to religious and spiritual belief and practice (pages 31–48)

Religious organisations (pages 31–35)

Wallis suggested religious organisations may have one of the following relationships to the wider society:

➤ *World-accommodating* – accepting the dominant norms and values of society, with members living similar lifestyles to other members of society.

➤ *World-rejecting* – in opposition to the world, rejecting many of the dominant norms and values of society, and replacing them with alternative beliefs and practices.

➤ *World-affirming* – accepting society as it is, and offering individuals the opportunity for self-improvement within it.

Churches and denominations

➤ Churches and denominations are organisations which have a bureaucratic and hierarchical structure, with rules and regulations. They are world-accommodating. Churches claim a monopoly over religious truth.

➤ Bruce suggests that the concept of 'the church' is really outdated in most Christian countries now, and should only be applied when a single religious organisation dominates society and can reasonably claim to be administering to all members of society.

➤ Most Western societies now have religious pluralism, with a wide diversity of religions and religious organisations, and none dominate or serve all members of society.

➤ Churches and denominations are becoming more alike, and, with religious pluralism, the term 'denomination' should now include churches as well.

Sects and cults

Whereas churches and denominations are generally seen as fairly respectable and mainstream organisations, sects and cults are seen as more deviant. This is because the media associate them (often quite unfairly) with groups seen as extremist and manipulative, as brainwashing their members and as harmful to both their own members and the wider society.

Sects are very tightly knit, closed groups with strict control of members; cults are very loosely knit groupings, open to all, highly individualistic, based on personal choice and with little control over members.

Stark and Bainbridge identify three types of cult:

1. *Audience cults* – provide little beyond information services of some kind for individuals, and there is little if any organisation or involvement of followers.

2. *Client cults* – sell services to customers, e.g. therapies of various kinds, and are more organised.

3. *Cult movements* are highly organised and often wealthy. They involve a wide range of activities, support and personal involvement and commitment, e.g. Scientology.

New religious movements (NRMs) (pages 35–39)

New religious movements (NRMs) consist of a diverse range of sects and cults that have emerged since the end of the Second World War in 1945, and particularly since the 1960s.

World-rejecting NRMs are the most controversial sects:

➤ They are concerned with spirituality and/or the supernatural.
➤ They gain support mainly from young adults, who are first-generation converts.
➤ They are very small and short-lived, with a high turnover of members.
➤ They maintain tight control over members, who are often required to make a sharp break with conventional life, and significant lifestyle changes.
➤ They are led by a charismatic leader with power over other members.
➤ They are certain that they hold the only correct 'truth'.
➤ They are hostile to wider society: a sharp divide between 'us' – the 'good and godly' group – and 'them' – the outsiders.
➤ They are treated with suspicion or hostility by wider society, particularly the media.
➤ They often hold Millenarial/doomsday beliefs that some form of sudden extra-worldly or supernatural intervention will change the world.

World-accommodating NRMs:

➤ They are mainly offshoots of mainstream Christian churches and denominations.
➤ Religion is seen as a personal matter.
➤ Members live conventional and conforming lives outside their religious activities.

World-affirming NRMs are mainly cults:

➤ They often lack many of the features associated with traditional religious organisations – e.g. theology, religious buildings and services, and rituals and moral codes.
➤ They are more like therapy groups.
➤ They provide techniques and knowledge that enable individuals to access spiritual powers within themselves to solve personal problems or become successful in existing society.
➤ Followers are consumers, buying services for sale to anyone who can afford them.
➤ Followers live otherwise conventional lives, and the services they buy are meant to help them to do this more successfully than ever.

EXAM TIP:

The different types of religious organisation can be used as examples to evaluate whether religion acts as a conservative force or a force for social change – e.g. churches v. sects and cults.

New Age groups (pages 39–41)

New Age beliefs refer to a wide diversity of mind–body–spirit ideas, interests and therapies that first became prominent in the 1980s.

➤ The New Age lacks the features of traditional religious organisations – e.g. an organised structure, leaders, premises, doctrines and rituals.
➤ It is not really a movement – more a loose-knit network of like-minded individuals who might keep in touch through social media.
➤ New Age ideas are mainly spread through the media and New Age shops.
➤ Anyone can take part (if they can afford it) – supporters are consumers, who subscribe to alternative spirituality through the commercial marketplace, e.g. buying therapy sessions, services, books, magazines, etc.
➤ New Age groups are examples of world-affirming client cults.

Heelas, and Bruce, see the New Age consisting of:

➤ *Detraditionalisation* – the rejection of traditional religions and spiritual authority.
➤ *An emphasis on the self*, which is essentially good and divine.
➤ *The only authority is the self and personal experience*.
➤ *Self-spirituality* – everyone becomes their own spiritual specialist, dipping into whatever beliefs and practices they fancy.
➤ *A holistic approach* – the mind, body, spirit, the environment and the supernatural all connected.
➤ *The global cafeteria* – people can pick 'n' mix from a vast range of beliefs, therapies and techniques drawn from across the globe.
➤ *Therapy* – New Age ideas are designed to be therapeutic: to make you more successful, healthier and happier.

> **EXAM TIP:**
>
> New Age religion is a good example to use in an answer on secularisation, or the postmodernist view of the role of pick 'n' mix religion and consumer culture in forming people's identities.

Reasons for the appeal and growth of sects and cults, new religious movements and New Age spirituality (pages 41–45)

Explanations for joining apparently deviant cults or sects could be because some or all offer:

➤ Practical solutions for those seeking to escape from difficult circumstances.
➤ Theodicies of disprivilege (Weber) and compensating rewards (Stark and Bainbridge) for those who are deprived, marginalised or alienated in existing society.
➤ The ability to pick 'n' mix beliefs, drawn from a wide range of new beliefs and religious groups made accessible through the internet and other media in a media-saturated globalised world (Baudrillard).
➤ A means of overcoming a sense of relative deprivation.

➤ New and clearly defined belief systems and supportive groups in periods of anomie – uncertainty and insecurity – created by rapid social change.
➤ A means of protesting against existing religious values and organisations or those of society as a whole.
➤ A source of identity or a lifestyle choice in postmodern society.
➤ A sense of security and independence for those facing status frustration.
➤ A means of achieving a happier and more successful personal, spiritual and working life (Heelas).
➤ A means of filling the spiritual 'vacuum of meaning' (Heelas) left by the lack of spirituality, firm beliefs and commitment in mainstream religions in a society which is undergoing secularisation.
➤ New universes of spiritual and supernatural meaning (Berger) where there has been a 'disenchantment with the world' (Weber).
➤ A means of overcoming the crisis of meaning (Bauman) and loss of faith in metanarratives (Lyotard) in postmodern society through more individualistic packages of belief.

EXAM TIPS:

➤ Don't miss the opportunity to score marks by assuming sects, cults, NRMs and New Age movements are all the same – try to distinguish between them.
➤ Make sure that the reasons you select to explain why people might join a sect, cult, etc., are appropriate to the type of sect or cult it is – e.g. poor people probably couldn't afford to buy the services in New Age client cults to help overcome marginalisation.
➤ The reasons behind the growth of NRMs, New Age movements and other sects and cults, and why people join them, are often linked to secularisation, as some people seek out a spirituality that has been lost in wider society. You can use this in specific questions on sects, cults, etc., but also in questions on secularisation. You'll pick up marks along the way (as long as it's relevant to the specific question asked).

The dynamics of sects (pages 46–48)

Niebuhr suggested that sects would be short-lived and would eventually either lose their sect-like characteristics and turn into denominations – e.g. Methodism and the Quakers – or disappear altogether. Some reasons for this are:

1. It may be difficult to sustain the enthusiastic fervour, commitment and strict discipline of sect members among children of the first generation of converts. Barker suggested that the heavy demands in world-rejecting NRMs lead people eventually to leave the sect. Sects will then either gradually wither away, or seek to retain members by 'cooling down' – becoming less sect-like and more like a world-accommodating denomination.
2. Sects that are founded and led by a single charismatic leader may lose support and disappear once the leader dies.
3. The variety of personal reasons and social circumstances which originally attracted people to the sect may, after a period of time, disappear and make sect membership redundant.
4. Religious diversity in postmodern societies, and growing individualism, mean more people want to experiment without long-term commitment to sects. Pick 'n' mix shopping in the spiritual supermarket may mean that religious sects have a short shelf-life.

5. The sect's promises may not come true, e.g. the predicted Judgement Day may not happen, undermining the beliefs of the sect.

Are all sects necessarily short-lived?

Aldridge argues that the idea that death or denomination are the only options for sects is false.

➤ Many sects have existed a long time while still retaining their features as sects.
➤ Not all sects depend on charismatic leadership.
➤ Many sects have been successful in socialising their children into acceptance of the sect's beliefs and practices, while also converting adults.
➤ Sects can maintain strict standards of conduct over long periods of time.

Examples of long-standing established sects include the Jehovah's Witnesses, the Amish and the Seventh-Day Adventists.

Bryan Wilson suggests that whether a sect can retain its sect status or will turn into a denomination will depend on what its members see as being required in order to be 'saved'.

➤ *Conversionist sects* were the most likely to develop into a denomination. These are sects which think that the best way to save the world is to be engaged with it and to convert individuals.
➤ *Introversionist sects* are unlikely to survive in denominational form. These believe that salvation can only be achieved by total withdrawal from the world. Trying to convert people would pollute, corrupt and destroy the fundamental beliefs of the sect.
➤ *Adventist or revolutionary sects* believe only sect members will be saved when the apocalypse comes. They may try to spread their beliefs, but cannot take on denominational form without abandoning the very beliefs, values and exclusivity on which the sect is founded.

TOPIC 4

The relationship between different social groups and religious/spiritual organisations and movements, beliefs and practices (pages 49–66)

Gender and religion (pages 49–54)

Women, in nearly all faiths, are more likely than men to have religious beliefs and to practise their religion (the exception is Islam). Compared to men, women are more likely:

➤ To express a greater interest in religion.
➤ To have firmer beliefs and stronger commitment.
➤ To involve themselves in religious rituals and worship.
➤ To be involved with all types of religious organisation, including NRMs and New Age cults.

Why are women more religious than men?

1. *Socialisation, motherhood and femininity*
   ⟼ *Gender socialisation* means females are brought up to be more caring and nurturing than males (Parsons and the expressive role). Greeley suggests that caring tends to be associated with a more religious outlook. Bruce suggests that this tends to lead women into greater involvement in all types of religious organisation.
   ⟼ *The guardians of family life and family traditions* are typically women. They take on the major responsibility for looking after the family, including their children's moral development by introducing them to approved social values, including religious beliefs.
   ⟼ *Women associate God with love, comfort and forgiveness* (compared to men who see God as power and control), Davie suggests, which is linked with traditional femininity and family roles.
   ⟼ *Women are more exposed than men to the ups and downs and changes of life*. Davie suggests that these factors give women a closer association with birth and death than men have, and these are central issues for many religions.
2. *Women live longer than men*. They are more likely to be widowed and living on their own as they grow older, and turn to religion for the support and sense of community it provides.
3. Women are more likely than men to face *social deprivation and marginality* in a patriarchal society, and to experience personal or family problems more acutely. Religion can provide some support.
4. *Status frustration* may be experienced by some women, who lack personal fulfilment or status due to being confined to the home or hindered in careers by the constraints of housework and childcare. Religious participation, particularly in religious sects or New Age cults, may help to overcome or compensate for this.

Patriarchy and religion

Feminists argue that many existing religions are patriarchal, such as in the following ways:

➤ *Religious scriptures* – Women are either invisible or occupy subordinate positions to men in most sacred texts.
➤ *Religious doctrines* – The teachings of many of the world's religions contain an ideology emphasising women's traditional roles as wives and mothers.

> *Being barred from the priesthood* (or equivalent).
> *The (stained) glass ceiling* – Women are often found at the bottom of the career ladder in religious ministries, facing the same 'glass ceiling' that they face in many other organisations.
> *The veiling of women*, by head coverings like the hijab and niqab, or full body covering with chadors and burqas, in some Islamic cultures has been interpreted as a powerful symbol of patriarchy, keeping women invisible and anonymous. (Note: some feminists argue that the veiling of women can be interpreted as a form of resisting patriarchy, by freeing women from the male gaze and sexual harassment in patriarchal cultures.)
> *The portrayal of women as morally polluting and corrupting*, and as sexual predators. Sexuality is presented as something that should be linked only to reproduction, and this reinforces women's primary roles as mothers. Women's menstruation is often regarded as polluting.
> *Women have fewer rights than men in many religious laws and customs* – e.g. in their access to divorce, and how many marriage partners they may have.

Feminists differ in their attitudes to religion

> *Liberal feminists* are likely to aim for more equality for women within existing religions, by seeking to remove obstacles that prevent them from taking on positions of authority.
> *Radical feminists* see most contemporary religions as existing for the benefit of men, and either present a fundamental challenge to religion altogether or seek to reshape it by recapturing the centrality of women in religion of early times.
> *Marxist feminists* focus on the way religion acts as a means of compensating women, particularly working-class women, for their double exploitation through their status as being both working-class and women.

The declining participation of women

Despite women's generally higher participation in nearly all forms of religious activity, women's levels of participation in the main UK Christian churches and denominations are declining at a faster rate than men's. Explanations for this include:

> *The women's movement and feminism*, which have led women to question the roles of women as wives and mothers with which the traditional Christian churches, and other religions, have been associated.
> *Changing sexual values and attitudes*, with a much more sexually diverse and permissive society. The attitudes of most religions to these seem old-fashioned and out-of-touch, driving younger women away.
> *The changing roles of women*, with most women now in paid employment. Work has displaced religion as a focus of activity and as a source of identity, as well as reducing the time available to pursue religious activities.
> *Family diversity* – contemporary societies have a growing diversity of family types and living arrangements. Such arrangements have met with disapproval or discouragement from the traditional churches, further alienating the involvement of women.

Ethnicity and religion (pages 54–61)

As a result of immigration, Britain is now characterised by religious pluralism, with a diversity of religious faiths.

Compared to the White British ethnic majority, the major Black and Minority Ethnic (BME) groups in Britain (African Caribbeans, Bangladeshis, Indians and Pakistanis) are, in general:

➤ Significantly more likely to hold religious beliefs (though they share some similarities in that younger people are less religious than older people – though the opposite is the case among Muslims).

➤ Far more likely to identify with and to practise a religion (though, like the White British population, women are more committed than men).

➤ More active in trying to establish state-funded faith schools with an ethos that reflects their religious beliefs and principles (particularly Muslims).

Black and Minority Ethnic group religions

➤ *African Caribbeans* are predominantly Christian, and mainly practise in the Pentecostalist and charismatic traditions. Rastafarianism is also found, particularly among young men, and often gives them very distinctive group identities. Modood found that, unlike in Asian communities, religion amongst African Caribbeans, as in the White British population, is much less important to their ethnic identity, and is mainly a matter of individual choice.

➤ *South Asians* predominantly belong to three main religions – Islam, Hinduism and Sikhism. Some of the values associated with these religions are under pressure and difficult to sustain in the UK, particularly among younger people – e.g. conflicts with equality laws, including gender and gay equal rights, and laws against sex discrimination in work and education.

Why are BME groups more religious?

1. Bruce suggests religion acts as a focal point *for community identity and cohesion*, in two ways:
   ⮕ *Cultural defence* – a way of protecting the values, language and traditions of the community, which may be under threat in some way.
   ⮕ *Cultural transition* – a way for immigrant groups to ease the period of upheaval and adjustment as they make the transition into a new culture.
2. Due to *social deprivation and marginalisation* through racism, higher levels of unemployment and Islamophobia, people may turn to religion as a compensator and as a secure and solid source of identity, status and community, which they find lacking in mainstream society.
3. More *tightly knit extended family structures* in Asian communities, combined with generally closer community life, may result in pressure to conform to religious values and behaviour.
4. Religion in BME groups can provide individuals with many markers of *social identity*. By asserting an identity drawn from religious elements of their cultures, members can resist the denial of status and the devaluing of their own culture by racism. Jacobson and Mirza each separately found that among young British-born Muslims, Islam is becoming a significant marker of identity, as a Muslim identity provided them with stability, security and certainties when they faced much uncertainty in other aspects of their lives.

EXAM TIP:

In questions on religion and ethnicity, you can gain valuable marks for knowledge and understanding, and application, by explaining higher rates of religiosity by applying ideas like Marx's view of religion as the 'opium of the people', Weber's 'theodicies of disprivilege' and Stark and Bainbridge's 'compensators'.

Age and religion (pages 61–65)

Compared to younger people, older people (aged 65+) are:
➤ More religious – *except* for young Muslims who are more religious and committed than older Muslims.
➤ More likely to believe in God.
➤ More likely to identify themselves as religious and see religion as important in their lives.
➤ More likely to participate in mainstream religious activity.

Heelas found that the majority of those involved in New Age ideas and activities, which might be expected to appeal more to less traditionally minded young people, were middle-aged or older.

Older people and religion

The greater religiosity of older people is often explained by three main factors:
1. *Disengagement* – As people get older, they become detached (disengaged) from the integrating mechanisms of society, such as participation in paid employment. They may face growing privatisation in their lives, with increasing social isolation as partners and friends die. Participation in religious organisations provides a social support network to overcome this.
2. *Religious socialisation* – Older people are more likely to have had a greater emphasis placed on religion through the education system and family socialisation in the 1940s, 1950s and 1960s when they were younger.
3. *Ill-health and death* – Older people tend to be faced with declining health, and death looms on the horizon. These are the very things that religion concerns itself with, so older people engage with religion for meaning, answers and support.

Younger people and religion

The lower religiosity of young people is often explained by:
1. *The declining attraction of religion* – Many young people find the mainstream religious organisations boring, old-fashioned, out-of-touch, and holding values they find alien. Religion is seen as very 'uncool' in many young peer groups, which exerts social pressure not to be religious. Leisure has become a much bigger part of life, and shops, clubs and pubs all open for very long hours, including on Sundays.
2. *The expanded spiritual marketplace* – Lynch suggests young people are turning away from conventional ideas of religion as there is now an expanded 'spiritual marketplace'. This involves growing exposure and access to a wide diversity of religious and spiritual ideas from which young people can pick 'n' mix and consume, as with other products, to form their identities. Young people's religiosity may be finding expression outside traditional religions and religious organisations.

3. *The privatisation of belief – believing not belonging*: Davie suggests that young people may still have some general spiritual or religious beliefs, but see them as a private matter. They may not feel they identify with, or belong to, any particular religion or set of beliefs, or admit to them in surveys. Davie expressed this in the words 'believing without belonging'.

4. *Secular spirituality* – Lynch suggests that young people may now be finding religious and spiritual meanings inspired by experiences in non-religious or secular life, rather than through traditional conceptions of religion, e.g. celebrity culture, clubbing, nature/the environment, can take on the form of the 'sacred' in their lives (think: Durkheim's idea of civil religions).

5. *Secularisation and the decline of metanarratives* – There has been growing secularisation and disenchantment in Western societies, and young people are the most likely to be hit first by this process.

6. *Declining religious education* – Bruce points out that religious education is in terminal decline, e.g. Sunday schools have practically disappeared, and religious education in schools is transformed into secular moral or personal education. This means that the majority of young people don't get any religious education at all (unlike today's older people when they were young).

Social class and religion (page 66)

Social class is not a very significant factor in analysing religion. The following generalisations about the links between social class and religion might be made:

➤ *The upper and upper-middle classes*, especially women, tend to be over-represented in traditional religious organisations such as the Church of England. They are more likely to be regular attenders than working-class people. Churchgoing (in all Christian faiths) is largely a middle-class pursuit. This may be partly because of the more conservative ideologies of churches.

➤ *Affluent members of the young middle class* (particularly women), like young professionals, are the group most likely to be attracted to New Age ideas, spirituality and therapies and to world-affirming NRMs. This is because followers are customers – spiritual shoppers who have to spend money to buy into the products and services associated with these cults.

➤ *The lower-middle and upper-working class* are over-represented among Catholics and Methodists. Denominations tend to attract higher proportions of working-class members than churches (except for the Catholic Church).

➤ *Those in the poorest social groups* are the least likely to attend traditional churches and denominations. World-rejecting sects gain their strongest support from the most deprived and marginal social groups. This may be explained by their social disadvantage – through the Marxist idea of religion acting as the 'opium of the people', or the Weberian idea of a theodicy of disprivilege.

EXAM TIP:

When answering questions on religion and social groups, to get top marks remember to apply studies and theories to the specific issues raised by the question. Don't just write everything you know in general terms about gender, ethnicity, age or social class, and religion.

TOPIC 5
The significance of religion and religiosity in the contemporary world, and globalisation and the spread of religions (pages 68–88)

The secularisation thesis (pages 68–71)

Bryan Wilson defined secularisation as 'the process whereby religious thinking, practice, and institutions lose social significance'.
➤ *Religious thinking* – The influence of religion on people's beliefs and values.
➤ *Religious practice* – The things people do to carry out their religious commitment.
➤ *Religious institutions* – The extent to which religious institutions have maintained their influence in wider society.

Problems of measuring secularisation
1. *How religion is defined in the first place influences what indicators are used to measure the extent of secularisation.*
2. *Reliability and validity* – Do historical statistics on religion (against which secularisation over time is measured) meet contemporary standards of accuracy in data collection? Does the way questions are asked change the information obtained? Do different religious organisations use the same methods of counting membership?
3. *Measuring decline* – Secularisation means that society was once more religious than it is now. This is not easy to establish – historical records about the strength of religion in the past are sparse; data collection methods weren't as reliable; and there were no opinion polls or interviewers carrying out surveys.

> **EXAM TIP:**
>
> In any question on secularisation, remember that a key element of the debate is how religion is defined and measured in the first place.

The meaning and interpretation of evidence on secularisation
➤ *High participation doesn't necessarily mean belief* – People may attend a local church for non-religious reasons, e.g. social support, to appear respectable or to get their children places in a faith school.
➤ *Low participation doesn't necessarily mean lack of belief* – People might treat religious beliefs as a private matter and not be recorded in attendance statistics.
➤ *Survey results depend on the questions being asked* – e.g. a question like 'What is your religion?' encourages people to name a religion as it assumes people have one, though people might not be religious at all.

➤ *Statistics on religious practice are difficult to interpret* – e.g. to be counted as 'practising' a religion in a sect a person must show very high levels of commitment, but mainstream churches demand very little commitment for a person to be counted.

➤ *Different denominations use different criteria of membership*, so apparently similar types of figures may be recording different things.

The causes of secularisation (page 71)

➤ Religious organisations are increasingly seen by many as conservative, old-fashioned and out of touch with contemporary society.

➤ Many functions once performed by religious organisations have been taken over by the welfare state – e.g. education and welfare.

➤ Traditional religious organisations and their teachings have been undermined by the growth of alternative spiritual organisations, like sects, cults and New Age spirituality.

➤ Changing leisure patterns and more consumer-based lifestyles have meant that Sundays have become a time for leisure outings and shopping rather than religious observance.

➤ The growth of scientific explanations and the application of technology have undermined religious faith and beliefs. Comte and Weber saw rationalisation of the modern world leading to growing disenchantment.

➤ Postmodernists suggest more people are picking 'n' mixing beliefs as they go shopping in the spiritual supermarket for whatever mix of beliefs suits their personal lifestyle choices.

➤ Religious pluralism in contemporary societies means religion no longer commands the respect of the whole of society, and is no longer able to perform integrating functions and contribute to the maintenance of social cohesion and stability.

The evidence for secularisation (pages 71–78)

Evidence for the decline of religious thinking and belief

➤ *Fewer people believe in God.*

➤ *Religious belief has been marginalised* – Bruce suggests that religion and related beliefs are now, for most people, only a last resort, concerned with those areas of human life over which science and technology have no control, such as incurable illness.

➤ *Religious morality has little effect on people's behaviour.*

➤ *Beliefs have fragmented* – There is no longer one set of beliefs which most people share, but a wide diversity of religious faiths and other beliefs competing with religion.

➤ *Religious metanarratives have been displaced* in postmodern consumer-driven societies. People are shopping around in the spiritual supermarket, creating their own pick 'n' mix, do-it-yourself cocktail of beliefs, which may have little religious meaning to those involved in them.

➤ *The myth of belief in a 'spirit or life force'* – Bruce suggests that, although many people still claim to believe in a 'spirit or life force', this simply represents a halfway house towards secularisation, in which people move away from religious belief, but can't yet bring themselves to admit that they are nonbelievers.

➤ *Declining religious knowledge.*

Evidence for the decline of religious practice

➤ *Declining membership in all the major Christian denominations*.
➤ *Declining attendance* – Only around 2% of the population attend religious services on most Sundays – it was about 40% in 1851.
➤ *Declining numbers of religious marriages and baptisms* – Less than a third of marriages now involve a religious ceremony (two-thirds in 1966); fewer than one-fifth of babies are now baptised (two-thirds in 1950).
➤ *The near-extinction of Sunday schools* – A century ago, half of all children attended them.
➤ *The myth of belief without belonging* – Bellah and Davie both claim that a decline in religious practice does not necessarily mean a decline in belief – people still believe but just don't do anything about it. Voas and Crockett dispute this, and argue both belonging and believing are falling, and the majority of those who don't belong either don't consider themselves as religious or have no belief in God at all.
➤ *The myth of resacralisation* – Some argue the growth of NRMs and New Age spirituality is evidence of the renewal of religious belief and practice. Bruce argues this is incorrect – tiny numbers of people are involved, and any growth is insignificant compared to the decline of the major denominations.

Evidence for the decline of religious institutions

Religious institutions today have become increasingly marginalised. For example:
➤ *Church buildings are closing and crumbling today*.
➤ *The status of the clergy has declined*; they are poorly paid and hard to recruit.
➤ *Religious education has declined*, and in schools is now more like personal development or social studies.
➤ *Church of England schools struggle to find enough Christian headteachers*.
➤ *Major Christian festivals*, like Christmas and Easter, have little religious meaning to most people in British society.
➤ *Religious institutions have 'disengaged' from society*, as Martin puts it – e.g. the welfare state now provides education, welfare benefits, health and social care that were once a near-monopoly of churches.
➤ *Globalised media (especially the internet) and free education* have eliminated the authority and monopoly of knowledge once enjoyed by religious institutions.
➤ *Religious institutions are no longer closely associated with the state* and have little influence over social policies.
➤ *Religious institutions have lost their monopoly over the ceremonies marking the 'rites of passage'*, such as birth, marriage and death.
➤ *Institutional religion has become fragmented by growing religious pluralism*, and can no longer provide a single universe of meaning or act as a social glue binding people together.
➤ *Religious institutions themselves have become secularised* – what Herberg called 'secularisation from within' – by compromising and watering down their beliefs.
➤ *Religious institutions have been undergoing what Lyon calls a process of 'Disneyisation'*, as they dilute and simplify themselves to market themselves as being as inoffensive and neutral as possible – just like the Disneyland theme parks.

The evidence against secularisation (pages 78–81)

Evidence against the decline of religious thinking and belief

➤ *Many people still show signs of religiosity* – Surveys show that around 70% of people still have some elements of religiosity in their thinking.

➤ *Resacralisation* – Heelas et al. argued that there is a process of resacralisation (a revival of religious belief) and a 'spiritual revolution' as people reorient themselves to a more individualistic spirituality centred on the self, e.g. towards New Age mind–body spirituality and world-affirming NRMs like Scientology.

➤ *Christian religious beliefs remain strong* – e.g. Pentecostalism, Evangelical Christianity and Christian fundamentalism (particularly in the USA) hold very strong beliefs and are growing.

➤ *High levels of belief are still shown in BME religions in the UK*, such as Hinduism, Sikhism and Islam.

Evidence against the decline of religious practice

➤ *Belonging without believing* – People may once have attended church, not out of belief, but because it was a social necessity in the community. The decline in church attendance today, therefore, may only mean a decline in the social pressure to attend church, rather than a decline in belief.

➤ *Believing without belonging* – Bellah et al. and Davie suggest there has not been a decline in belief, but only a shift from participation in public religious services to more private worship.

➤ *Not all denominations and faiths are declining* – There has been an increase in membership of some Christian groupings, such as Pentecostalism, of Islam and Hinduism among BME groups, and of NRMs and New Age movements.

➤ *Many people continue to make use of religious ceremonies for the 'rites of passage'* such as death (about 90% of funerals involve a religious ceremony of some kind), and, to a declining extent, baptism and marriage.

Evidence against the decline of religious institutions

➤ The Church of England (C of E) remains the established (or 'official') church in England; the British monarch must be a member of the C of E, is head of the C of E and is crowned by the Archbishop of Canterbury; C of E bishops still have seats in the House of Lords (the 'Lords Spiritual').

➤ The C of E is extremely wealthy, and it is one of the largest property owners in the UK. The Roman Catholic Church is the world's largest Christian denomination, and retains extensive powers and influence over the state in several European countries and in many South American countries.

➤ Black and Minority Ethnic (BME) group religious leaders are increasingly influential, particularly in Muslim communities, and are often consulted by governments in relation to social policies relating to those communities.

➤ Religious institutions remain very influential in education in Britain – e.g. C of E and Catholic faith schools, with a growing number being provided by other faiths.

➤ Religious institutions are now more focused on spiritual matters than at any time in the past. Though the influence of religious institutions may have been weakened in many areas by disengagement from secular society through structural differentiation, this might also strengthen the place of religion in people's lives, as religion avoids 'pollution' from involvement in non-religious affairs.

➤ Religious institutions remain very important in BME communities, providing a focus of social and cultural life as well as religious life. They are very important symbols of identity in BME communities, and Bruce suggests they act as important means of cultural transition and cultural defence in such communities.

EXAM TIP:

When answering questions on secularisation, remember that secularisation has a range of different meanings – e.g. decline in belief, practice and institutions. Measuring secularisation depends on how you define religion in the first place. Discuss evidence from a range of views, e.g. not just church attendance statistics (practice) but beliefs, and power of religious organisations too – and give theories, arguments and evidence/examples both for and against.

Secularisation in a global context (pages 84–85)

➤ *The secularisation thesis may be misleading and Eurocentric*, as it focuses only on the secularisation that is occurring in the UK and much of Europe.
➤ *It is misleading to think secularisation is a universal, global process* – in the United States and in many other countries, religious participation remains high, and in some countries religion is actually growing in strength and commitment.

The continuing significance of religion in the world
➤ *Religion remains strong in BME communities* in the UK.
➤ *Religious belief and practice remain high in many countries, and are growing in others.*
➤ *Religion is still a dominant social and political (as well as religious) force in a number of societies*, where religion is so deeply embedded in the culture that it is practically impossible to remain unaffected by religion in everyday life.
➤ *Islamic and Christian fundamentalism have become significant forces in the world today* – Bauman saw fundamentalism offering firm truths and certainty in a risk-laden and uncertain postmodern world.
  ➥ *Christian fundamentalism*, particularly in the United States, is politically active in the New Christian Right, and often wields substantial political influence.
  ➥ *Islamic fundamentalism* – Bruce suggests Islamic fundamentalism may be seen as a rational means of cultural defence of traditional Islamic beliefs and values threatened with elimination by the combined global influences of Western cultural imperialism, the Americanisation of the world's culture and the dominance of Western corporations in the world economy.

EXAM TIPS:

➤ Remember that secularisation is not occurring to the same extent in all countries of the world. Try to give some evidence of the growing significance of religion – e.g. the growth of Islamic and Christian fundamentalism.
➤ Watch the wording of questions on secularisation. If the question refers to the UK, focus on that. If it asks about secularisation generally, bring in examples from other countries or international trends.

Religious market theory

Religious market theory (also known as rational choice or market supply theory) suggests that religious organisations are like businesses that compete in the spiritual marketplace for customers. Stark and Bainbridge, and Stark and Finke, reject the secularisation thesis, and argue:

➤ There is a basic and constant demand for religion, as people have an essential need for certain compensators and rewards that only religion can provide.

➤ Though demand for religion may be constant, whether people choose to participate in religious organisations will depend on the supply – the quantity, quality and attractiveness – of the religious products that are made available to them.

➤ When they decide whether or not following a religion is in their interests, people make a rational choice based on the costs and benefits of that choice:

⮕ *Costs* – time commitment, financial costs or any tensions with wider society.

⮕ *Benefits* – spiritual fulfilment, future salvation, a useful social network or gaining social status.

➤ Religious participation will be highest when there is a wide diversity of religious organisations, competing with one another to offer the greatest rewards at the lowest costs.

➤ Religious pluralism creates a competitive religious market and there is a greater likelihood that everyone will find a faith that fits his or her beliefs as potential customers go shopping for faith in the spiritual supermarket, and this increases the take-up of religion.

➤ Stark and Finke suggest that, despite low participation rates, secularisation is not occurring in Europe. It is not that there is no demand for religion, but simply a lack of supply – people don't have enough options to choose from to cater for their beliefs.

Criticisms of religious market theory

➤ It doesn't explain high levels of participation even when there is little choice – e.g. in Islamic and Christian Orthodox countries where one single religion has a near-monopoly backed by the state.

➤ It doesn't allow for the wide diversity of NRMs and New Age movements, which haven't halted the decline in participation in Europe.

➤ It doesn't recognise what Herberg called 'secularisation from within', where competition, marketing and Disneyisation have 'dumbed down' religion (reduced the costs) to such an extent that religion has become more a part of social life rather than an expression of any real religious belief or commitment.

Existential security theory

Existential security refers to the extent to which everyday existence is secure, in the sense of income, food, healthcare, education, welfare, etc., so that people can take it for granted and don't have to worry too much about day-to-day or future survival.

➤ Norris and Inglehart argue that one major function of religion is to provide a sense of well-being and predictability when existential security is lacking.

➤ Virtually all prosperous advanced industrial societies are more secular than poorer developing nations, as they provide high levels of existential security.

➤ The poorest countries have the greatest demand for religion as they face the lowest levels of existential security.

➤ The United States – one of the world's richest countries – has high levels of religious participation, but might be expected to be much more secular. Norris and Inglehart suggest higher levels of religiosity are because of sharp inequalities in US society, combined with inadequate social welfare and healthcare systems. There are high levels of poverty for the poorest groups, and even the non-poor can face crippling medical bills if they fall ill.

Some points to consider in evaluating the secularisation debate

➤ Secularisation is contested – there are debates over defining it, measuring it, and its extent.
➤ Some define religion in terms of traditional religious beliefs; some as belief in a 'spirit' or 'life force'. The narrower the definition, the more likely you are to find secularisation.
➤ Are beliefs, practice and institutions all declining equally?
➤ Are NRMs and New Age ideas replacing traditional religions – and are they all really religious?
➤ A watering down of the definition of religion may itself be an indicator of secularisation – as Bruce put it, a halfway house on the road to disbelief.
➤ Is religion simply changing or reorienting itself and appearing in new guises?
➤ Is the secularisation thesis Eurocentric? Is the secularisation thesis ethnocentric?
➤ There's been a rise in fundamentalist religious beliefs in Islam and Christianity – is this a form of cultural defence in the face of growing secularisation? Or a sign of strengthening religious belief?

Globalisation and the spread of religions (pages 85–88)

The impact and consequences of globalisation on religion

➤ *Deterritorialisation and transnational religions* – Meyer suggests religions and religious beliefs are now less tied to particular countries or geographical locations, or linked to the histories, cultures or identities of particular nations and ethnic groups. Followers of every religion are now found in nearly every country in the world.
➤ *The global spread of a range of religious and spiritual ideas, and greater religious and cultural diversity* in many countries.
➤ *More opportunities for pick 'n' mix religion* – The internet has enabled new spiritual shopping opportunities to develop in the globalised user-oriented spiritual supermarket.
➤ *A 'clash of civilisations' and 'culture wars'* – Huntington suggests globalisation can lead to a 'clash of civilisations' between the lifestyles, beliefs and cultures of different religions as they come into ever-closer contact with one another. Kurtz says this can spur 'culture wars' between religions, and sometimes between modernising and traditional groups within the same religion.
➤ *Declining religious freedom* – Governments may interfere with and regulate religious practices, partly to avoid community conflicts, but also to protect dominant cultures from what they perceive as threats posed to their traditions and values by other 'alien' religions.
➤ *The rise of fundamentalism as cultural defence* – Bruce suggests Christian and Islamic fundamentalism have emerged to protect traditional religious values which are threatened by the modernising, secularising and corrupting influences of cultural imperialism, e.g. the Western treatment of sexuality; the use of women as sex objects; attitudes to divorce and gender roles.

GENERAL EXAM TIP:

Remember that two out of the three exam questions on Beliefs in Society involve an Item to refer to. You *must* refer to that Item to achieve top-band marks. For 10-mark ('Applying material from Item I, analyse two') questions, you must refer *only* to ideas or issues that are raised in the Item. For 20-mark ('Applying material from Item J, and your knowledge, evaluate') questions, you must refer to the Item and your knowledge gained elsewhere in your studies of Beliefs. Remember the Item is there to help and guide you, so use it.

By the time you go into the exam, you should know all the material listed on page 89 of the textbook. You should also know the key terms listed on page 90 – using them correctly will help you gain marks for knowledge and understanding. You can check their meaning on-the-go by going to the online glossary by following the link at www.politybooks.com/browne. Put it on your phone for ready reference.

3
GLOBAL DEVELOPMENT

TOPIC 1
Development, underdevelopment and global inequality (pages 94–113)

Defining development (page 95)

Most sociologists concern themselves with development as the goal of achieving a desirable society by deliberate policies aimed at economic growth, and raising living standards.

1. *Economic development* generally involves economic growth (a bigger economy) accompanied by rising living standards.
2. *Social development* focuses on the everyday experiences and opportunities that people have and their general happiness and well-being – e.g. educational opportunities; health and access to healthcare; democracy; human rights; and gender equality.
3. *The reduction or elimination of poverty* – combining successful implementation of economic and social development. Amartya Sen argues that development is about overcoming poverty because it is necessary to have a minimum living standard to take part in everyday life, and this allows people to develop their potential and increases human freedom.

Measuring development (pages 95–101)

Economic development
This is usually measured by increases in Gross National Income (GNI) – the total value (in US dollars) of goods and services produced in a country in a year. This is usually expressed as GNI 'per capita' (per person in the population) to allow for differences in the size of populations between countries.

GNI per capita can be a misleading measure of development because:
➤ *It does not measure social development.*
➤ *It is an average for the whole population*, and so might disguise inequalities in its distribution.
➤ *It only counts what happens in the 'official' economy*; some important activities are not counted – e.g. growing food for one's own consumption. Storey argues these are often activities carried out by women, so that GNI can be seen as gender-biased.
➤ *It tells us nothing about the nature or side-effects of development* – e.g. environmental degradation; rising crime rates; and the loss of community.
➤ *It does not show whether economic growth is sustainable.*

> **EXAM TIP:**
>
> In an exam question or stimulus Item, the terms GDP (Gross Domestic Product) and GNP (Gross National Product) may be used instead of GNI. Although there are some technical differences between these three terms, they are not significant in terms of the exam, so you shouldn't be concerned and you can treat them as the same thing. But when you're writing your answers, use whichever term the question uses.

Social development

Commonly used measures include:

> ➤ *Education* – e.g. the percentage of children attending school; literacy rates.
> ➤ *Health* – e.g. life expectancy; infant and maternal mortality rates; the number of doctors and hospitals in relation to population.
> ➤ *Democracy* – e.g. free and fair elections.
> ➤ *Gender equality* – differences between males and females in education, health, politics etc.

Combined measures of economic and social development

> ➤ *The Human Development Index (HDI)* produced by the United Nations combines measures of economic and social development to give an HDI score by which countries are ranked.
> ➤ *The Gender Inequality Index* (GII) – measures the disadvantages faced by girls and women.
> ➤ *Gross National Happiness* – includes spiritual and psychological aspects of development.
> ➤ *Happy Planet Index* – includes ecological footprints, well-being and life expectancy.
> ➤ *Good Country Index* – tries to quantify the contribution each country makes to 'the common good of humanity' rather than their own leaders, businesses and citizens.

Poverty

> ➤ *The Multidimensional Poverty Index (MPI)* is used by the UN to measure poverty, considering health, education and living standards.
> ➤ *Income of less than US$1.25 a day* ($1.90 from October 2015), adjusted for purchasing power, is used by the World Bank – about 1.2 billion live in poverty on this definition.
> ➤ *The Millennium Development Goals (MDGs)* were a set of eight targets and measures set by the UN in 2000 to halve extreme poverty (alongside other development measures) by 2015. These were continued by the Sustainable Development Goals (SDGs) in 2015, with a view to eliminating extreme poverty in 15 years.

Some evaluative points on defining and measuring development

> ✓ *Measures can be useful* – they enable comparisons of the levels of development between different countries, and lay the basis for explaining these differences.
> ✗ *There are different ways of defining and measuring development and some measures of development are arbitrary.*
> ✗ *Statistics may be unavailable, or of doubtful validity or reliability.*
> ✗ *Not all important aspects of development can be measured quantitatively* – e.g. well-being and happiness.

✗ *GNI per capita doesn't tell us about* – the distribution of wealth; whether a country's resources are being used for social development.

> **EXAM TIPS:**
>
> ➤ In appropriate questions, remember that 'development' is a contested or controversial concept. Try to include some evaluation of the strengths and weaknesses of different approaches, to gain marks for knowledge and understanding, and for analysis and evaluation.
> ➤ Aim to gain marks for application by giving examples of particular countries or development issues raised during your course.

Terminology (pages 101–103)

➤ *First World and Third World* – These terms are now used more rarely as 'Third World' is generally regarded as out-of-date, as it is no longer sensible to treat all the countries previously in that category as a single group.
➤ *North and South (or Global South)* – The developed, industrialised countries are mainly in the northern hemisphere and the poorer, underdeveloped or developing countries are mainly in the southern hemisphere (but not exclusively – e.g. Australia and New Zealand).
➤ *West* – Another term used to describe the most industrialised and wealthiest countries.
➤ *Majority and minority world* – Two-thirds or more of the world's population (the majority) live in poorer countries, whereas the richer industrialised capitalist world represents a privileged minority of the world's population.
➤ *Undeveloped, underdeveloped, developing and developed countries* – Describes or interprets the stages of development of different countries.
➤ Terms referring to countries at different stages of economic development:
  ➠ MEDCs – **M**ore **E**conomically **D**eveloped **C**ountries, with the highest standards of living.
  ➠ LEDCs – **L**ess **E**conomically **D**eveloped **C**ountries, e.g. Bangladesh.
  ➠ LLEDCs – **L**east **L**ess **E**conomically **D**eveloped **C**ountries (countries lagging behind the main LEDC countries), e.g. sub-Saharan Africa.
➤ *The bottom billion* – A term used by Collier because the least developed countries together contain around a billion people (in 2007, at the time Collier wrote his book).

> **EXAM TIP:**
>
> For knowledge and understanding, try to use the terminology (correctly) in Global Development answers. Watch out for any terms used in questions so your answer is about the things the question is asking about.

Theories of development 1: modernisation theory (pages 103–106)

Modernisation theory has been the dominant theory of development over the past 50 years. It suggests poorer countries would develop if they changed from traditional to modern societies by adopting superior and modern Western capitalist values and culture, and that modernisation would overcome cultural and economic barriers to economic growth inside their countries. This includes transformations such as:

➤ Strong community bonds → individualism.
➤ Religious/superstitious beliefs → rational decision-making.
➤ Patriarchy → more gender equality.
➤ High birth rates → lower birth rates and population growth.
➤ Living in farms/villages → urbanisation.
➤ Simple division of labour → complex division of labour.
➤ Subsistence agriculture → commercial manufacturing.

Rostow argued that societies need to pass through five stages of economic growth. Overseas aid was crucial in providing assistance for poorer countries to modernise and move through these five stages.

Stage 1 Traditional societies – subsistence farming; limited wealth; and traditional values hold back social change.

Stage 2 Preconditions for take-off – Western aid, values and practices begin to take hold, establishing the conditions for development.

Stage 3 Take-off – economy grows as modern values and practices pay off; new entrepreneurial class emerges which is willing to take risks in investing in business; more large-scale production and exports; wealth begins to 'trickle down' and reach the mass of the population.

Stage 4 The drive to maturity – society becoming modernised; economic benefits continue; investment in education, health services and media leads to rising living standards.

Stage 5 The age of high mass consumption – economy at Western levels; high standards of living (for most); access to education and health; most people living in cities.

Hoselitz emphasised that developing countries needed to modernise socially and culturally as well as economically, through:

➤ Urbanisation – cities could act as centres of Western values and spread them to rural areas.
➤ Education – Western-style schools, and bringing future rulers to schools and universities in the USA and Western Europe.
➤ The media – to spread modern Western ideas, e.g. family planning and democracy.

Evaluation of modernisation theory

✓ Western standards of economic growth and of consumption remain the aspiration of many in LEDCs.
✓ The rich countries continue to use development aid to try to help poorer countries develop.
✗ The clear distinction between 'traditional' and 'modern' is questionable: traditional characteristics are found in highly developed economies.
✗ It is ethnocentric: the only route to development is to adopt Western culture and values.
✗ It ignores the downsides of modern societies.
✗ It assumes LEDCs need to adopt Western values and need outside aid and expertise. This downgrades local culture, knowledge and expertise.

- ✗ It assumes that foreign aid and economic development is always a good thing. It ignores corruption, environmental destruction and the role of multinational Western companies in exploiting LEDCs for their own benefit.
- ✗ It focuses too much on the internal economic and cultural barriers to development, and ignores the external factors – e.g. exploitation by richer countries hindering development.

EXAM TIP:

Remember that top marks are most likely to be awarded to students who can show evaluation skills by giving a range of arguments and counter-arguments, tied to theories and evidence/examples.

Theories of development 2: neoliberalism (pages 112–113)

Neoliberalism replaced modernisation theory as the guiding 'official' approach to development in the 1980s. Like modernisation theory, it says the obstacles to development are internal to underdeveloped countries, pointing to economic policies and institutions which limit the free market.

Policies for development

- ➤ *Reducing the role of the state and 'parastatal' (state-run) institutions* as they put too much 'red tape' in the way of development.
- ➤ *Privatisation* – selling off state-owned companies, e.g. water and power.
- ➤ *Cutting government subsidies* which keep the prices of essentials, such as food and fuel, low.
- ➤ *Cutting state spending*, especially on welfare, so that the state would be less important in the economy.
- ➤ *Cutting taxes* – leaving people free to spend their money rather than the government taxing and spending it.
- ➤ *Free trade* – removing tariffs and restrictions on imports and exports.
- ➤ *Trade is better than aid* as too much aid is siphoned off by corruption, isn't spent as intended, supports inefficient businesses and distorts the free market.
- ➤ *Integration into the global economy*.

Evaluation of neoliberal policies

- ✓ They provide a clear set of policies for modernising and developing free market capitalist economies.
- ✗ They don't work – countries were making greater economic and social progress before the imposition of neoliberal policies.
- ✗ Dependency theorists argue they simply open up countries to greater exploitation, particularly by transnational corporations.
- ✗ Foreign investment rarely reaches the poorest countries.
- ✗ Free trade disadvantages poor countries, as they can't compete against much more advanced, stronger and efficient Western businesses, particularly the large multinational corporations.

EXAM TIP:

It's possible exam questions may use the term 'New Right' instead of 'neoliberalism'. Don't let this bother you – you can treat them as the same thing. But when you're writing your answers, use whatever term the question uses.

Theories of development 3: dependency theory (pages 106–109)

Dependency theory, associated with Frank, developed in the 1970s as a response to modernisation theory. It focuses primarily on the external causes of underdevelopment, rather than the internal cultural and economic factors in modernisation theory.

➤ It is a view of development from the perspective of LEDCs – 'a view from the South' – rather than from the perspective of MEDCs – 'a view from the North' – as in modernisation theory.

➤ It is a neo-Marxist theory of development – a group of rich core countries (the metropolis) in the minority world exploit a much larger group of periphery countries (satellites) in the majority world.

The stages of dependency

1. *Stage 1 – Mercantile capitalism* (fifteenth and sixteenth centuries). European merchants began to plunder, loot and trade with the undeveloped countries of the South. The slave trade began, with Britain at the centre of the triangular trade between West Africa, the Americas and Europe. This boosted Britain's economic growth.
2. *Stage 2 – Colonialism* (seventeenth to twentieth centuries). Western European nations took direct political control of lands around the world. The colonies provided markets for manufactured goods produced by the West, and were exploited for cheap food, resources, labour and cash crops for export to the colonial power.
3. *Stage 3 – Neo-colonialism* (mid twentieth century onwards). Many colonies achieved political independence. The developed countries still held economic control and continued to exploit the former colonies through cheap access to raw materials and markets for Western manufactured goods. The ex-colonies came to rely on aid, continued to be underdeveloped and remained in a state of dependency.

What prevents development?

➤ Developing countries are now in a very different situation from the original undeveloped Western countries, and cannot follow in the footsteps of the West as modernisation theorists suggest.

➤ The spread of capitalism will lead to greater underdevelopment, not more development. The MEDCs have made the poorer countries poor, and it is in their interests to keep them that way by kicking away the ladder towards development.

➤ Neo-colonialism locks underdeveloped countries into a chain of dependency, preventing development through:
    ➠ Exploitative one-sided relationships of unfair and unequal terms of trade.
    ➠ Inappropriate political, educational and healthcare systems and institutions, inherited from colonialism.

- Dependency on aid with conditions attached.
- Political alliances by which developed countries dominate developing countries.
- 'Buying off' the elites of poorer countries by allowing them to share in the profits, to discourage them from adopting policies that would benefit the majority of the people.
- The power of transnational corporations.
- Global finance and huge debt burdens.

How can underdeveloped countries develop?

For dependency theorists, the only solution to dependency is to escape from the capitalist system and the 'master–servant' relationship by:

- Development led by the state itself, not by national or international private interests or the needs of foreign capital.
- Isolation – self-reliance, with little contact with the rest of the world.
- Adopting economic policies to bring about development formed around nationalism, national unity and self-reliance, rather than a reliance on aid.

Evaluation of dependency theory

- ✓ It recognises the importance of the history of underdeveloped countries in creating dependency, which modernisation theory regards as unimportant.
- ✓ It recognises that the development of the metropolis causes the underdevelopment of the satellite (poorer) countries.
- ✓ It shifts the focus of barriers to development away from the internal economic and cultural factors in traditional societies towards the economic policies of rich countries.
- ✗ It doesn't recognise other causes of underdevelopment, e.g. cultural factors, economic corruption and mismanagement, inter-ethnic conflicts.
- ✗ It doesn't provide many practical solutions to LEDCs on how to develop.
- ✗ It is pessimistic in that it sees any development would be limited.
- ✗ It's out-of-date – there are some countries that were formerly colonies that have been very successful in developing their economies under capitalist principles, e.g. India and South Korea.
- ✗ It ignores some long-term benefits of colonialism in some countries – e.g. Western medical advances, and infrastructural developments like roads and railways.
- ✗ Aid from rich countries can bring benefits, not just dependency and harm.

Theories of development 4: world systems theory (pages 110–111)

This is a modified version of dependency theory, also based in Marxism, with a similar emphasis on external economic policies rather than internal factors, developed by Wallerstein in the 1970s as a response to criticisms of dependency theory:

- It argues that focusing on governments is the wrong level of analysis – governments have declined in power, transnational corporations are more powerful than ever. Global corporations and global capital override national boundaries and governments have little power to control them.
- It accepts that the poorest countries are not necessarily permanently trapped in a cycle of dependency and underdevelopment – some can undergo economic development.

➤ It suggests that to understand why countries are rich or poor, we need to examine global economic institutions and corporations which form a unified capitalist system – the modern world system (MWS) made up of three zones:

⟶ *The core* – MEDCs, which control world wages and production of manufactured goods.

⟶ *The semi-periphery* – countries with some advanced urban sectors, but rural poverty resembling the periphery.

⟶ *The periphery* – the least developed countries, providing raw materials and cash crops to the core and semi-periphery.

The MWS is a dynamic system. Countries can move between the three zones (but most don't) because capitalism does not respect national borders; capital will move to wherever money is to be made, so the MWS continually changes as capitalism searches for profit.

Evaluation points

✓ It focuses on capitalism as a global system, not just a relationship between individual countries.

✓ It recognises that global capital and corporations transcend national boundaries in their search for profit.

✓ It recognises that underdevelopment and dependency are not always permanent – some countries can move from the periphery to the semi-periphery zones.

✗ It has many of the same weaknesses as dependency theory – e.g. a focus only on external capitalist exploitation, rather than on internal barriers to development.

EXAM TIPS:

➤ To gain marks for application, and for knowledge and understanding, apply different theories of development, even in questions that aren't explicitly about theories – e.g. on gender or education and development.

➤ Gain marks for application, and for knowledge and understanding, by giving examples – e.g. of policies or particular countries – and refer to the names of researchers or theorists.

➤ In questions on why some countries have managed to develop and why some remain underdeveloped, remember to refer to both types of countries.

➤ You can evaluate theories by referring to other theories – e.g. questions about modernisation theory can be evaluated by reference to dependency theory.

The impasse in development theory and post-development theory (pages 111–112)

No theory has been able to explain adequately the patterns of development and underdevelopment in the contemporary world. This has been made more acute by:

➤ *The growth of postmodernist ideas*, which began to undermine the two metanarratives of Marxism and development.

➤ *The emergence of post-development theory*. This questioned whether development – with its emphasis on economic growth and Western materialism and consumption – was necessarily progress. It emphasised the ethnocentric assumptions of Western superiority – 'West is best' – and argued that there could be no universal model of development.

> *The growing focus on globalisation*, which began to overlap with or displace development theories.
> *The growth of environmentalism*, and concerns that development tied to industrialisation would cause lasting environmental harm and would not be sustainable.

People-centred development and environmentalism (pages 111–112)

People-centred development

This is sometimes described as 'grassroots development', or as a 'bottom-up' approach rather than a 'top-down' one. It has the following features:

> *Sustainability* – e.g. using locally sourced renewable resources, and local knowledge and skills.
> *Community participation*.
> *Social justice* – e.g. democratic decision-making and the involvement of all groups – especially women, who have often been excluded.
> *Meeting people's basic needs*.
> *Funding by non-governmental organisations*, running small-scale projects decided by local communities.

Evaluation of people-centred development

✓ It can greatly improve the lives of groups of poorer people in local communities.
✗ Favoured by neoliberals, it reduces the role of the state, which can enable governments to avoid taking responsibility for promoting development.
✗ It is unlikely to lift a whole country out of poverty, as it is small-scale.

Environmentalism

This approach argues that development through economic growth damages the environment, e.g. diminishing resources, harmful use of pesticides, pollution from industries and that we should focus on sustainable development, which may involve less growth and a reduction in Western patterns of production and consumption. (See also pages 65–66 of this book.)

EXAM TIP:

Always remember that the best answers are likely to be those that keep a very close focus on the question, and draw on a range of up-to-date examples.

TOPIC 2

Globalisation and its influence on the cultural, political and economic relationships between societies (pages 115–124)

Globalisation refers to the growing interconnectedness of societies across the world. This has been brought about by factors such as:

➤ Faster and more frequent communications.
➤ Cheaper, and more, travel.
➤ The growth of a global economy.
➤ The global spread of neoliberal free market capitalism and free trade.
➤ The development of global organisations.
➤ The development of global social movements.

Economic globalisation (pages 115–117, 120)

Economic globalisation involves growing trade and economic connections between different parts of the world. Frobel described the 'new international division of labour' (NIDL), in which design and knowledge remain in the developed world, but manufacturing production moves to LEDCs and is then exported (mainly) to the MEDCs.

Evidence for a single fully integrated global economy includes:

➤ *The spread of capitalism (the 'free market') and neoliberal policies* around the world.
➤ *The growth and power of transnational corporations* (TNCs), which produce, market and sell products in global markets, and purchase their supplies from a wide range of different countries (so that labour and production costs are as low, and profits as high, as possible).
➤ *The spread of what Ritzer called 'McDonaldisation'* – the organising principles of a fast-food restaurant – efficiency, calculability, predictability and control – come to dominate and standardise many aspects of economic and cultural life globally.
➤ *The globalisation of international finance and banking.*
➤ *The reduced control of national governments over their economies*, as power shifts in favour of international financial and banking institutions, and multi- or transnational corporations.

Limits of economic globalisation

➤ There are still many national companies, and even the largest corporations often have national bases.
➤ Nation-states still play important roles in controlling the direction taken by the world economy.
➤ Groups of countries, e.g. the European Union, can still provide basic rights and protection for workers, and limit the power of TNCs.
➤ Hirst and Thompson see no evidence yet of a fully developed global economic system.

> **EXAM TIP:**
>
> You could draw on Wallerstein's world systems theory, which sees the world's economy as a unified capitalist system – the modern world system – to provide theoretical support for economic globalisation.

Political globalisation (pages 117, 120–121)

Evidence for political globalisation includes:
- *The global spread of Western-style liberal democracy, human rights and individual freedom.*
- *The erosion of the power of elected national governments* – Decisions are increasingly made by unelected and unaccountable TNCs, and global or supranational political entities such as the European Union or the United Nations.
- *The increase in global decision-making*, as national governments face global problems they cannot resolve alone – e.g. climate change, terrorism, the drugs trade, refugees.
- *The rise in new transnational social movements*, that operate across several countries or globally, organised around global issues – e.g. debt relief; the environment; health; climate change; or global inequality. National boundaries no longer restrict political activity.

Limits of political globalisation
- *National governments still have considerable power* – e.g. to wage war, raise taxes and decide social policies. It is national governments that decide whether or not to create or support international government organisations (IGOs).
- *The spread of liberal democracy may not be as real as it appears* and Western democracies still tolerate and support undemocratic regimes which they regard as allies.
- *There has been an assertion of strong national, ethnic and religious identities to resist globalisation* – e.g. Britain's vote to leave the EU in 2016; Islamic fundamentalism.
- *McGrew argues that, although nation-states are not in terminal decline, there is plenty of evidence of a transformation of politics.*
- *There may be less, not more, democracy* – the national political parties and governments citizens vote for are no longer able to take some really important decisions. These are increasingly made at a global level by elites who are not accountable to the general population, or by TNCs, who are accountable only to shareholders.

> **EXAM TIP:**
>
> Examiners are impressed by candidates who can apply their knowledge to contemporary events. Keep an eye on the news for current examples of political globalisation to refer to in your answers – e.g. TNCs that avoid paying taxes to national governments, or political campaigns by global social movements, e.g. on LEDCs' poverty or debt, or the environment.

Cultural globalisation (pages 118, 121–123)

Evidence for cultural globalisation includes:
➤ The existence of worldwide media, information and communication systems.
➤ The global spread of Western (especially American) consumer culture and patterns of consumption – e.g. McDonald's, Coca-Cola, hip hop and rap music.
➤ More cultural homogenisation – cultures across the world becoming more alike.
➤ The globalisation of religions, which are less tied to specific geographical locations – e.g. Christianity and Islam are now found in most countries of the world.
➤ The global dominance of the English language.
➤ The spread of Western values – e.g. about families, relationships and lifestyles; gender equality; and human rights.
➤ Cosmopolitan lifestyles, drawing on cultural and ethnic identities from all over the world.
➤ World sport.
➤ World tourism.

Evaluation of cultural globalisation
✓ The cultural flow is not always one-way from North to South. Reverse cultural flows have brought South to North – e.g. Bollywood cinema, world music, Asian martial arts, Pokemon and Hello Kitty, etc., have all become valued parts of Western culture.
✓ Global migration means that Southern cultures have significant presences within MEDCs, contributing to more diverse and richer cultures.
✓ New hybrid 'third' cultures may emerge that combine elements of different cultures enabling non-Western cultures to survive in a new form – e.g. glocalisation; keeping traditional cultures alive through 'authentic' spectacles for tourists to gaze at.
✓ The expansion of the internet and global telecommunications have greatly increased the access of many of the world's people to information and ideas from everywhere.
✗ Cultural globalisation is cultural imperialism: Western or American culture and values are imposed on non-Western cultures.
✗ The main global mass media and communications corporations are all based in the North.
✗ Western culture may be degrading or destroying local cultures and values in developing countries.

Theoretical perspectives on globalisation (pages 119–120)

McGrew identifies three theoretical approaches to globalisation.

The neoliberals
Neoliberals (also referred to as positive globalists or optimists) welcome globalisation as a positive force because:
➤ The worldwide expansion of the capitalist free market leads to global economic growth, the spread of modern (i.e. Western) values, the eradication of poverty, and the spread of democracy.
➤ The production of wealth will eventually 'trickle down' to the whole population, bringing higher standards of living for all.
➤ In the long run, there will be no losers, only winners, from globalisation.

The radicals

Radicals are neo-Marxists, associated with Frank's dependency theory and Wallerstein's world systems theory. They see globalisation as a negative force because:

➤ Economic globalisation mainly benefits the already rich MEDCs.
➤ It has mainly furthered the interests and profits of TNCs, and has led to the emergence of what Sklair called the 'transnational capitalist class'.
➤ It has increased global inequality and widened the gap between the rich and poor. In those countries that have developed, wealth has not 'trickled down' but remains in the hands of wealthy elites.
➤ It is based on high consumption and the spread of consumerism, which is not environmentally sustainable.
➤ It is based on what Galtung called 'structural violence', where some groups are exploited by the systematic denial of their rights – e.g. because of their gender, ethnicity, religion or caste.
➤ Cultural globalisation is cultural imperialism.
➤ Unelected and unaccountable TNCs have replaced elected governments as the driving force of globalisation.
➤ The North's gaining of wealth based on intensifying the poverty of the South creates growing threats of terrorism, rising numbers of undocumented (illegal) economic migrants and refugees.

The transformationalists

Transformationalists, such as Cohen and Kennedy, sit between the neoliberals and the radicals. The outcomes of globalisation are uncertain. They argue:

➤ Globalisation may be controlled and used to promote development.
➤ It may be possible for people and countries to reject some negative, and embrace positive, aspects of globalisation.
➤ Globalisation may not be unstoppable – it may even slow or go into reverse.
➤ There is not a homogeneous global culture imposed through cultural imperialism, but new hybrid cultures blending different cultures (glocalisation).
➤ Reverse cultural flows mean that the developing world influences the culture of the West – it's a two-way process.
➤ The world is still unequal, but globalisation (particularly cultural globalisation) is transforming the old hierarchies of North/South and First World/Third World.

EXAM TIPS:

➤ The different theoretical perspectives on globalisation can be used to evaluate its advantages and disadvantages.
➤ If you get a question on one of the theories, you can use the other theories to evaluate it.
➤ To show you can apply theories, always try to give examples to illustrate the theoretical issues you are discussing.

TOPIC 3

The role of transnational corporations, non-governmental organisations and international agencies in local and global strategies for development (pages 125–134)

States and development (pages 125–126)

➤ *Development states* – states that focus on development goals – have sometimes proved successful in leading development and economic growth. Leftwich argues development states played an essential role in the few recent examples of successful industrialisation and economic growth – e.g. the Asian Tigers, or China today. Such states tend to be authoritarian, but this is less acceptable today, as aid and debt relief are often dependent on states being democratic.

➤ *Predatory states* hinder development. These are states where corrupt politicians and civil servants abuse their positions and prey on their own people. They plunder aid and the country's resources for their own self-enrichment, sometimes in collusion with rich countries.

➤ *Governments of LEDCs have few resources to achieve development*.

➤ *Neoliberals* believe the role of the state should be mainly limited to maintaining a stable and secure society in which private businesses and the free market can operate without state regulation.

➤ *Marxist dependency theorists* favour state-led development; however, they argue that many states are controlled by the ruling class to serve its own interests, and its allies in the developed North. For the state to help development, it needs to be transformed by socialism to represent the interests of the majority.

Transnational corporations (TNCs) and development (pages 126–128)

➤ Transnational corporations (TNCs) are huge, very powerful, globalised businesses. They are sometimes called multinational corporations (MNCs). Examples include Nestlé, HSBC, Toyota, Shell, Unilever, Sony, Amazon and Walmart:
  ⟹ Their operations transcend national borders.
  ⟹ They produce and sell around the world.
  ⟹ They use global supply chains.
  ⟹ They employ people in many different countries.

➤ Globalisation and the new international division of labour have created more, and larger, TNCs than ever before.

➤ TNCs' prime purpose is to make profits for their shareholders, not to develop poorer countries.

➤ Export Processing Zones (EPZs) or free trade zones are set up in many countries to attract investment by TNCs by offering them special inducements – e.g. tax exemptions; the removal of normal workplace protections for workers. This is because governments regard the presence of TNCs as beneficial to their countries' long-term economic development.

Modernisation theory and neoliberalism stress the benefits of TNCs for development

➤ *Cultural change* – more modern values promoting development and aspiration.
➤ *Investment* – money; resources; technology; expertise; and job creation.
➤ *Educational improvements*, to provide skilled workers.
➤ *More jobs in local businesses* to supply and service the TNCs.
➤ *More jobs and training for women*, promoting gender equality.
➤ *Providing infrastructure* from which local people can also benefit.
➤ *Encouragement of international trade*, and opening up new markets.

Dependency theory stresses the disadvantages of TNCs

Dependency theorists argue the overall effect of TNCs is to weaken and exploit workers in developing countries, and strengthen capitalism.

➤ *Exploitation of workers* – Poor working conditions and low pay, use of child labour and other abuses.
➤ *A 'race to the bottom'* – A term used by Kerngahan to describe the way LEDCs compete with each other to attract TNCs by allowing ever-worsening legal protections, wages, benefits and conditions for workers; ever fewer environmental regulations or tax requirements.
➤ *The capital-intensive nature of some TNC activity* means it does not create as many jobs as sometimes claimed.
➤ *Exploitation of the environment* with harmful consequences for local people.
➤ *Exploitation of local markets* – e.g. mis-selling of goods, out-of-date goods and harmful goods.
➤ *The best-paid jobs go to expatriates* from the developed world rather than to local people.
➤ *Few financial benefits for the developing country* – Profits are exported and local taxes avoided, leaving few resources for governments to tackle poverty and fund healthcare, clean water, etc.
➤ *Products are for export to Western markets*, so local people are unable to buy or afford them.
➤ *TNCs have little loyalty to particular countries* – when labour is cheaper elsewhere, they will move on.
➤ *Bio-piracy* – TNCs are able to patent traditional medicines and sources of food, making money from resources that ought to belong to developing countries, and also eliminating domestic firms that sold these products.
➤ *Exploitation of consumers in the West*, by giving misleading impressions that the companies' policies are socially and environmentally friendly.

Reasons why TNCs are able to act in unethical ways

➤ *The economic and political power* of the largest TNCs enables them to ensure policies are made that favour them, or to force or blackmail governments into overlooking wrong-doing.
➤ *They often operate through smaller, subsidiary companies* – so any wrong-doing is blamed on the subsidiary, letting the parent company off the hook.
➤ *There is little incentive to act ethically* – Laws are hard to apply and enforce globally. Any fines for breaking regulations and laws are tiny as proportions of profits, and in any case the cost can be passed on to consumers. Imprisonment for corporate crimes is very rare.

EXAM TIPS:

➤ To gain high marks, when examining the role of TNCs in development, apply the different theories – e.g. neoliberalism, modernisation theory, dependency theory, etc. Use these theories for evaluation too.
➤ Don't forget to look at both the benefits and disadvantages of TNCs in development, and try to give examples of the behaviour of specific TNCs to gain extra marks for application.

International non-governmental organisations (INGOs) and development (pages 128–131)

➤ *Non-governmental organisations (NGOs)* are often non-profit or charitable organisations that are economically and politically independent from government or profit-making businesses.
➤ *International non-governmental organisations (INGOs)* are NGOs that work internationally on a range of humanitarian, development and environmental issues in LEDCs.
➤ INGOs, such as Oxfam, play a vital role in emergencies, raising funds from the public for disaster relief. Most also work successfully at providing development aid in local projects.

Strengths of INGOs in helping development
➤ Less bureaucratic than governments – can mobilise resources and act quickly, and respond flexibly to local needs.
➤ Worldwide track records of success of working on small-scale, achievable projects, in partnerships with local people.
➤ Good knowledge of needs through involvement of local people.
➤ Able and willing to take risks.
➤ Seen as trustworthy – political neutrality and independence from local political power structures or government policy agendas.
➤ Not driven by profit (unlike TNCs).
➤ Continuity (unlike government aid, which can be affected by elections).
➤ Responsive to beneficial intentions of donors, on whom they rely for funding – keeps them focused.

Criticisms of INGOs
➤ Effectiveness limited.
➤ Sometimes work too closely with governments or rely on government funds – undermining independence, neutrality and trust among local people.
➤ Work hampered by the political agendas of governments.
➤ Sometimes have links with TNCs.
➤ Unclear accountability – who are they responsible to?
➤ Inappropriate spending of funds – e.g. spending too much on administration and media publicity, rather than aid.
➤ Portray people in developing countries as helpless victims and objects of pity (not least to raise funds in Western charity collections).

➤ Not always prioritising the right things – e.g. some faith-based INGOs have been accused of being too concerned with spreading their religious beliefs.
➤ Being too concerned with good publicity and building a successful media brand.

INGOs and global civil society
➤ Civil society refers to the network of businesses, political groups and voluntary organisations that exist between individuals/families and the state.
➤ Globalisation has led to the emergence of a global civil society, including INGOs and global social movements opposed to neoliberal globalisation.
➤ The anti-globalisation movement comes together at the World Social Forum and supporters are often found protesting at meetings of the neoliberal World Trade Organization (WTO), the World Bank and the International Monetary Fund (IMF).

International governmental organisations (IGOs) and development (pages 131–133)

States cannot solve development problems alone, and so they cooperate to set up a number of transnational organisations – international governmental organisations (IGOs).

The United Nations (UN)
➤ Has a wide variety of programmes and agencies, many of which are concerned with economic and social development.
➤ Establishes global targets for development and poverty reduction.
➤ Tends to be more radical and pro-South than the IMF, the WTO and the World Bank.

The European Union (EU)
The EU and its member countries are the world's largest donor of development aid.

The Bretton Woods Institutions
These are largely under the control of MEDCs, particularly the USA, and are heavily influenced by neoliberalism. They face a lot of political opposition because they are not seen as neutral, but as acting in the interests of the world's most powerful and richest countries.

The International Monetary Fund (IMF)
The IMF is the lender of last resort for countries in debt. IMF loans are conditional on countries adopting IMF neoliberal economic policies – structural adjustment programmes (SAPs).

Evaluation of the IMF's role in development
✓ It is fairly sensible to have an IGO to regulate the global economy, and help countries in debt.
✓ It is useful to enable developing countries to access funding and expertise to help with their economic development and reduction in poverty.
✗ It adheres strictly to neoliberal policies, and SAPs don't work in developing countries:
➠ They promote TNCs rather than domestic industries.
➠ Deregulation of employment rights leads to worse working conditions.

⟾ They cut government spending on education and health.

⟾ They reorient the economy to export markets rather than domestic needs.

⟾ When any development does occur, it increases inequality – the already better-off gain more, and the poor face even greater poverty.

✗ It imposes the same conditions on all, regardless of the country's level of development or its resources – 'One size fits all.'

✗ It deals mainly with short-term economic problems, and is less interested in longer-term development.

The World Bank

The World Bank has a clearer development and poverty reduction role than the IMF. It gives loans to governments of developing countries at low rates of interest, or zero interest for the poorest countries.

➤ In the past, it has been restricted to lending for specific projects, such as dams, which were often inappropriate for wider development.

➤ It works closely with the IMF and SAPs, so many of the criticisms of the IMF also apply to the World Bank.

The World Trade Organization (WTO)

The WTO pushes neoliberal reforms in the area of trade – the removal of trade barriers restricting free trade between countries.

➤ In practice, poorer countries are not involved in important discussions.

➤ It leads to unfair trade between developing and developed countries. Developing countries are often forced by SAPs to open up their countries to Western exports, but the WTO is relatively ineffective in making rich nations open up their markets to the products of developing countries.

➤ It gives free trade priority over all other considerations, including sustainable development.

TOPIC 4

Development in relation to aid and trade, industrialisation, urbanisation, the environment, war and conflict (pages 135–156)

Aid (pages 135–138)

➤ 'Aid' refers to financial grants and loans (which have to be repaid) to developing countries. It can also include military supplies, and medical and technical assistance.
➤ Aid comes from two main sources:
  ⅢⅢ➤ INGOs, who collect money from the public in the West for development aid – e.g. Oxfam and Christian Aid.
  ⅢⅢ➤ Official Development Assistance (ODA) – loans and grants either directly from government to government or channelled through IGOs, e.g. the World Bank.
➤ Aid is often tied or conditional – either to be used for a particular purpose or conditional on implementing particular policies.
➤ Aid typically goes from rich to poor countries.

The case for aid
➤ *Aid from the North can provide a helping hand*, enabling developing countries to reach prosperity and mass consumption, as modernisation theory suggests.
➤ *Aid saves lives* – in emergencies, disasters, famines, earthquakes, etc.
➤ *Aid stops things getting worse* or makes things better than they would otherwise have been.
➤ *Aid works* – it has led to great improvements in education, healthcare and infrastructure which otherwise would not have been affordable.
➤ *Aid increases world security* by reducing threats of poverty-driven social unrest; illegal economic migration; wars; production of illegal drugs for sale in rich countries.
➤ *Aid is morally and ethically right*.

The case against aid

The neoliberal view
➤ *Aid creates a culture of dependency* – states come to rely on handouts, taking away their initiative, and willingness to help themselves.
➤ *Aid does nothing to change cultural values* – poor countries stay poor because of their own failed values, such as laziness, corruption or inefficiency.
➤ *Aid interferes with the free market* – it's a form of subsidy which discourages the efficiency, competitiveness, free enterprise and investment necessary to encourage development.
➤ *Aid is money down the drain* – if a project is viable, it should be able to attract private investment so that aid is unnecessary.
➤ *Aid fosters corruption and poor governance*. Moyo, from the developing country of Zambia, argues aid should be phased out, and replaced by encouragement of entrepreneurship and the free market.

The neo-Marxist view

➤ *Aid is imperialism* – Hayter says aid is nearly always conditional, and enables rich countries to exercise power over, and control the economies of, poorer ones.

➤ *Most aid doesn't alleviate poverty* – its real purpose is to strengthen the international system which damages the interests of the poor and increases inequality.

➤ *Aid creates jobs and export markets for countries that provide the aid.*

➤ *Most aid doesn't go to the people or countries who really need it*, but to those who are willing to cooperate with and give political support to the donor countries.

Evaluation of aid – does it do more harm than good?

✓ The right kind of aid – small-scale, aware of local needs, controlled at a local level, usually given by an NGO – can be very positive.

✓ Aid in a disaster or emergency can be vital.

✗ Aid is not enough to solve the problems of poverty.

✗ Aid overall results in money flowing from, not to, the South – e.g. African countries send more money to the West in payment of interest on loans than they receive in aid.

> **EXAM TIP:**
>
> Remember that top marks are most likely to be awarded to students who can show evaluation skills by giving a range of arguments and counter-arguments, tied to theories and evidence/examples – e.g. modernisation theory supports aid, and neo-Marxists and neoliberals don't. Try to distinguish between different types of aid – it is unlikely that anyone will object to unconditional aid for poor countries that are hit by natural disasters, but conditional aid with strings attached might be viewed differently, e.g. by neo-Marxists.

The debt crisis and development (138–140)

Dependency theorists argued that inadequate, embezzled or inappropriate foreign aid, and the history of colonialism, meant LEDCs needed to borrow money to fund development.

Modernisation and neoliberal theories believed lending money to LEDCs would enable them to develop and pay the interest on these loans, and eventually repay them.

Economic recession in richer countries in the 1980s cut the export markets of poorer countries, and SAPs failed to produce the predicted economic growth.

A growing debt crisis – LEDCs hadn't the money to repay interest on the loans, and had to borrow more to cover the interest payments. More countries went into ever deeper debt. Many countries were spending more on interest payments on loans than they received in aid.

Debt boomerangs – George showed that the debt crisis could also cause problems in the North, what she called the 'debt boomerang'.

The Highly Indebted Poor Countries Initiative (HIPC) was launched in 1996 by the IMF and World Bank, in response to rising international protests by global social movements. This allowed some debts to be reduced or written off, provided the countries adopted IMF- and World Bank-approved economic policies.
↓
A new debt crisis? In 2016, loans to LEDCs were increasing again, and it is likely a new debt crisis will arise, and many countries will continue facing extreme poverty and a lack of development due to the burden of debt.

Trade (pages 140–143)

The view of modernisation theorists and neoliberals
➤ Trade was key to the economic growth of developed countries in the past; today's developing countries should become more involved in international trade so they can develop too.
➤ The way to develop trade is through trade liberalisation and free trade.
➤ Countries who produce goods at competitive prices will succeed and develop; those who are inefficient and uncompetitive will stagnate and be forced to change.
➤ Free trade is more effective in boosting development than aid.
➤ Increased wealth in developing free trade economies eventually 'trickles down' to the poor. (See pages 57–58 for why SAPs failed to boost development.)

The view of dependency theorists and radicals
➤ Trade is one of the ways in which the North ensures the neo-colonial exploitation of the South.
➤ Developing countries remain heavily dependent on the export of a few primary products. The major share of the profits from these exports goes to those businesses in the North that ship, process, package and sell the products. Even the tiny amount of money producers make is at risk from falling world prices, or from changing fashions or tastes in the North.
➤ The terms of trade between Northern and Southern countries have negative impacts on development:
  ⏵ The rich world uses its dominance in the world trade system to ensure that the prices that producers in the developing world can get are low, leaving little to fund development or reduce poverty.
  ⏵ Free trade is imposed on LEDCs through SAPs, but MEDCs don't apply those same rules to themselves. They protect their own producers from cheaper foreign goods by making the exports of LEDCs uncompetitive.

Fair Trade
Growing opposition to unfair trade is found in the Fair Trade movement. This is trying to alter the terms of trade so that producers in developing countries receive a higher proportion of the profits from their goods, and that their goods are produced ethically.
➤ Neoliberals oppose Fair Trade because it interferes with the operation of the free market, and they argue it is unfair as it gives privileges to the relatively small number of producers who meet the criteria to take part in Fair Trade schemes.
➤ Some progressive people also question whether the Fair Trade logo is a marketing device used by big businesses to sell products by deceiving customers into thinking the company is more ethical than it actually is.

Industrialisation (pages 143–145)

Industrialisation is the move from traditional agriculture and small-scale workshops to mechanised agriculture and large-scale factory production.

Import substitution industrialisation (ISI)
ISI involves replacing imported goods by home-produced goods. This was used by many LEDCs (e.g. Mexico, Argentina, Brazil and India) in the 1950s and 1960s to try to develop their economies and become less dependent on imports from the developed world.
- Advantages of ISI for developing countries:
  - Helps them to become less dependent on MEDCs.
  - Gives them more control over their economies.
  - Enables them to reinvest profits and develop their economies.
- Disadvantages:
  - It wasn't very successful: any savings from domestic production of goods were balanced by the costs of importing the necessary raw materials.
  - The protection of infant industries through tariffs on imports leads to inefficiency and lack of innovation.
  - It could lead to retaliation – with exports to MEDCs facing similar high tariffs, so their goods become uncompetitive in Western markets.

Export-oriented industrialisation (EOI)
EOI was a strategy begun in the 1970s, and involved industrialisation by producing specialised manufactured goods in areas in which there was a relative advantage enabling them to be marketed cheaply in the developed world.
- Advantages of EOI for developing countries:
  - Encourages development by enabling tax incomes on profits for paying off debt, reinvestment for economic growth, and higher standards of living.
  - Worked well for Japan, and for the newly industrialising countries (NICs), particularly the 'Asian Tigers' of South Korea, Taiwan, Singapore and Hong Kong, which made rapid progress in the late twentieth century.
- Disadvantages:
  - The focus on export industries was often at the expense of promoting domestic markets, other sources of economic growth, and social development. The model was reliant on export markets remaining strong – e.g. strong demand in Western countries.
  - There were special circumstances in Japan and the Tiger economies which did not apply to other countries and might explain their success.
  - LEDCs often do not have access to the capital investment and skills required for EOI, which means TNCs take advantage of cheap labour to produce exports, with few benefits for the economic growth of LEDCs.
  - The success of Japan and the Asian Tigers reduced opportunities for other developing economies to succeed, because there are fewer opportunities left to exploit.

Other opportunities for industrial development

Agriculture

Some LEDCs have concentrated on agriculture, rather than industry, for development – e.g. exporting cash crops, Fair Trade produce and exotic 'superfoods' in demand in Western countries.
- Industrial-style techniques were often used, but with the downside of environmental problems caused by heavy use of pesticides and insecticides.
- Production and export are often controlled by TNCs, with the disadvantages for wider development that involves.

Data processing, software development and customer services

Globalisation opened up some new opportunities for LEDCs in data processing and software development for Western companies. Global communications technology has enabled Western customer services to be outsourced to LEDCs where labour is much cheaper and less regulated – e.g. Western companies using India-based call centres.

Tourism

International tourism is often regarded as the third-largest industry in the world, after oil and vehicle production.
- With globalisation, mass tourism is no longer restricted to predominantly developed countries, and non-Western destinations have grown in popularity, particularly the cheaper countries of the developing world.
- Developing the tourist industry offers a number of advantages for LEDCs, including more jobs and more income for the local economy.
- But it also has disadvantages:
  - Environmental damage.
  - Growing inequality, between those who benefit from tourism and those who don't.
  - Tourism is seasonal, leaving un- and underemployment for parts of the year.
  - Relying on one industry is risky as a development strategy as tourist numbers may decline suddenly.
  - Hotels import much of the food they serve and the materials they use, so little benefit to the local economy.
  - Profits often do not remain in the country, but in the hands of foreign tour operators.

Evaluation of industrialisation as a development strategy in poor countries
- Industrialisation can bring its own problems – e.g. environmental damage.
- Industrialisation is often not accompanied by matching social development – e.g. improved educational and social security systems, improved rights and conditions for the workforce, and democratic systems of government.
- Any benefits often go to foreign businesses (TNCs) or to local elites.
- It can be fragile and unsustainable development when it depends on a single industry or product.

Urbanisation (pages 146–149)

Urbanisation is driven by push and pull factors, as people seek the better healthcare, education and employment opportunities of urban centres, and move away from poverty and lack of opportunity in rural areas.

Modernisation theorists

Modernisation theorists see urbanisation in poorer countries as being essential for the cultural and economic change required for development because it:

➤ *Provides a labour force* concentrated in one place for factories and businesses.

➤ *Promotes cultural change and modern values* – it removes people from the traditional values of rural life and exposes them to Western values essential for development.

Dependency theorists argue:

➤ Many cities in developing countries are not a response to industrialisation; they were established or grew dramatically under colonial rule, because they were used as administrative centres and as staging posts in exports of raw materials and cash crops.

➤ A two-tiered social system grew up under colonialism, with colonial administrators and local elites having much higher living standards than the mass of the population. These inequalities have not changed under neo-colonialism, and TNCs have replaced the colonial powers.

➤ Urbanisation creates growing social inequality and social problems hindering development. Urbanisation in LEDCs today involves:

⟿ *Cities divided into wealthy elites and a mass of people living in poverty.*

⟿ *High levels of un- or underemployment* – more people than jobs means many rely on insecure, part-time, self-employed and/or low-paid casual work.

⟿ *The growth of urban squalor, and shanty towns*, where people live in makeshift homes vulnerable to earthquakes and flooding, and lack access to water, sanitation, waste disposal facilities, education, healthcare and other resources typically associated with Western cities.

➤ LEDCs cannot follow the same path to development as MEDCs did in the past. Colonialism has made it impossible for them to do so. Today's cities in LEDCs are made up of a poor and marginalised population who lack basic rights. In contrast, the poor in the growing Western cities of the nineteenth century were united by collective working in factories and workshops, and often organised in trade unions – Marx's potentially class-conscious revolutionary proletariat.

Differences between urban and rural poverty in developing countries

➤ The living conditions of the poor in the cities of LEDCs are often worse than for those who live in rural areas.

➤ Because of SAPs, many city services (such as water) have been privatised, so are inaccessible to the poor, who can't afford them. In rural areas, poor people are more likely to have access to free natural water supplies, and free traditional remedies.

➤ People in rural areas also benefit from having family members in cities who send home some of their earnings.

The environment (pages 149–152)

➤ Development can have negative impacts on the environment – e.g. global warming and climate change; land, air and water pollution; toxic waste; deforestation; desertification; loss of biodiversity; permanent loss of non-renewable resources.

➤ The Brundtland Commission report in 1987 coined the term 'sustainable development' with the aim of trying to ensure that development met the needs of the present without compromising the ability of future generations to meet their own needs.

➤ Although poorer people are the least responsible for environmental problems, they are affected by them more than wealthier people – e.g. they are more likely to live on land that is vulnerable to flooding, or close to sources of pollution, and they lack the resources to move or to change their situation.

The view of neoliberals

➤ The solution to environmental problems is in the extension of the free market.

➤ Capitalism may have contributed to environmental problems, but it will generate solutions to the problems through 'technological fixes' – e.g. wealthy corporations developing electric cars.

➤ Privatisation of public goods can resolve problems – e.g. private owners of water supplies and land would be more likely to protect such resources by promoting sustainable use as this would secure their future profits.

The view of neo-Malthusians and modernisation theorists

➤ Continuing population growth threatens the environment, especially in developing countries. Those who damage the environment most in developing countries, especially in rural areas, are the poor.

➤ Population growth means that more and more marginal land has to be farmed, with loss of soil and eventual desertification.

➤ These problems are internal to developing countries, and social and cultural change and economic modernisation are needed to resolve them.

The view of anti-Malthusians and dependency theorists

➤ Many of the causes of environmental problems in LEDCs are rooted in the unequal global distribution of resources, in which rich countries consume a far greater share of resources and generate far more waste than poor countries do.

➤ The exploitation of the developing world's resources to maintain mass consumerism in the West underlies many environmental problems in LEDCs.

➤ Western pressure to attract investment from TNCs leads some LEDCs to weaken environmental controls.

➤ The use of the best agricultural land by TNCs for cash crop production pushes small farmers onto marginal, unsustainable land.

➤ The solution to environmental degradation is for Western countries to reduce their consumption levels, and their ecological footprints; LEDCs can achieve some economic growth, but it is not environmentally sustainable for them to aspire to Western lifestyles.

War and conflict (pages 152–156)

Most of today's wars are civil wars, and occur in some of the poorest developing countries; they are what Kaldor calls 'new wars'. Kaldor argues that new wars are a result of globalisation, and to some extent a reaction against it.

Why are there so many civil wars in the poorest countries?

➤ *Neo-Malthusians*, like Kaplan, argue that uncontrolled population growth and overpopulation, urbanisation, and resource scarcity and depletion are leading to a struggle to survive, manifested in civil wars in developing countries.
➤ *Modernisation theorists*, such as Ayoob, argue that civil wars are part of the process of creating modern states. Civil wars will become less common as countries begin to adopt modern (Western) values, free trade and democracy.
➤ *Dependency theory* sees civil wars arising from external factors in a global context:
  ➡ Duffield argues globalisation has increased inequalities. This leads to more poverty, frustration and desperation.
  ➡ Hanlon argues some developing states are weak and politically unstable so cannot control the resulting breakdown in social order.
  ➡ Changes in terms of trade can adversely affect people and create poverty.
  ➡ The cheap and easy availability of arms, particularly through the arms trade controlled by transnational criminal networks.
  ➡ Aid can contribute to the conditions for war if most of the benefits go to one group and so increase inequalities.
  ➡ Ethnic conflicts can be exploited by politicians and others seeking power. These are often rooted in, and legacies of, colonialism.
  ➡ Interference by other (mainly developed) countries – e.g. by supplying arms; by engineering military coups.

The effects of war on development

Wars have negative consequences for development, and these can last for many years after wars are over.

➤ *War is expensive* – it absorbs money that could be used for development.
➤ *War often makes trade impossible.*
➤ *War destroys the infrastructure necessary for social and economic development.*
➤ *War creates poverty* and undermines poverty reduction. Humanitarian aid agencies working to alleviate poverty find working in war zones difficult.
➤ *War damages the environmental infrastructure.*
➤ *War kills and harms health long after conflicts cease*, because of destroyed health services, food and water supplies, and life in refugee camps.
➤ *War destroys security and effective government*, which Collier argues are essential for both social and economic development.

EXAM TIPS:

➤ On questions on the link between wars and development, evaluate by putting wars in the context of different perspectives on development, e.g. dependency theory, modernisation theory, neo-Malthusianism, etc.
➤ Don't just limit yourself to analysing the view prompted in the question or the text in the Item. Be prepared to make explicit evaluation by offering alternative explanations for conflicts in poor countries.
➤ Always give a conclusion, based on your arguments, and with an explicit link back to the question.

TOPIC 5

Employment, education, health, demographic change and gender as aspects of development (pages 157–172)

Employment (pages 157–159)

Formal-sector work

The formal sector is the officially recognised and recorded sector of the economy.

➤ It is generally characterised (compared to the informal sector) by fairly stable employment, higher wages, more regulated conditions and better workers' rights.

➤ It includes work in the public sector, e.g. as teachers or in health services; and for TNCs, or for local businesses supplying TNCs. Formal-sector work is in short supply and is highly sought-after in most LEDCs.

Working for TNCs

➤ Compared to the informal sector, and the local formal sector, TNCs offer relatively good pay and conditions to those they directly employ, though the most highly paid work is often performed by foreigners or in the developed world.

➤ TNCs tend not to employ many workers directly, and much of their work is subcontracted out to local firms.

➤ Local firms supplying TNCs compete in a 'race to the bottom' to gain TNC business by supplying at low prices. This may lead to poor conditions for workers.

Informal-sector work

The informal sector is the unrecorded informal economy.

➤ It features insecure and temporary work; irregular wages and low pay; self-employment in petty trading, or in micro-enterprises, operating on a very small scale and often established with micro-credit (very small loans).

➤ Work is often labour-intensive, unregulated, may be illegal, and tax may not be paid.

➤ The extent and nature of informal-sector employment means there are very large numbers of people in LEDCs who are underemployed, unable to work to their full potential and unable to work themselves out of poverty.

➤ Many people in developing countries, particularly in rural areas, support themselves through subsistence agriculture – growing food for their own consumption, or by hunting, fishing and gathering.

Especially disadvantaged groups

➤ *Children*

    ➦ In developing countries, children are often an economic asset to families – e.g. helping on the family farm; selling produce at a market; employment in the informal sector.

    ➦ Children working hinders social development – e.g. children may work in the informal sector rather than going to school.

➠ Child labour has been a serious problem in developing countries. The use of child labour is now diminishing, due to international campaigning.

➤ *Older people* – The idea of retirement belongs to the formal sector, and there are unlikely to be state pensions. Many poorer older people will have no option but to keep on working for as long as they are physically able.

➤ *Disabled people* – In the absence of state support, disabled people rely on family and community, or may generate income by begging.

➤ *Women* – In some cultures it is unacceptable for women to work outside the home. Women are often reliant on husbands and fathers to earn money; for women alone, such as widows, making money may be very difficult. Even in the formal sector, women are often taken advantage of, working for lower wages than men and in poor conditions.

Globalisation and employment

➤ *Economic migration* – increasing numbers of people from LEDCs seek work in the North, where pay and living standards are much higher. Some are well trained and qualified, e.g. as doctors; others are unqualified. Some work legally, others not; some are abroad only for a short period, and others stay for many years. Many poor economic migrants, as well as refugees from war, famine and political persecution, risk their lives to reach what they hope will be a better and safer life in the North.

➤ *Remittances* – These are transfers of money by migrant workers back to family and friends in their country of origin. These are an increasingly important feature of economies in LEDCs. Harris described remittances as 'one of the most successful mechanisms for redistributing the world's income in favour of poorer countries'.

Education (pages 159–162)

Modernisation theory
Modernisation theorists argue that Western-style education is essential to development because:

➤ It spreads modern values and enables a break with traditional values that act as obstacles to development.

➤ It provides human capital – the knowledge and skills possessed by a workforce that enable it to contribute to development.

➤ It trains future political and business leaders to foster development.

Dependency theory

➤ Sees Western-style education as a form of cultural imperialism, imposing Western values.

➤ Argues that education was one of the main ways colonial powers exercised control over their colonies. Under neo-colonialism, Western-style education systems are about social control, and providing passive workers and consumers for capitalist economies from which only elites benefit.

➤ Education can be helpful for development, but only if it encourages students to be critical thinkers who challenge existing inequalities, and enables them to transform developing economies to work for the majority of people.

Other benefits of education for economic and social development

➤ Universal education in the North was associated with economic growth, rising living standards and improvements in health.
➤ Education, especially for literacy and numeracy, gives people some control over their own lives, and makes it more difficult for them to be exploited.
➤ Education of girls has positive outcomes in improving the health and nutrition of families and their chances of employment, limiting the number of children women have, and reducing infant and maternal mortality rates.

Problems of education in contributing to development in LEDCs

➤ When a country has limited resources, it may choose to educate a minority for leadership and management posts if the majority do not need an education for their work.
➤ A country may decide to achieve economic growth first, seeing education as something to fix later.
➤ Education may simply make people more discontented and rebellious if they cannot use their education to improve their lives; some may choose to emigrate to other countries, reducing the prospects for development in their own countries.
➤ There is still gender inequality in education. Girls are less likely than boys to go to school.
➤ There is social inequality in education – poorer children are less likely to attend school than those from wealthier families.
➤ Teachers are not well paid, so teaching is not an attractive career.
➤ Schools are under-resourced: very large classes; inadequate buildings with few facilities; few textbooks; and little science or other practical equipment.
➤ Some schools may charge fees that only well-off parents can afford.
➤ War disrupts education; schools are sometimes attacked and teachers and pupils killed or kidnapped.
➤ Pupils may have a lot of time off school because of illness and infectious disease outbreaks.
➤ Even for pupils who do well at primary level, there are often not enough secondary places available.
➤ Walking a long distance to school may be necessary.

EXAM TIPS:

➤ When you get questions on the links between education and things like industrialisation, modernisation and development, bring in different perspectives on development – e.g. dependency theory and modernisation theory.
➤ You could also apply your earlier studies on education – e.g. the functionalist or Marxist perspectives on the links between education and the economy; education as a route to social mobility; education providing human capital; education and values of achievement and meritocracy, etc. But make sure you apply these to the specific demands of the question.

Health (pages 162–165)

In general, poor countries have poor health, as shown by high rates of child and maternal mortality, and poor life expectancy.

➤ 'Diseases of poverty' – diseases arising because victims are malnourished and poor – are more common. These are infectious diseases such as diarrhoea, and bacterial and viral diseases such as polio, cholera, hepatitis and typhoid, which are often big killers and have largely been wiped out in MEDCs.

➤ Malaria is a huge problem – it affects millions of people, and kills hundreds of thousands every year, many children under age 5.

➤ Accidents and injuries have more serious consequences in LEDCs because victims are less likely to receive prompt and effective treatment (if they receive any).

➤ Women, children and rural populations are the main victims of death and disease.

Major factors underlying poor health

➤ *Poverty* – lack of income; inadequate diets/malnutrition; poor housing; lack of affordability of healthcare

➤ *Poor hygiene* – lack of piped, clean water and of sewage and waste disposal facilities encourage the spread of infectious diseases.

➤ *Lack of education and literacy*, particularly health education, means a lack of understanding of the causes of diseases, and ways of preventing them.

➤ *Lack of access to healthcare* – free public health facilities are often rare and of poor quality, and may be a very long way away.

➤ *A lack of facilities* – hospitals, treatment centres and ambulances, and shortages of medicines and medical equipment.

➤ *A shortage of skilled health workers.* There is little financial incentive to work in poor rural areas – or indeed in developing countries at all, hence the 'brain drain' of doctors, nurses and other health professionals to the North.

Applying the theories

Modernisation theory

➤ Health patterns of LEDCs will follow those of the developed world as they modernise economically and socially.

➤ LEDCs should draw on aid and expertise from the developed world, drop traditional medical practices and concentrate on Western-style healthcare.

➤ LEDCs are still at the stage MEDCs were at centuries ago. Modernisation will enable them to make an epidemiological transition. Improvements in nutrition, hygiene, sanitation and education will move LEDCs towards a period when death rates from infectious diseases will be negligible, infant and child mortality low and life expectancy much higher.

Dependency theory

➤ There is no reason to assume that today's LEDCs can simply follow the path of the rich world.

➤ Modernisation by adopting a Western-style system in cities can leave the poor and those in rural areas with little access to healthcare.

➤ Health in LEDCs is made worse by the effects of cultural imperialism, debt, aid, trade and the activities of TNCs and IGOs:

⟶ The adoption of lifestyles of the rich world (e.g. diets heavy in fats and sugars, smoking and less physical activity), leading to increases in 'diseases of affluence' – e.g. cancers and heart disease.

➠ Imposed neoliberal policies such as cuts in public spending give states little scope to act effectively to improve health.

➠ Pharmaceutical TNCs are reluctant to make their medicines available at prices people can afford or to allow LEDCs to manufacture their own generic versions.

➠ Pharmaceutical TNCs focus their research on medicines that will make them most money, not the ones which are most needed.

➠ Pollution and environmental damage caused by TNCs can affect health.

EXAM TIPS:

➤ In any question on health and development, be sure not only to describe what the influences are, but also to explain how they affect health – e.g. lack of research by pharmaceutical TNCs, or the cost of their drugs, means treatments aren't available or affordable for some of the major diseases experienced by LEDCs; or unsafe recycling of e-waste can cause health problems like cardiovascular disease, DNA damage and cancer.

➤ As always, for high marks, put your answers in the context of theories – e.g. modernisation and dependency theories – applied appropriately to the question. And weigh the theories against one another for evaluation.

Demographic change (pages 166–169)

Demography refers to the study of human populations, such as their size and structure; demographic change is about how these change over time.

➤ World population growth has accelerated rapidly in the last 100 years. Most of the increase has been in LEDCs.

➤ Today's MEDCs, during the period of industrialisation and urbanisation, went through a demographic transition from high birth and death rates, and low life expectancy (large numbers of young people and few elderly people) to low birth and death rates, and higher life expectancy (growing numbers of older people, and proportionately fewer younger people).

➤ The demographic transition in MEDCs was driven by:

➠ *The changing status of children*, from being an economic asset to becoming an economic burden – e.g. having to be supported through compulsory education; banning of child labour.

➠ *The reduced need for families to have many children* – more were surviving into adulthood, so birth rates fell; growing welfare provision meant people were no longer dependent on their children to look after them as they grew older.

➠ *Improvements in public hygiene and health education*, reducing child and adult death rates from infectious and other diseases.

➠ *Improved healthcare, health education, medicines and medical advances.*

➤ Modernisation theorists expect there to be a similar demographic transition in LEDCs, as they go through the same process of modernisation as developed countries did.

➤ Many of today's LEDCs are passing through the demographic transition but the birth rate is still high, and many LEDCs still have high population growth.

➤ Just because MEDCs went through a demographic transition, we can't assume that it is inevitable. Hewitt and Smyth argue some countries may get stuck in the transition phase – the 'demographic trap'.

The Malthusian view and modernisation theory

Malthus, at the end of the eighteenth century, argued that the world's population would inevitably grow faster than the food supply and that it was therefore essential to curb population growth. Modern followers of Malthus's ideas are referred to as neo-Malthusians and the approach has also been taken up by modernisation theorists. They argue:

➤ Population growth in LEDCs is leading to poverty; famines and malnutrition; uncontrollable urbanisation; resource depletion; and environmental damage.

➤ Kaplan argued these factors undermine already weak states and lead to instability, causing parts of the poor world to collapse into anarchy and civil wars – a process he referred to as the 'New Barbarism'.

➤ High birth rates and population growth are the biggest obstacles to Western-style social and economic development and poverty reduction. Controlling population growth through reducing birth rates should therefore be the main objective of modernising governments and development aid (promotion of family planning, availability of contraception, free access to abortion, financial incentives to reduce family size).

The anti-Malthusian view and dependency theory

Dependency theorists adopt an anti-Malthusian view: poverty and lack of development are the causes, not the consequences, of high population growth.

➤ Colonialism and neo-colonialism have created a situation, as Adamson argues, where poverty makes high birth rates a rational choice by parents:
   ⟼ Children are economic assets as they can work and earn money.
   ⟼ In the absence of a welfare state, high infant and child mortality rates encourage poor parents to have more children to ensure some survive to support them in old age.

➤ Aid that focuses on controlling population is misguided – the way to tackle population growth is to tackle poverty, reduce infant and child mortality, and provide better public welfare, health and education.

➤ The education of women is of central importance in reducing birth rates because:
   ⟼ They gain status through education, rather than having lots of children.
   ⟼ They are more able to work to support their children, rather than relying on their children for work and income.
   ⟼ They are better able to look after the health of their children, reducing mortality.
   ⟼ They are likely to have better access to, and willingness to use, contraception.
   ⟼ They are more empowered, and more likely to take decisions about their own fertility, or negotiate with their husband, rather than accepting his patriarchal authority.

➤ The real cause of hunger and malnutrition in LEDCs is not over-population or lack of food, but the unequal distribution of the world's resources, and economic exploitation by MEDCs.

Gender (pages 169–172)

Women in LEDCs face a series of disadvantages compared to men:

➤ Less education.
➤ More poverty – the feminisation of poverty.
➤ Poorer health – including maternal mortality, less access to healthcare, and lower life expectancy.
➤ Poorer pay in employment, even when they do the same work as men.
➤ Harder work – a triple burden of paid or unpaid work, domestic labour and emotional work, including care of children.
➤ Subordinate positions in households and communities – a product of patriarchy and patriarchal attitudes.
➤ Exclusion from positions of power.
➤ Owning far less land and property.
➤ Having less control over their lives.
➤ Forced marriage and marriage at a very early age ('child brides').
➤ More violence – this includes traditional practices such as female genital mutilation.
➤ Aid benefits men more than women – e.g. agricultural training programmes are offered more to men than to women, because it is assumed that men are more suited to technical and scientific training.

Steps towards improving women's position

➤ The promotion of gender equality is now widely recognised by feminists, the UN, IGOs, INGOs and global social movements as a central issue in development – e.g. the UN's Human Development Report includes a Gender Inequality Index.
➤ The Millennium Development Goals of 2000–15, and the Sustainable Development Goals of 2015–30 which replaced them, include the promotion of gender equality, the empowerment of women, better educational opportunities for women, and improvements in maternal health, and reductions in maternal and infant mortality.
➤ Microcredit schemes offered by banks and INGOs have also been targeted at women, providing small loans (microloans) to enable them to access resources, to empower them and improve their lives.

Gender and the effects of globalisation

➤ *Emigration* – Ehrenreich and Hochschild describe how millions of women leave LEDCs each year to work as nannies, maids and sex workers in MEDCs.
➤ *Risks of trafficking* – Globalisation and transnational criminal networks have led to an increase in trafficking of women and girls from LEDCs, for cheap labour and the Western sex industries – often in conditions of modern slavery.
➤ *Backlashes* – Globalisation has produced a backlash in which supposedly traditional values and practices are reasserted, e.g. by Islamic fundamentalists who associate women's rights and education with Western values.
➤ *Exploitation by TNCs* – It is mainly women who work in the sweatshops producing goods for sale by TNCs in Western consumer markets.

Applying the theories

➤ *Modernisation and dependency theories* developed before second-wave feminism in the 1960s and 1970s. They had little to say about gender issues. Both can be seen as part of the 'malestream' sociology of that time.

➤ *Modernisation theory* was closely associated with the sociological perspective of functionalism, which saw the modern family at that time as the patriarchal nuclear family, where women played expressive roles in the home, while men played instrumental roles as family breadwinners.

➤ *Dependency theory* focused on relationships between countries rather than social groups, and both here and in world systems theory there is little discussion of women.

➤ *More recent feminist theories* have placed much greater emphasis on women's role in development. Their importance has been recognised in challenging and modernising traditional patriarchal values and male power, which act as obstacles to development.

➤ *Socialist feminists* emphasise new form of exploitation of women arising from the global spread of capitalism. Companies pay little and treat female workers poorly. Training and job security are rarely provided. Often, in patriarchal societies, the money goes straight to a man.

EXAM TIP:

In appropriate questions on gender and development, you should refer to the various disadvantages women face in the development process – e.g. in education, health, allocation of aid, traditional values, etc. You can analyse/evaluate these by referring to the ways things are changing, e.g. in sociological theories, and by the extent to which NGOs and IGOs are now recognising gender as a significant element in the development process.

GENERAL EXAM TIP:

Remember that two out of the three exam questions on Global Development involve an Item to refer to. You *must* refer to that Item to achieve top-band marks. For 10-mark ('Applying material from Item K, analyse two') questions, you must refer *only* to ideas or issues that are raised in the Item. For 20-mark ('Applying material from Item L, and your knowledge, evaluate') questions, you must refer to the Item and your knowledge gained elsewhere in your studies of Global Development. Remember the Item is there to help and guide you, so use it.

By the time you go into the exam, you should know all the material on page 173, and the key terms listed on page 174 of the textbook. Knowing the key terms and using them correctly will help you gain marks for knowledge and understanding. You can check their meaning on-the-go by going to the online glossary by following the link at www. politybooks.com/browne. Put it on your phone for ready reference.

4
THE MEDIA

TOPIC 1
The relationship between ownership and control of the media (pages 179–190)

Traditional and new media (pages 179–180)

➤ 'Traditional media' refers to mass media that communicate uniform messages in a one-way, non-interactive process to very large mass audiences, e.g. traditional radio and TV broadcasting, and print newspapers.
➤ 'New media' refers to *interactive* digital technology and media products, and social media, which enable people to create, share and exchange information and develop social networks.
➤ The distinction between traditional and new media is becoming blurred as mass media companies are increasingly using new media, including social media.

Formal controls on the media (pages 181–182)

➤ *The law* – e.g. libel laws, laws against inciting religious or racial hatred.
➤ *Ofcom* (the Office of Communications) – the official media regulator.
➤ *The BBC Trust*, together with Ofcom, regulates the BBC, and seeks to ensure the BBC remains independent of any pressure and influence from any source.
➤ *The Independent Press Standards Organisation* (IPSO) monitors standards of journalism in newspapers and magazines – e.g. issues such as accuracy and invasion of privacy.

How governments influence and control media output (pages 182–183)

➤ By official government press conferences and briefings of journalists.
➤ Leaks and off-the-record briefings to journalists.
➤ The use of government spin doctors, who try to manipulate the media and news stories.
➤ Refusal to issue broadcasting licences to those whom it deems are unfit and unsuitable.
➤ The use of filtering and surveillance software to block access to some internet sites.
➤ Electronic surveillance of emails, monitoring of websites and intercepts of mobile calls.

Ownership of the media (pages 183–186)

Features of media ownership

Bagdikian highlighted that a handful of global media companies and moguls – what he called 'Lords of the Global Village' – dominated the world's mass media. The features of media ownership include:

➤ *Concentration of ownership* of all kinds of media in the hands of a few very large companies.
➤ *Vertical integration* – ownership of all aspects of a single medium, e.g. a film production company that also owns the cinema chains showing the films.
➤ *Horizontal integration* – media owners have interests in a range of media.
➤ *Diversification* – media companies have interests in a wide variety of products besides the media, e.g. Virgin media, trains, airline, bank, etc.
➤ *Global conglomeration* – owners have global media empires.
➤ *Synergy* – media companies package and sell their products in different forms to mutually promote sales and maximise profits, e.g. a film may also involve a book, a music CD or download, a computer game, toys, etc.
➤ *Technological convergence* – several media technologies are combined in a single device, e.g. a smartphone used to make calls, text, watch films, surf the web, play games, listen to music, read books, take photos, etc.

Bagdikian suggests this raises three questions:
1. Are the media simply spreading a limited number of dominant ideas (the dominant ideology) that protect the interests of the dominant class in society?
2. Do the owners of the media control the content of the media?
3. What effects do the media have on the audiences they aim at?

Ideology, control of the media, and media content (pages 186–191)

The manipulative or instrumentalist approach to media content

This is a traditional Marxist approach, adopted by writers like Miliband. This suggests that:

➤ Media owners directly influence media content, and manipulate it to protect their interests and spread the dominant ideology. For Marxists, the media promote incomplete and distorted 'preferred readings' of news stories which the ruling class would like audiences to believe.
➤ Editors, managers and journalists have little choice other than to operate within the boundaries set down by the owners as they depend on them for their jobs.
➤ Media audiences are fed on a dumbed-down mass diet of undemanding, trivial and uncritical content, which stops them focusing on and challenging serious issues.
➤ The Leveson Inquiry in 2012 uncovered a range of links between media owners and governments, with media support given to political parties in return for government policies favourable to the interests of media owners.

Evaluation of the manipulative/instrumentalist approach

➤ It assumes media audiences are passive and easily manipulated.

➤ Pluralists argue there is a wide range of opinion in the media. The media's owners are primarily concerned with making profits. This means attracting large audiences to gain advertisers, and the only means of doing this is to provide what the audiences – not the owners – want.

➤ The state regulates media ownership so no one person or company has too much influence.

➤ Pluralists and neophiliacs (optimists who welcome and embrace new media) suggest the rise of interactive digital media and of citizen journalism has undermined the ability of media owners to control media content.

The dominant ideology or hegemonic approach to media content

This is a neo-Marxist approach, associated with the work of the Glasgow Media Group (GMG). This suggests that:

➤ Mass media spread a dominant ideology legitimising the power of the ruling class.

➤ The media present the values and beliefs of the dominant ideology as reasonable and normal, and form a consensus around them. This ensures what Gramsci called the 'hegemony' or dominance in society of ruling-class ideology, so ruling-class ideas become part of everyday common sense. Ideas or behaviour outside the established consensus are presented as not to be taken seriously.

➤ Media managers and journalists have some professional independence from owners, but still generally choose to support the dominant ideology. This is because they are predominantly white, middle-class and male, and thus act in keeping with the dominant ideology.

➤ The GMG suggests that the media act in two related ways to protect the dominant ideology:
  ⮕ *By gatekeeping* – deliberately and routinely excluding reports on some issues.
  ⮕ *By agenda-setting* – encouraging audiences to think about some events/issues rather than others.

➤ Media managers and journalists also need to attract audiences and advertisers if they are to produce profits for the owners. This means that sometimes journalists develop critical, anti-establishment views to attract audiences. This also helps to maintain the illusion that routine media content is generally objective and unbiased.

Evaluation of the dominant ideology or hegemonic approach

➤ It underrates the power and influence of the owners – owners do appoint and dismiss editors who step too far out of line, and journalists' careers are dependent on gaining approval of their stories from editors.

➤ Agenda-setting and gatekeeping suggest a direct manipulation of audiences more in keeping with the manipulative or instrumentalist approach.

➤ Pluralists suggest the rise of the new globalised interactive digital media and citizen journalism has undermined the traditional influence of media owners and journalists, and put more control into the hands of media users.

The pluralist approach to media content

➤ Media content is driven by the fight for profits through high circulation and audience figures. The only control over media content is consumer choice.

➤ There is a wide diversity of competing media, catering for a huge range of audience interests and ideas.

➤ Competition for audiences prevents any one owner or company from dominating the media, and media regulators, like Ofcom, also act to prevent this happening.

➤ The media are generally free of any government or direct owner control. Journalists have some professional honesty and independence, and have to work to satisfy and maintain their audiences.

➤ Audiences are not passive; they can choose whatever interpretation suits them, and can accept, reject, reinterpret or ignore media content in accordance with their own tastes and beliefs.

➤ The new globalised digital media, including social media, enable all sorts of views to be represented through citizen journalism. Media owners and their journalists no longer have a monopoly on media content.

Evaluation of the pluralist approach

➤ While managers, journalists and television producers have some independence, they work within constraints placed on them by the owners. They cannot always simply respond to audience wishes.

➤ Even if they have some professional independence, the main sources of information for journalists tend to be the most powerful and influential members of society, who are most likely to be interviewed on TV, appear on chat shows, be quoted in newspapers, etc.

➤ Only very rich groups have the resources required to launch major media to get their views across independently of the media corporations and established journalists.

➤ The pressure to attract audiences actually *limits* media choice. Curran, and Barnett and Seymour, found media competition for audiences leads to a 'race to the bottom' – media content becomes unchallenging and bland (e.g. tabloidisation, 'infotainment').

➤ Hegemonic theorists argue that people have been socialised by the media. The media themselves may have created their tastes, so that what audiences want is really what the media owners want.

EXAM TIPS:

➤ In questions on media ownership and control of media content, evaluate one approach, e.g. Marxist manipulative approach, using and contrasting the other approaches, e.g. neo-Marxist and pluralist.

➤ To show you can apply the theories (and gain marks for application), always try to give examples drawn from recent media reports.

TOPIC 2
The media, globalisation and popular culture (pages 192–200)

Globalisation and the media (page 192)

➤ Globalisation means societies across the world have become more interconnected.
➤ Media corporations now operate on a global scale and own media across the world.
➤ Electronic media shrink barriers of space and time so that the world has become like what McLuhan referred to as a 'global village'.

Popular culture (pages 192–194)

➤ The large media corporations produce cultural products designed to be sold on the global mass market to make profits. The media are now spreading a mass culture on a global scale.
➤ This has led to a growing globalisation of popular culture: people in many countries of the world are now exposed to the same cultural products and media content.

Postmodernists argue . . .
➤ The global reach of contemporary media and the huge expansion of the media-based creative industries have made a huge range of media and cultural products available to everyone.
➤ Strinati argues this has made the distinction between high and popular culture meaningless: high culture is no longer the preserve of cultural elites, and people now have a wide diversity of cultural choices and products available to them and can pick 'n' mix from either popular or high culture.
➤ The media have transformed popular culture into high culture and high culture has been transformed into popular culture.
➤ Strinati rejects the suggestion that there is a single mass culture which people passively and uncritically consume, as suggested by Marxists, and points to a wide diversity and choice within popular culture, which people select from and critically respond to.

Marxists, and critical theorists of the Frankfurt School, argue . . .
➤ Global media businesses produce media products which are imposed on the masses for financial profit.
➤ Popular mass culture is a form of social control, giving an illusion of choice between a range of similar dumbed-down, standardised, trivial and uncritical media infotainment and escapist fantasy.
➤ This lulls consumers into an uncritical, undemanding passivity, making them less likely to challenge the dominant ideas, groups and interests in society.
➤ Marcuse suggested consumption of media-generated mass culture undermined people's ability to think critically about the world and the potential for revolutionary action to change society. Livingstone disagreed with the Marxist view. She argued there is much in popular culture that educates and informs the public about important or controversial social issues, and generates, rather than kills off public debate.

Global popular culture (pages 195–198)

➤ Flew suggests that globalisation and the evolution of new media technologies have played an important role in the development of a global popular culture.
➤ Sklair suggests powerful global media corporations, largely American-based, spread the same news, information, entertainment, consumer and cultural products to a global market. These have become part of the ways of life of many different countries. This encourages acceptance of the dominant ideology of Western capitalist societies, which Sklair calls the 'culture-ideology of consumerism'.
➤ Globalised media content and advertising have undermined national and local cultures. The process of cultural homogenisation means that what were once separate cultures become blended into one uniform culture.

The Marxist view of the media and the globalisation of popular culture

➤ Globalisation of popular culture benefits media owners, who gain colossal profits from exporting and advertising their products across the globe.
➤ Thussu argues that the globalisation of television and competition between media conglomerates for audiences and advertising have led to TV news across the world becoming more like 'global infotainment'. An emphasis on celebrities, crime, corruption and violence has replaced serious reporting of public affairs.
➤ This US-style infotainment is accompanied by the promotion of a false global 'feel-good factor' based on Western, and particularly US, consumerist lifestyles.
➤ This process of creating a globalised popular culture diverts people's attention away from more serious issues, and makes them less likely to challenge the dominant ideas and groups and interests in society, and encourages those from non-Western cultures to accept Western values and culture as superior to their own.

Cultural and media imperialism

➤ Marxists suggest that the domination of Western culture and values over non-Western cultures is a process of cultural and media imperialism. This is because Western culture undermines local cultures and cultural independence.
➤ Media imperialism has moved the world's cultures towards a global cultural homogenisation, in which the media-saturated global village is largely a North American and Western one.

The pluralist view of the media and the globalisation of popular culture

Pluralists reject the Marxist view.

➤ The global reach of modern media technology offers a huge range of media products. This gives consumers across the world a wide diversity of cultural choices.
➤ Compaine argues that global competition is expanding sources of information and entertainment, rather than restricting them or dumbing them down.
➤ Tomlinson argues that globalisation does not involve direct cultural imposition from the Western world, but that there is a hybridisation or mixing of cultures. People pick 'n' mix and draw on both Western/global cultures and their own 'glocalised' local cultures. This means there is more, not less, cultural diversity in the world.

➤ The flow of cultures is not necessarily only from the West – e.g. Bollywood-style media productions have spread from East to West.

➤ New media technology enables consumers to create and distribute their own media products, and to generate their own popular culture, rather than being the passive victims of Western media conglomerates.

➤ Rather than people being doped into passivity, as some Marxists argue, consumers and audiences now have more choices and knowledge available to them than ever before in history. This makes it ever more difficult for any one set of ideas or culture to dominate in the world.

The postmodernist view of the media (pages 198–200)

➤ Society is now what Baudrillard called media-saturated, meaning our view of the world is created and defined by the media.

➤ Media images are what Baudrillard called 'simulacra' – reproductions and copies which appear to be showing real events, but have no connection with those real events. The replacement of reality by simulacra creates a hyperreality – a view of the world which is created and defined by the media. The image of an event becomes more real than the event it is meant to be depicting.

➤ The media no longer reflect reality but actively create a hyperreality, leaving audiences confused about what is real and what is media-created.

➤ Strinati emphasises the importance and power of the globalised media in forming our sense of reality, shaping consumer choices, and dominating the way we form our personal identities.

➤ Globalised media have brought to the world's population greater awareness and access to a diversity of cultures for shaping their own identities and lifestyles.

Criticisms of postmodernist and pluralist views of the media (page 199)

➤ Postmodernist views assume that people are passively submerged in media hyperreality; they do not allow for the fact they can discuss, interpret, ignore or reject media imagery and messages.

➤ Media images and representations of gender, age, ethnicity, disability and so on do not open up new choices of identity and lifestyle, but simply present and reinforce stereotypes.

➤ Many people, particularly in the poorest social groups and the poorest countries of the world, simply do not have access to new media or cannot afford to embrace the opportunities and choices offered.

➤ Marxists emphasise the myth of choice alleged by postmodernists and pluralists. Transnational media conglomerates control the major media and forms of communication and influence.

EXAM TIPS:

➤ In a question on the media and popular culture/globalisation, remember there is a debate between Marxists who emphasise cultural imperialism – a negative view; pluralists who emphasise cultural diversity and hybridity – a positive view; and postmodernists who focus on globalised cultures and wider identity choices, but also on media imagery and hyperreality distorting the world – a sort of ambiguous third position. Evaluate any one of these approaches by reference to the others.

➤ Always remember to give contemporary examples to show you can apply your theories, and give a firm conclusion based on your arguments and linking it back to the question.

TOPIC 3

The processes of selection and presentation of the content of the news (pages 201–213)

The social construction of the news (page 201)

➤ Media news is manufactured and packaged like any other consumer product.

➤ The GMG (Glasgow Media Group) has shown that the selection and presentation of media news stories is not a neutral process. The selection, production and packaging of the news are influenced by a range of practical, social and political factors. These are summarised in figure 1.

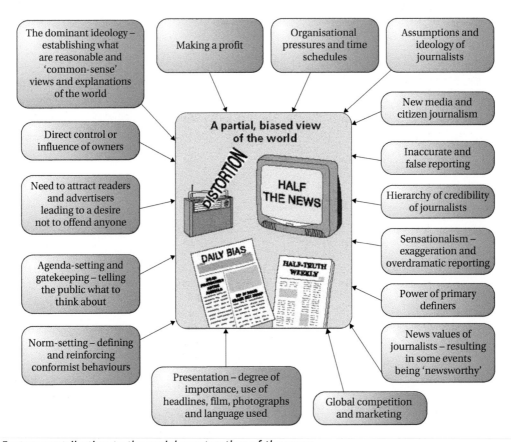

Figure 1 *Factors contributing to the social construction of the news*

The influence of owners (page 201)

➤ Owners occasionally give direct instructions to news editors.
➤ The owners, via editors, influence the resources made available to cover news stories.
➤ Journalists, and particularly editors, depend for their careers on not upsetting the owners.
➤ The owners are concerned with making profits, and this depends on attracting large audiences. In an increasingly competitive global media environment, this often means news is turned into unthreatening, unchallenging, inoffensive and bland 'infotainment'. Media owners may thus encourage this sort of media output.

Making a profit (page 202)

➤ In a highly competitive global media market, Bagdikian suggests that news reports will try to avoid offending advertisers, with some stories repressed or killed off altogether, as Curran, and Barnett and Seymour, found.
➤ It is important to appeal to a wide variety of audience tastes. Minority or unpopular points of view are unreported or ridiculed; serious hard news journalism is 'dumbed down'; news is sensationalised and popularised by tabloidisation, and transformed into infotainment.
➤ Profit motives often mean the media adopt a very conservative, uncritical approach to the news. Marxists argue this helps to maintain the hegemony of the dominant ideas in society.

Globalisation, new technology and citizen journalism (pages 202–203)

➤ In the competitive global market, news providers need to compete to survive. It is therefore crucial for media companies to be right up-to-date, appeal to audiences, and diversify how they present their news.
➤ New technology means news is instantly available from practically anywhere in the world twenty-four hours per day. The mainstream media news organisations can no longer rely only on their TV news bulletins or their daily newspapers to attract audiences, as people are now tweeting, texting and surfing the web for news that interests them.
➤ Citizen journalists now have greater opportunities to shape mainstream news – e.g. by spreading news stories and information via Facebook, Twitter or YouTube.
➤ Bivens suggests such grassroots alternative sources of news and information can help to overcome or bypass suppression of stories, or biased or inadequate news reports, in established media.
➤ Citizen journalism also suits the mainstream news media's own needs, as they can obtain news items and supporting video cheaply, compared to sending out their own reporters and news cameras.

Practical and organisational constraints (pages 203–204)

➤ People now expect to be able to access up-to-date news at all times and wherever they happen to be – e.g. through their phones, tablets and laptops.
➤ The intensity of news has changed, with news breaking rapidly on social media like Twitter. Mainstream news media must respond to this changed situation if they want to attract audiences.

➤ Competition means journalists have to work within very tight time schedules to meet ever-shortening deadlines which means taking shortcuts in news gathering; getting a news story first becomes more important than getting it right; more churnalism and less journalism.

Agenda-setting, gatekeeping and norm-setting (pages 204–205)

Agenda-setting
➤ Journalists and editors lay down the list of subjects, or agenda, for public discussion when they select which items to include, and which to exclude, when reporting the news.
➤ Those who own, control and work in the media have a great deal of power in society, as the news media are in a position to tell audiences what issues to think about.
➤ The GMG suggests agenda-setting supports the spread of the dominant ideology.
➤ The desire of media organisations to make money, to attract large audiences and hence advertising, and the organisational pressures generated by rolling news in the framework of global competition, mean that some news items are more likely to be ignored or treated less favourably than others, for fear of offending owners, audiences and advertisers.

Gatekeeping
➤ The media's power to refuse to cover some issues and to let others through is called gatekeeping.
➤ The GMG suggested owners, editors and journalists frequently exclude items because they are damaging to the values and interests of the dominant social class.
➤ Sometimes the media do not cover issues because journalists and editors think they lack interest for readers and viewers, or because of practical constraints.

Norm-setting
McCombs suggests that the news media now increasingly tell us not only *what* to think about, but also *how* to think about certain subjects, emphasising and reinforcing conformity to social norms. Norm-setting is achieved in two main ways:
➤ *Encouraging conformist behaviour* by positive media reports – e.g. not going on strike, obeying the law, conforming to gender stereotypes, etc.
➤ *Discouraging non-conformist behaviour*, by seeking to isolate those who do not conform by making them the victims of unfavourable media reports – e.g. by giving extensive sensational and negative treatment to stories about crime, murder, riots, benefit fraud, illegal immigrants, etc.

Presentation of the news (page 206)

The way news items are presented may be important in influencing how people view stories:
➤ The physical position of a news story on a website or in a newspaper; the order of importance given to stories in TV news bulletins; the choice of headlines; whether there is accompanying film or photographs.
➤ The images selected and how they represent the people involved.
➤ The use of emotive language.

Inaccurate or misleading reporting and moral panics (pages 206–207)

➤ Inaccurate reporting may arise because of the organisational pressures on time so stories aren't properly checked and verified.

➤ False reporting and the media's tendency to exaggerate and dramatise events are devices used to make a story more interesting to attract audiences.

➤ False, inaccurate or exaggerated and sensationalised reporting can sometimes generate a moral panic (Stan Cohen) – a wave of public concern and anxiety about some exaggerated or imaginary threat to society.

➤ Moral panics show the media's power to define what is normal and what is deviant, unacceptable behaviour, and to reinforce a consensus around the core values of the dominant ideology, while at the same time making money through attracting audiences.

➤ Exaggerated, sensationalised and distorted reporting can lead to deviancy amplification – actually creating or making worse the very deviance the media condemn.

➤ McRobbie and Thornton suggest that media-generated moral panics are now becoming less common. New media practices mean most events have such short shelf-lives in sustaining audience interest that they are unlikely to be newsworthy for long enough to become a moral panic.

➤ Pluralists and postmodernists argue there is now such a huge diversity of media reports and interpretations of events (including citizen journalism) that people are now much more sceptical of mainstream media interpretations and less likely to believe them.

News values (pages 207–210)

➤ Galtung and Ruge showed that journalists operate with values and assumptions – called news values – that guide them in deciding which events are newsworthy enough to attract audiences.

➤ Some news values: unambiguity; unexpectedness; negativity; meaningfulness; personalisation.

Journalists construct the news in other ways too . . . (pages 210–211)

➤ The GMG has pointed out that journalists tend to be mainly white, male and middle-class, and they broadly share the interests and values of the dominant ideology.

➤ *Hierarchy of credibility* – Becker suggested journalists attach the greatest importance and credibility to the views of powerful and influential individuals and groups ('primary definers') rather than ordinary people.

➤ Manning suggests journalists are under increasing pressure from market competition to use primary definers as a cheap and readily available source of news.

➤ Journalists tend to be somewhere in the moderate centre ground of politics, and so ignore or treat unfavourably what they regard as 'extremist' or 'radical' views.

➤ To reduce time and costs, journalists often produce articles based on information provided by news agencies, government press releases, spin doctors, public relations consultants and so on, without checking facts or digging out the news themselves. This has been described as 'churnalism'.

Is media news just propaganda? (pages 211–212)

Marxists argue . . .

➤ The social construction of the news means it gives only a partial and biased view of the world.

➤ What counts as 'the news' is a manufactured product that reflects the interests of powerful groups, and is produced within a framework of the dominant ideology.

➤ Herman and Chomsky regard media news as little more than a propaganda system for the elite interests which shape and control it.

➤ Ownership and control, market forces, the media's profit orientation, and dependence on advertisers influence what journalists do, what they see as newsworthy and the ideas they take for granted as they do their work.

Pluralists and postmodernists disagree with the Marxist view . . .

➤ Media competition means the news contains a diversity of views, so there is no consistent bias in favour of any particular ideology.

➤ Media competition and the need to attract audiences mean that journalists do occasionally expose injustice, or corruption in government and business, and therefore are not always or simply in the pockets of the powerful.

➤ Agenda-setting, gatekeeping and news values reflect audience choices, not journalists' choices.

➤ The rise of the new media and citizen journalism has begun to undermine the power of the mainstream media organisations, and enables alternative views to those of the media establishment being made available to millions of people across the globe.

➤ Postmodernists might argue all news is just socially constructed hyperreality, so none of it bears much relation to reality anyway.

> **EXAM TIPS:**
>
> ➤ In any question on the social construction or selection and presentation of the news, the role of journalists, etc., try to refer to as many (relevant) factors as you can.
> ➤ Evaluate them using other factors – e.g. practical constraints are more significant than ideological factors; news values reflect audience choices and market forces, not journalists' manipulation or the imposition of the dominant ideology.
> ➤ Work competing Marxist/pluralist/postmodernist theories into your answer.
> ➤ Remember to give contemporary examples from news reports to show you can apply your theories and arguments.
> ➤ Give a firm conclusion/overall judgement based on your arguments, and link it explicitly back to the issue posed and wording in the question.

TOPIC 4

Media representations of age, social class, ethnicity, gender, sexuality and disability (pages 214–239)

Media representations and stereotyping (pages 214–215)

➤ Media representations often conform to and create stereotypes – generalised, oversimplified views of the features of a social group.

➤ The GMG argues that media representations and stereotypes are formed within the context of the dominant ideology of society and generally reinforce it.

➤ Media representations are part of the media gaze – the way the media establishment views society and represents it in media content.

➤ The media gaze is generally from the perspective of the predominantly male, able-bodied white upper and middle class who own and control the media, and produce media content.

➤ A feature of the media gaze is what Gerbner and Gross, and Tuchman, called 'symbolic annihilation': some groups are omitted, under-represented, condemned or trivialised in the media, or only appear in a limited number of stereotyped roles.

➤ Gauntlett cautions that there is a diversity of media, a diversity of representations and a diversity of audiences, and it therefore can't be assumed media representations will either be consistent or have the same – or any – effects on audiences.

EXAM TIPS:

➤ When answering questions on media representations of particular social groups, try to avoid just repeating media stereotypes. Achieve some balance and evaluation by recognising how and why changes and improvements are occurring alongside traditional representations.

➤ Apply theories, and use terminology – e.g. symbolic annihilation; stereotype; media gaze.

➤ A useful opening paragraph is to expand and explain the issue raised in the question, including any specific terms that are used there – e.g. stereotypes.

Media representations of age (pages 215–217)

Representations of children

➤ Children (up to the age of about 14) are generally represented in a positive way – e.g. cute, brilliant, little angels (little devils in sitcoms).

➤ They are often represented as consumers of toys and games in advertising; as accessories to enhance their parents' image; and as symbols representing innocence.

Representations of youth

➤ Youth (from around age 15 to the early 20s) are often the subject of negative media stereotyping as a problem group.

➤ They are often represented in the context of crime and deviance. Such images are typically associated with young working-class males, with an over-representation of young Black Caribbean males.

➤ They are often labelled as folk devils and used as scapegoats in the media for social problems, creating moral panics.

➤ Young people are major users of new media. Negative stereotypes in the mainstream media may increasingly be combated by young people themselves by texting, tweeting, YouTube and the other devices of citizen journalism. This means that mainstream media organisations may over time be forced to change their traditional media stereotypes of young people.

Representations of older people

➤ Older people – say in their late 50s onwards – are often either largely invisible in the media, or presented in quite negative ways. Typical stereotypes include: figures of fun; being forgetful and difficult; in ill-health; being a burden, and stubborn and grumpy.

➤ Stereotypes are often more positive for older men than women.

➤ The growing numbers of older people in the population with money to spend – the 'grey pound' – mean we might expect more positive images of ageing to emerge as media conglomerates pursue the growing older people's market.

> **EXAM TIP:**
>
> When you get a question on media representations or stereotyping of age, include the differences between age groups, explain why these stereotypes exist and why they might be changing.

Media representations of social class (pages 217–221)

➤ The mainstream media gaze results in:
  ⮕ More favourable stereotypes of the upper and middle classes than the working class or the poor.
  ⮕ An over-representation of the upper and middle classes and an under-representation of the working class.
  ⮕ The portrayal of the working class in a more restricted range of roles than the middle class.

➤ Jones suggests the media give the impression that the values and lifestyles of the middle class are the norm; the working class and the poor/underclass are presented as in some ways abnormal/deviant and/or as figures of fun.

➤ Media news values mean the rich and famous are more newsworthy than similar stories about working-class people. The poor only become newsworthy when they are used to highlight the individual failings of undeserving people – e.g. as benefit 'scroungers' or as criminals.

➤ The neo-Marxist GMG points out there is little media content that explicitly discusses class privilege, class inequality and power differences.

Representations of the working class
- The working class and the poor are typically stereotyped in negative ways.
- Neo-Marxists like the GMG see such negative representations as the media acting against groups which challenge or don't conform to the dominant ideology.
- The working class is often presented most positively in the stereotypical and romanticised context of traditional working-class close-knit communities.
- Jones suggests the dominant media representation of the working class today is the demeaning and hostile 'chav' stereotype, which merges the working class with the poor. Shildrick argues this reinforces the popular impression that the poor are poor because of their own failings – the 'undeserving poor' – and neutralises any public sympathy for their plight.
- Lawler suggests media representations of the working class provide one way for the middle class to secure and maintain its identity, through a sense of its own superiority over white working-class culture.
- Such representations of the working class reinforce the cultural hegemony of the dominant class and a perception of the normality of middle-class life.

Representations of the middle class
- The middle class and its lifestyles receive the greatest exposure in the media, and representations are generally positive.
- Middle-class tastes and lifestyle are presented in drama, sitcoms, advertising, magazines and newspapers as the norm to which everyone should aspire.
- Such positive representations confirm and promote the dominant ideology and help to legitimise the existing class structure and class inequalities.

Representations of the upper class
- The upper class is generally presented as being 'well bred', cultured and superior.
- The lavish lifestyles of the upper class often provide media content for mass audiences.
- *Pluralists* see such media representations as simply providing what media audiences want.
- *Neo-Marxists* like the GMG see such representations as a celebration of hierarchy and wealth which promotes the dominant ideology.

> **EXAM TIP:**
>
> When you get a question on media representations or stereotyping of social class, include some references to the different social classes, explain what these stereotypes are, and why they exist. Give examples from contemporary media.

Media representations of ethnicity (pages 221–226)

- Neo-Marxists like the GMG point to the way representations of Black and Minority Ethnic (BME) groups are filtered through the gaze – what Stuart Hall called 'the white eye' – of a predominantly white middle-class-dominated media establishment.
- BME interests and representations feature mostly in specialised programmes on minority group issues.
- BME groups have been under-represented in heavyweight roles, such as those of political commentators or experts, or in subjects of a serious nature.

Media stereotypes of ethnicity

➤ BME people are frequently used as scapegoats for social problems, and portrayed in negative stereotypes such as: criminals; threats to British culture; causes of social problems, conflict and trouble; lacking in skills.
➤ Negative media stereotyping in recent years has also been applied to white people from Eastern Europe. These groups have been (wrongly) blamed by the media for virtually every problem that has beset Britain.

Explanations for stereotyping of ethnicity

➤ Pluralists argue media representations of ethnic minorities reflect the news values of journalists, who are providing what media audiences want.
➤ Cottle suggests that media stereotypes of ethnicity enable majority white audiences to construct and secure their identity by defining themselves – 'us' – as different from and superior to BME groups – 'them'.
➤ Neo-Marxists like the GMG argue negative media stereotypes are the result of a predominantly white media establishment, ideology and news values. Media stereotyping and scapegoating of BME groups reassert and reaffirm ruling-class hegemony in society generally by:
  ⮞ Fuelling racism.
  ⮞ Dividing the working class.
  ⮞ Diverting attention away from the structure of inequality in society.
  ⮞ Reinforcing the hegemony of the dominant white ideology and culture.

Changing stereotypes of ethnicity?

➤ There is a growing acceptance in the media of BME groups as a mainstream part of British society.
➤ There are more black and Asian figures appearing in music, arts, TV dramas and soaps, and as TV presenters.
➤ BME groups have more access via new media, and satellite and cable TV, to programmes relevant to them. This puts pressure on mainstream media organisations to be more responsive to their needs to retain media audiences and advertising revenue.
➤ Young people from BME groups are greater users of the new media than the average in the UK, enabling them to counter negative ethnic stereotypes and reports in mainstream media.

EXAM TIPS:

➤ In questions on ethnicity and the media, include what the stereotypes are – it's also worth mentioning the way negative stereotyping is also being applied to white migrants from Eastern Europe.
➤ Show application by drawing on contemporary examples – e.g. the media treatment of refugees and asylum seekers.
➤ Include reasons why these stereotypes might exist (including theories like neo-Marxism and pluralism) and what effects they might have on media audiences.
➤ Evaluate by some discussion of how and why stereotypes might be changing.
➤ Always give a conclusion, summing up your response to the specific issue raised in the question – a useful device is to use the same wording as used in the question.

Media representations of gender (pages 226–233)

➤ Neo-Marxists like the GMG, and feminists, argue that representations of gender are filtered through the media gaze of a predominantly male-dominated media establishment.
➤ Mulvey argued that media representations of women reflected the male gaze, whereby women are portrayed as sexual objects for men's satisfaction.
➤ Feminists suggest the media tend to be patriarchal and spread a patriarchal ideology.
➤ Tuchman argued women face symbolic annihilation in the media – by being omitted altogether, or under-represented, or represented in a limited range of stereotyped roles.

The media and the social construction of gender differences

➤ Connell argues that gender identities are in part constructed by the media reproducing culturally dominant stereotypes of men and women ('hegemonic masculinity' and 'hegemonic femininity').
➤ The media create and reinforce these hegemonic gender stereotypes through advertising.

Female stereotypes

Women are portrayed:

➤ More in the private sphere of the home than in the public world of the workplace and the street.
➤ In a narrow range of gender-specific roles.
➤ As emotional and unpredictable.
➤ As WAGs – the wives and girlfriends of men.
➤ As sex objects – part of what Naomi Wolf calls the 'beauty myth' – thin, pretty and sexually attractive to men.
➤ As home-makers and mothers.
➤ As ball breakers – a negative stereotype of sexually active, selfish, independent and ambitious career-minded women who don't depend on men.

Male stereotypes

Men are portrayed:

➤ More in the public sphere outside the home.
➤ In a wide range of roles, often carrying higher status than women's.
➤ As jokers – who use laughter to avoid displaying seriousness or emotion.
➤ As jocks – who show aggression to demonstrate power and strength.
➤ As strong silent types – who are in control, act decisively, and avoid weakness by not talking about their feelings or showing emotion.
➤ As big shots – who are economically and socially successful.
➤ As action heroes – who are tough, strong and show extreme aggression and often violence.
➤ As buffoons – who are totally inept at parenting or housework.

Theoretical explanations for media gender stereotyping

➤ *Pluralists* – Stereotyping occurs because that is what media audiences want.
➤ *Liberal feminists* – Stereotyping occurs because of the under-representation of women and lack of equal opportunities in male-dominated media organisations. Stereotyping will diminish as women break through the glass ceiling in media organisations.
➤ *Marxists and Marxist feminists* – Stereotyping is driven by patriarchal ideology, and the need for media organisations to make profits, by attracting advertisers who use stereotypes to sell their products.
➤ *Radical feminists* – Stereotyping occurs because society is patriarchal. Media-generated stereotypes of femininity discourage women from making the most of the opportunities available to them, and undermine any threat to male dominance in society.

Changing representations of gender

➤ McRobbie argues that a new form of popular feminism – 'girl power' – has emerged, shown in young (pre-teen and teenage) women's magazines and websites. These promote female assertiveness, self-confidence, independence and ambition.
➤ Inness found women were being presented more in TV dramas and films as powerful 'tough girls', and 'action heroes', taking on roles that were once the preserve of men.
➤ Gauntlett suggests that the media are providing a wider range of representations of masculinity beyond traditional hegemonic masculinity.
➤ The use of male bodies as sex objects in advertising, in much the same way that women's bodies have always been used.
➤ Men's magazines are also covering concerns that were once restricted to women – e.g. diet, health and cosmetics.

Explaining changing representations

➤ McRobbie suggests that, in postmodern society, there is much more fluidity and flexibility in gender identities, weakening traditional stereotypes.
➤ The changing position of women in society and their growing success in education and the job market have created a growing social expectation that women and men should be treated equally. This has made traditional stereotypes seem outdated.
➤ The growth in the presence and influence of women in media management and production.
➤ The power of advertisers, who are tapping into a new lucrative men's market for consumer cosmetics.
➤ The need of media organisations to retain advertising revenue and profits by attracting a changing media audience, particularly among women, for whom traditional patriarchal stereotypes have diminishing relevance to their lives.

But don't forget the limits of these changes when evaluating . . .

➤ Gender stereotypes still thrive in the media.
➤ New media technology has led to the exploitation of women as sex objects and as victims of sexual violence more extensively than ever.

EXAM TIPS:

➤ When tackling a question on gender and the media, stay focused on the question, but you don't have to agree with a particular view that the question suggests, as long as you give good arguments and evidence for not doing so.
➤ Apply your arguments, explanations and theories to both female and male representations (unless the question only specifies one of them), and illustrate them with examples.
➤ Evaluate by criticising different theories and explanations, and by considering to what extent stereotypes are changing or disappearing.
➤ Reach a conclusion and overall judgement based on your evidence and arguments, linking it back to the wording of the question.

Media representations of sexuality (pages 233–235)

Representations of heterosexuality
➤ Heterosexuality has been the dominant view of 'normal sexuality' within hegemonic masculine and feminine stereotypes.
➤ Women's sexuality in the media has been defined largely by their physical attractiveness and sexual appeal to men.
➤ Men are also becoming represented more as sexualised objects in much the same way as women.
➤ A new 'metrosexual' male stereotype has emerged in the media – heterosexual men who embrace their feminine side, are fashion-conscious, use skincare products, etc.

Representations of homosexuality
➤ The media are controlled by middle-class white, predominantly heterosexual, men, so the media view of homosexuality is formed through a heterosexual media gaze.
➤ The fear of loss of profits if investors, advertisers or media audiences are offended has meant that lesbian, gay, bisexual or transgender/transsexual (LGBT) sexuality has been traditionally treated by the media as deviant and perverse.
➤ Women were stereotyped as butch lesbians; gay men as effeminate, camp and flamboyant, or as macho camp.
➤ News values have meant that LGBT sexuality was traditionally portrayed as marginal to society.
➤ Gross argues the media have often symbolically annihilated LGBT sexuality by excluding it altogether, or trivialised, condemned or made fun of it.
➤ When LGBT characters have appeared in the media, they are usually cast and defined in terms of their sexual orientation, rather than being normal characters who also just happen to be LGBT.

Changing representations of sexuality
➤ There is a growing acceptance and tolerance in media representations of a diversity of sexual orientations (though mostly lesbians and gay men).

➤ The popularity of gay media celebrities would seem to confirm that media representations and audience reactions are beginning to change.

➤ The camp gays/butch lesbians stereotypes have largely disappeared.

➤ Pluralists would suggest these changes have arisen because media companies are responding to changing audience attitudes, and are actively courting a large and affluent LGBT consumer market – the 'pink pound'.

➤ Postmodernists would argue there is growing fluidity and flexibility around identities – including sexual identities – in postmodern societies. Whether you're heterosexual or LGBT isn't such a big deal anymore.

➤ Gill cautions that, to avoid the risk of offending heterosexual audiences or of putting off advertisers, mainstream media still represent LGBT sexuality only in a 'sanitised' way – e.g. gay men are still only rarely portrayed kissing, touching or having sex (unlike heterosexual men).

➤ Gill suggests the opposite applies for lesbians. They rarely appear in advertising and other media in anything other than a highly sexualised manner, which appeals to heterosexual male fantasies.

➤ Such representations have the triple effect of:
  ⯈ Appealing to the gay and lesbian market.
  ⯈ Not offending heterosexual media audiences and advertisers.
  ⯈ Not challenging heterosexual ideology, but actively securing its continued hegemony as the norm.

Media representations of disability (pages 236–239)

➤ Those who control the media industry are predominantly white, middle-class and able-bodied men, so the media gaze which forms representations of disability is that of the able-bodied.

➤ Media stereotyping plays a major role in forming people's views about disability, often through negative stereotypes, which may give distorted impressions of disability to those without direct experience.

➤ Disabled people are under-represented in media content, to such an extent that they face symbolic annihilation.

➤ Disabled people are rarely portrayed in media content as anything other than disabled people. They are seldom represented as a perfectly normal part of everyday life, as workers, parents, etc., who happen to have an impairment as well.

Media stereotypes of disability

➤ Barnes identified the following media stereotypes of disabled people:
  ⯈ *As pitiable or pathetic* – e.g. in TV charity appeals.
  ⯈ *As sinister or evil* – e.g. as nasty criminals in films.
  ⯈ *As super cripples* – e.g. in media coverage of the Paralympics.
  ⯈ *As laughable or an object of ridicule* – e.g. the 'village idiot'.
  ⯈ *As a burden* – the view of disabled people as having to be cared for by others.
  ⯈ *As non-sexual* – lacking sexual feelings.

➤ Briant et al. of the GMG found that disabled people were becoming even less likely to be portrayed in sympathetic and deserving terms, and more likely to be portrayed as undeserving: as benefit 'scroungers', etc.

EXAM TIP:

In questions on the media and disability, you may conclude the media do still produce negative stereotypes or ignore disabled people. But try to apply some examples of positive representations of disability or signs of progress from your own media consumption.

GENERAL EXAM TIP ON MEDIA REPRESENTATIONS:

It can't be assumed that media stereotypes necessarily have an effect on media audiences – e.g. people who have their own experiences to draw on might challenge or dismiss the stereotypes. The following section covers a series of theories about the effects of the media on audiences. You could gain extra marks by referring to some of these theories in your evaluation of media stereotyping.

TOPIC 5

The relationship between the media, their content and presentation, and audiences (pages 240–253)

Methodological problems (page 240)

➤ It cannot be taken for granted that the media have any effect on audiences, or that everyone will react to a media text in the same way.

➤ A media text is polysemic – people exposed to the same media texts do not interpret and react to them in the same way.

➤ The media is only one agency influencing people's views. It is very difficult to disentangle the effects of the media from the whole range of other factors influencing people.

➤ It is hard to establish, with the spread of the new media, which particular media cause any alleged effects.

➤ It is practically impossible to establish what people's beliefs, values and behaviour might have been without any media influence.

➤ Contemporary society is media-saturated – everyone is exposed to some form of media, and for all their lives. This makes it almost impossible to compare different effects between those who have been exposed to the media and those who haven't.

Media effects models: active and passive audiences (page 241)

➤ *Passive audience models* assume media audiences are passive 'cultural dopes' who mindlessly consume and accept media texts.

➤ *Active audience models* assume media audiences actively interpret or criticise media texts, give them different meanings and interpretations from that intended, or simply ignore or reject them altogether.

The hypodermic syringe model – a passive audience approach (pages 241–242)

➤ This suggests that the media act like a hypodermic syringe injecting media texts into audiences.

➤ Audiences are seen as unthinking, passive receivers of these media texts. They are unable to resist the messages that are 'injected' into them.

➤ Audiences are filled with the dominant ideology, sexist and racist stereotyped images, and they immediately act on these messages.

Evaluation of the hypodermic syringe model

➤ It assumes the entire audience is passive and homogeneous (sharing the same characteristics) and will react in the same way to media content.

➤ It assumes audiences are gullible and easily manipulated.
➤ It assumes the media have enormous power and influence, overriding all other agencies of socialisation and people's own experiences.
➤ There is little evidence that media content has the immediate effects on audiences the model suggests.

The two-step flow model – an active audience approach (pages 242–243)

Katz and Lazarsfeld suggest that:
➤ The key factor affecting audience responses is the influence of 'opinion leaders' in the social networks to which people belong.
➤ Opinion leaders are those respected members of any social group who select, interpret and filter media texts (the first step) and then lead opinion about them in their social groups, and whom others listen to and take notice of (the second step).
➤ Audiences are therefore not directly affected by media texts, but are influenced by mediated – or altered and interpreted – messages received from opinion leaders.

Evaluation of the two-step flow model
➤ There are probably more than two steps in the media's influence.
➤ It stills rests on the basic assumption that the influence of the media flows from the media to the audience, and assumes that media audiences are more or less victims of media content.
➤ It does not recognise that people may have views, opinions and experiences of their own, regardless of what opinion leaders say.
➤ It doesn't explain why opinion leaders are directly influenced by media content when others in the audience are not.
➤ The rise of the new media diminishes the role of opinion leaders, as people receive a diversity of mediated messages from Facebook contacts, blogs, YouTube, etc.

The cultural effects model (the 'drip drip' effect) – an active audience approach (pages 243–246)

The neo-Marxist cultural effects model suggests that:
➤ Media texts are formed by, and spread, the dominant ideology in society.
➤ Audiences interpret the media they consume, and may respond in different ways depending on their social characteristics, such as their social class, gender or ethnicity, and their own experiences.
➤ Those without their own experiences to draw on to make judgements are more likely to accept what the media tell them.
➤ Nonetheless, the media gradually influence the audience over a period of time, gradually shaping people's taken-for-granted common-sense ideas and assumptions to match the dominant ideology.

Encoding/decoding and reception analysis
➤ Stuart Hall, from a neo-Marxist perspective, suggested media texts are 'encoded' with a dominant hegemonic viewpoint by those who produce them.
➤ Morley said media texts could be decoded or read in one of three ways:

1. *The preferred or dominant reading* – acceptance of the dominant hegemonic viewpoint.
2. *A negotiated reading* – the dominant reading is accepted, but amended to fit audiences' own beliefs and experiences.
3. *An oppositional reading* – outright rejection of the preferred or dominant interpretation of media content.

➤ Morley suggests that the particular reading that audiences adopt will be influenced by their own knowledge and experiences, the social groups to which they belong, and their social characteristics.

Selective filtering – an interpretivist approach

➤ Klapper's interpretivist selective filtering approach suggests that people actively engage with media content, and that there are three filters that people apply in interpreting that content:
1. *Selective exposure* – they choose to access media content that fits in with their existing views and interests.
2. *Selective perception* – they'll interpret a message in accordance with whether or not it fits in with their own views.
3. *Selective retention* – they'll only remember media messages that support their beliefs.

Evaluation of the cultural effects model

➤ Philo of the GMG argues the encoding/decoding and selective filtering approaches, and the idea that media texts are polysemic, exaggerate the extent to which audiences can give whatever interpretations they choose to media content.

➤ Most people accept the dominant media account unless they have access to alternative forms of information. Most people don't, and rely on very traditional news sources to form their beliefs and understanding.

➤ It assumes media personnel like journalists work within the framework and assumptions of the dominant ideology. It doesn't recognise that journalists have some independence in their work. They can sometimes be very critical of the dominant ideology and the existing arrangements in society.

The uses and gratifications model – an active audience approach (pages 246–248)

➤ Emphasises what audiences use the media for, rather than what the media do to influence audiences.
➤ McQuail and Lull argue that audiences use the media to satisfy their own desires and interests (gratifications) in different ways:
➡ *Diversion* – leisure, entertainment and relaxation.
➡ *Personal relationships* – keeping up with family and friends, meeting people, etc.
➡ *Personal identity* – keeping up with interests that they identify with.
➡ *Surveillance* – accessing information about things that might affect them.
➡ *Background wallpaper* – a distraction while doing other things.
➤ These various uses mean people make conscious choices, selections and interpretations regarding the media, which are likely to be influenced by a wide range of social factors.
➤ Different individuals and social groups have different needs, so it is very difficult to generalise about the effects of the media.

Evaluation of the uses and gratifications model

➤ It overestimates the power of the audience to influence media content.
➤ It underestimates the power and influence of the media and media companies to shape and influence the choices people make and the pleasures they derive from the media.
➤ It focuses too much on the use of the media by individuals, rather than the group settings suggested by the two-step flow and cultural effects models.

EXAM TIP:

Questions on the relationship between the media and their audiences are quite popular with examiners. Focus on any particular model of media effects mentioned in the question or Item, identify strengths and weaknesses, and use all the other theories to evaluate them. If the question doesn't identify any particular model, make reference to them all. A useful organising framework for your answer is provided by the passive v. active audience approaches. In your conclusion, reach a judgement on what model you find most convincing, but, as always, link this closely to the wording in the question, or the view expressed in the Item.

Violence and the media (pages 249–252)

➤ The uncertainty of the effects of violence in the media on violence in real life is shown by the different and contradictory conclusions reached:
  ➠ *Copycatting or imitation* – exposure to media violence causes people to copy it.
  ➠ *Catharsis* – exposure to media violence reduces real-life violence as people live out any violent tendencies in the media's fantasy world.
  ➠ *Desensitisation* – repeated exposure to media violence has gradual 'drip-drip' long-term effects making people less sensitive to seeing or using real-life violence and more accepting of it.
  ➠ *Sensitisation* – exposure to media violence makes people more sensitive to the consequences of violence, and less tolerant of real-life violence.
  ➠ *Psychological disturbance* – repeated exposure to media violence causes long-lasting psychological disturbance in some children.
  ➠ *Exaggeration* – exposure to media violence exaggerates the fear of real-life violence.

In research into whether violence in the media causes real-life violence, it is hard to establish:
➤ Whether more aggressive people choose to watch violent programmes (i.e. selective exposure).
➤ Whether violent programmes make viewers aggressive (i.e. media effects).
➤ Whether certain social circumstances both make people more aggressive and lead them to watch more violent television (i.e. a common third cause).

EXAM TIP:

The debate on the effects of violence in the media is a useful source of examples to apply in questions on the various media effects theories – e.g. linking copycatting to the hypodermic syringe model, or desensitisation to the cultural effects model.

TOPIC 6

The new media and their significance for an understanding of the role of the media in contemporary society (pages 254–269)

Features of new media (pages 254–257)

➤ *Technological convergence* – a single device combines various media technologies that were once separate.

➤ *Cultural convergence* – consumers seek out and share new information and make connections between dispersed contents from a range of media.

➤ *Interactivity* – the audience can actively interact with and customise the media. Jenkins suggests this interactivity has led to:

   ➡ *Participatory culture* – a media culture in which the public do not act as consumers only, but also as contributors or producers of media content.

   ➡ *Collective intelligence* – users of new media collaborate and share knowledge, resources and skills to build a shared or group intelligence.

➤ *Dispersal* – the new media are less centralised, more adapted to individual choices in their use, and integrated into everyday life.

The extent of new media and their users (page 257)

➤ Internet use now outstrips TV viewing across Europe, though in the UK people still watch TV a lot more than they use the internet.

➤ Most UK households now have internet access, over 80% of the population use the internet, and over half of adults have a social networking profile.

➤ Advertisers now spend more on internet advertising than traditional media advertising.

➤ Many national newspapers and TV stations now have their own websites, reaching millions more people than their printed papers or TV channels do.

Digital divides (pages 257–261)

➤ *Social class* – The middle and upper classes are the most likely to be frequent internet users.

➤ *Age* – Younger people are the greatest users, and this declines among older age groups.

➤ *Gender* – Playing computer games, watching videos online, and take up of smartphones are more popular among males; e-readers, making phone calls/texting, and use of social networking sites are more common among females.

➤ *The global digital divide* – Used most heavily and by the largest proportion of people in the Western world. Many of those living in the world's poorest countries lack access due to poverty.

Many of the digital divides in access to and use of new media are diminishing rapidly.

The effects of new media and new technologies on traditional or 'old' media (pages 261–263)

➤ *Loss of audiences* – a huge decline in printed newspaper sales, and a general downwards trend in viewing of TV news bulletins.
➤ *Convergence* – the growing use of new media by traditional media.
➤ *Synergy* – e.g. newspapers often refer readers to their websites.
➤ *The use of digital technologies* – e.g. enabling live video recordings at the scene of a news event.
➤ *The use of the new media to form the content of the traditional media* – e.g. newspapers and TV using the blogosphere and citizen journalism to research their own media reports.
➤ *Interaction with media audiences and changing consumer demands.*
➤ *Changes in journalism in traditional media*
  ➠ Huge increase in the quantity of information, and an increased speed of flow of news.
  ➠ Citizen journalism has made traditional media much more accountable. They risk widespread critical responses through social media if they produce biased or inaccurate reports.
➤ *Loss of control over news agendas*
  ➠ Those accessing news come increasingly via referrals from social media, giving more power to new media corporations.
  ➠ McNair suggests that top-down control, by media owners and by primary definers, is shifting more towards bottom-up control by ordinary people in the form of citizen journalists.
➤ *The rise of churnalism and infotainment in the traditional media* – a consequence of cost-cutting by media owners and time pressures arising from the intensity of 24/7 rolling news.

The significance of the new media in contemporary society (pages 263–269)

Curran and Seaton suggest there are two general views on the new media's significance in contemporary society:

The cultural optimist/neophiliac view

➤ *More informed consumers, wider choices and more user participation.*
➤ *Greater democracy:*
  ➠ Greater opportunities for ordinary people to influence, hold to account, protest at and organise against governments and corporations, and to initiate change in society.
  ➠ More freedom of ideas and expression, through citizen journalism, outside the control of established media.
➤ *More access to all kinds of helpful information from different sources.*
➤ *The world becomes what McLuhan called a global village* – users from around the world connect and interact with each other instantaneously, making the world like one village or community, promoting cultural diversity and understanding.
➤ *Social life and social interaction are enhanced* – people can expand their personal boundaries beyond geographical area and immediate social connections through social networking sites.

The cultural pessimist view

➤ *Problems of the validity of information* – hard to know whether reports are true or exaggerated.
➤ *Cultural and media imperialism* – the new media have led to the imposition of Western, and especially American, cultural values across the world, with the undermining of local cultures and cultural independence.
➤ *A threat to democracy*:
  ➡ More and more of what we know is dominated and controlled by the new media corporations which MacKinnon calls the 'sovereigns of cyberspace'.
  ➡ Political regimes and governments can monitor people's activity on new media, invading their privacy or even using it to control their populations and prevent political protest.
  ➡ Reinforcing the dominant ideology – the major media corporations dominate the web.
➤ *The lack of regulation* – which makes it easier to spread things like, e.g., child pornography.
➤ *Commercialisation and limited consumer choice*:
  ➡ Social networking sites enable targeted advertising based on detailed information about people's lives and interests.
  ➡ Barnett and Seymour, and Curran et al., showed how there is poorer-quality 'dumbed-down' media content to attract large audiences.
➤ *Increasing surveillance in everyday life* – e.g. mobile phone tracking to find out where people are, etc.
➤ *The undermining of human relationships and communities* – more social isolation, with people wrapped up in the virtual world of solitary electronic media.

EXAM TIP:

Depending on the question, a good way of structuring your answers to new media questions is to put them into the framework of the debate between cultural optimists/neophiliacs and cultural pessimists.

GENERAL EXAM TIP:

Remember that two out of the three exam questions on the Media topic involve an Item to refer to. You *must* refer to that Item to achieve top-band marks. For 10-mark ('Applying material from Item M, analyse two') questions, you must refer *only* to ideas or issues that are raised in the Item. For 20-mark ('Applying material from Item N, and your knowledge, evaluate') questions, you must refer to the Item and your knowledge gained elsewhere in your studies of the media. Remember the Item is there to help and guide you, so use it.

By the time you go into the exam, you should know all the material and key terms listed on pages 270–271 of the textbook. Knowing the key terms and using them correctly will help you gain marks for knowledge and understanding. You can check their meaning on-the-go by going to the online glossary by following the link at www.politybooks.com/browne. Put it on your phone for ready reference.

5
STRATIFICATION AND DIFFERENTIATION

TOPIC 1
Stratification and differentiation by social class, gender, ethnicity and age (pages 276–302)

Introducing stratification and differentiation (pages 276–278)

➤ Differentiation is the way in which people perceive and treat each other as different.
➤ Stratification is where this differentiation becomes the basis for dividing societies into a hierarchy of unequal social groups.
➤ Stratification systems may be based on religion, or more commonly on economic factors.
➤ A stratification system may be:
  ⮕ An *open system* – where individuals achieve their positions, and there is the opportunity for social mobility, where people can move between strata.
  ⮕ A *closed system* – where social position is ascribed (fixed) at birth, nothing can alter it and there is no chance of social mobility.
➤ Groups in the stratification hierarchy will have different amounts of power or authority:
  ⮕ *Power* – the ability of some individuals or groups to get their own way in particular situations.
  ⮕ *Authority* – when the exercise of power is seen as legitimate or justified, and so is accepted by others.
➤ Inequality is a feature of all stratification systems, and is becoming more widely used to replace the terms 'stratification and differentiation'. Inequality involves three interlinked ideas:
  ⮕ *Inequality of opportunity* – not everyone has the same chance to pursue success because of artificial, socially created barriers.
  ⮕ *Inequality of access* – not everyone has the same rights and opportunities to access the same valued goods or services of some kind, e.g. schools.
  ⮕ *Inequality of outcome* – not everyone achieves similar levels of rewards.
➤ Milanovic suggests there is 'good' inequality and 'bad' inequality:
  ⮕ *Good inequality* is that which enables people to achieve their potential and provides incentives that motivate them to do so.
  ⮕ *Bad inequality* is that which doesn't motivate people to achieve, but stops them achieving to preserve the social privileges of those already higher up the social hierarchy.
➤ Wilkinson and Pickett argue that societies which have high levels of social inequality have overall lower levels of general social well-being compared to those which are more equal.

The functionalist theory of stratification – a consensus perspective

➤ Functionalists see stratification as necessary and beneficial for the smooth and efficient running of society because, as argued by Davis and Moore:
  ⟹ All social roles (occupations) must be filled by those best able to perform them.
  ⟹ Certain jobs are more functionally important than others for society.
  ⟹ These jobs will require more talent or training.
  ⟹ Not everybody has these talents or is prepared to undergo the necessary training.
  ⟹ People must be motivated to make the necessary sacrifices (e.g. low pay during education and training) to train for these positions with the promise of future high rewards in terms of income, wealth, status and power.
➤ Society is meritocratic – it is based on a meritocracy where people occupy the most important social positions because of their greater talents, abilities, qualifications and skills.

Criticisms of functionalist theory

Tumin argues that Davis and Moore are wrong because:
➤ Some positions are functionally more important than they may appear to be.
➤ Inequality of opportunity in unequal societies prevents disadvantaged individuals from developing their talents and skills. The system of stratification itself prevents the pool of talent being larger.
➤ Training is not a 'sacrifice' that needs rewarding. The costs are usually borne by parents or the state, and being a student can be pleasurable.
➤ Higher pay is not the only motivator for people to undertake training for functionally important jobs.

Stratification may be dysfunctional and inefficient because:
➤ It limits the possibility of discovering the full range of talent in a society.
➤ It makes people at the bottom feel less important to society, thus giving them less motivation to participate in society or seek to improve themselves.
➤ Inequality can be a cause of hostility and conflict between people.
➤ Wilkinson and Pickett point out that, on almost every measure, the more unequal a society is, the more it suffers from social ills such as increased crime, ill-health and social disharmony.

EXAM TIP:

The functionalist theory of stratification is closely aligned with the views of the New Right, particularly in regard to the desirability of stratification, so you can refer to that from your wider reading in any question on the functionalist approach. A question on functionalist theory might also be 'disguised' as a question on the New Right approach to stratification, so watch out for that. You can also criticise/evaluate functionalist theory by reference to the conflict theories of Marx and Weber.

The Marxist theory of stratification – a conflict perspective

➤ The basis of all stratification systems is the private ownership of the means of production.

➤ Society is stratified into two basic social classes: the owners and non-owners of the means of production. The proletariat have to work for wages to live as they do not own the means of production.

➤ The bourgeoisie exploits the proletariat by paying them less than the value of what they produce – this produces profit for the bourgeoisie and causes class conflict.

➤ The owning class is a ruling class and maintains its power through what Althusser called:

⇒ *The repressive state apparatus* – those institutions concerned with mainly repressive, physical means of keeping a population in line, such as the army, law, police, courts and prisons.

⇒ *The ideological state apparatuses* (ISAs) – agencies that spread the dominant ideology, e.g. the family, religion, the education system and the media.

➤ Marx predicted that the two basic classes would become more polarised (with the working classes becoming poorer and poorer) and a resulting conflict between classes would eventually lead to the working class overthrowing the bourgeoisie in a communist revolution, creating a new system in which the means of production would be owned by everyone. It would be a classless society, with no exploitation and no class conflict.

The main criticisms of Marxist theory . . .

➤ Its predictions of class conflict and revolution have not come true.

➤ The working class has not got poorer.

➤ It over-emphasises social class as a source of inequality and conflict, and ignores other identities.

➤ There are more than two social classes (e.g. middle classes).

(There is more discussion of the Marxist theory of stratification on pages 137–8 of the textbook.)

The Weberian theory of stratification – a conflict perspective

➤ Weber criticised Marx for concentrating only on economically based class inequality. He argued that society was also stratified by status (based on esteem in the eyes of others) and party (based on access to and ability to influence political power and decision-making).

➤ For Weber, social class was based on market situation – the scarcity and value placed on people's skills in the labour market, and therefore how much they could sell their labour for. This meant there was a diversity of classes (not just two).

➤ Different classes have different life chances – the chances of obtaining those things defined as desirable, and of avoiding those defined as undesirable, in any society.

➤ Societies were stratified by:

⇒ *Social class* – groups sharing similar market situations.

⇒ *Status* – groups sharing a similar status, e.g. gender or ethnicity.

⇒ *Party* – groups that have or try to influence political power.

➤ Class, status and party may coincide. But status and party can also cut across class – e.g. black and white male workers may have a similar market situation (class) but be divided by the status difference of ethnicity.

➤ For Weber, class, status and party may each provide a basis for division and conflict in society, so the system of stratification is much more complex than Marx's simple two-class system.

➤ Weber's distinction between class, status and party has the advantage over functionalist and Marxist theories of being able to explain a wider range of inequalities in contemporary societies, such as those based around gender, ethnicity or age.

Feminist theories of stratification – conflict perspectives

➤ Feminists generally regard other theories of stratification as malestream theories in that they mainly focus on the position of men and assume that what is true for men is true for women as well.

➤ Feminists regard the concept of patriarchy – power and authority held by males – as an important element in explaining women's subordinate position in society.

➤ Patriarchy cuts across class differences.

➤ Walby argues women are kept in a subordinate position through six structures:
  ⟹ *The household* – in which women have the primary responsibility for domestic labour and childcare, limiting their access to and advancement in paid work.
  ⟹ *Paid work* – women get lower-paid and lower-status work.
  ⟹ *The state* – whose policies are primarily in the interests of men.
  ⟹ *Sexuality* – where different standards are expected from women and men.
  ⟹ *Male violence* – which is ignored, condoned or inadequately tackled.
  ⟹ *Cultural institutions* – which reinforce patriarchy and patriarchal ideology.

Radical feminism

➤ Radical feminists, such as Firestone, argue that biology is the basis for women's inequality and domination by men. Equality between the sexes can only occur when the family is abolished, childbirth is carried out independently of men, and women begin to live their lives separately and apart from men (separatism).

Criticisms of the radical feminist approach include:

➤ It assumes all women share common interests, but ignores inequalities between women, such as those of class and ethnicity.

➤ It doesn't recognise that gradual reforms have improved opportunities for women and weakened patriarchy.

➤ Separatism is a personal lifestyle choice, which is a means of escaping patriarchy rather than challenging it, and is unlikely to appeal to all women.

Marxist/socialist feminism

➤ Marxist feminism suggests that gender inequality arises primarily from the nature of capitalist society, not from an independent system of patriarchy. It is working-class women who suffer the worst consequences of this.

➤ Capitalism intensifies patriarchal inequalities in pursuit of its own interests in the following ways:
  ⟹ In the family, women are used as free labour in the form of unpaid domestic labour and childcare.
  ⟹ Women and children act as a brake on revolutionary ideas – men cannot afford to strike to improve their working conditions because their families would starve while the strike lasted.
  ⟹ When men come home from work stressed-out and angry, their wives and children calm them down, give them a reason for continuing to work and send them back the next morning, ready for another day's labour.
  ⟹ Women are used as a cheap labour force, and as a reserve army of labour, which can be called away from the home when circumstances demand.

➤ Equality of women with men will only come about through revolutionary change which challenges both capitalism and patriarchy.

Criticisms of the Marxist feminist approach include:
- ➤ It doesn't explain the fact that patriarchy has existed in all known societies.
- ➤ It is men – not just capitalism – who benefit from women's subordination.
- ➤ By emphasising the class differences between women, it deflects attention away from those problems shared by all women.

Liberal feminism
- ➤ Liberal feminists, like Oakley, suggest women's inequality arises primarily through factors like sexist stereotyping in the media; gender role socialisation; women's primary responsibility for housework and childcare; their dual burden in both paid employment and domestic labour; a lack of positive role models; and sex discrimination through outdated laws and attitudes.
- ➤ These generate a lack of equal opportunities for women, and keep women in a subordinate position to men.
- ➤ This strand of feminism is more optimistic about achieving equality for women through a gradual process of reform.
- ➤ The main criticism of liberal feminism is that it merely deals with reducing the effects of women's subordination, rather than challenging the fundamental causes. Radical and Marxist feminists suggest these lie in the structures of patriarchy and/or capitalism, and women's equality can only be brought about by revolutionary changes.

Black feminism
- ➤ Black feminism emerged as a result of concerns that many early feminist theories were ethnocentric and ignored the different experiences of patriarchal subordination among Black and Minority Ethnic (BME) women.
- ➤ Mirza argues that, although BME women suffer many of the same problems as white women, they have to contend with the additional problem of racism, which makes their life experience different.
- ➤ Liberal and radical feminists are critical of Black feminism because, by emphasising the ethnic differences between women, it deflects attention away from those problems shared by all women.

EXAM TIP:

Patriarchy is a key concept in feminist approaches – you should refer to it to gain marks for knowledge and application.

Postmodernist approaches to stratification

➤ Social structures, such as systems of stratification, have fragmented, weakened or ceased to exist.
➤ Social class, gender, ethnicity and age are of declining significance as sources of identity, and have been replaced by growing individualism, consumerism and individual choice.
➤ Pakulski and Waters argue that group solidarity, established through social class, gender, ethnicity or age, has declined. Stratification is now based more on a status ranking of freely chosen consumer lifestyles, and people can redefine their position and the image they project to others by changing their consumption patterns and lifestyles.

Criticisms of postmodernism

➤ Bottero argues that postmodernism ignores the objective constraints on people's behaviour caused by inequalities in wealth, income and education.
➤ Only the most well-off members of society have real consumer choice and the means of freely establishing their position through consumer lifestyles in the consumer-based stratification system.
➤ People are not always able to freely project any images they choose, as their plausibility to others is affected and imposed by social expectations and stereotypes surrounding, for example, gender, ethnicity and age.
➤ Many people continue to make choices in accordance with culturally defined norms and values derived from the social structure.

EXAM TIP:

In questions on a specific theory of stratification, e.g. functionalism, you can draw on the other theories for criticism and evaluation, but you'll also need to give criticisms of that theory in its own right. You could also use the postmodernist ideas of individualism and personal choice to criticise and evaluate functionalist, Marxist, Weberian and feminist theories.

Economic bases for stratification and differentiation (pages 300–302)

➤ The economic bases for differentiation are to do with the control of essential resources, usually water, people and land, or the means of producing desired goods.
➤ Control and ownership of people means slavery, whereby people are bought and sold like objects, forced to work for no pay and have their whole lives controlled by their owners.
  ⮕ It was once associated with the ancient world of Greece and Rome, but the slave trade contributed to the development of the European and US economies between the sixteenth and nineteenth centuries until its abolition in the UK and the USA in the nineteenth century.
  ⮕ Forms of modern slavery still exist: an estimated 35 million people worldwide are trapped in modern forms of slavery.
➤ Control and ownership of land is associated with the feudal system of medieval Europe.
  ⮕ Remnants of the feudal system are still found today in the UK and Europe through the ownership of large areas of land by aristocratic families.

➤ Ownership and control of the means of production refers to key resources like factories, land and machinery necessary to produce society's goods, on which everyone depends for their livelihood.
  ⟹ The stratification system is based on a fundamental division between those who own and control the means of production and those who don't. This has laid the basis for the contemporary system of stratification based on social class, and its accompanying social-class inequalities.

Sex/gender as a basis for stratification and differentiation (pages 289–291)

➤ Functionalist writers, such as Parsons, argue that the differences between the sexes are innate and biologically based:
  ⟹ Men are biologically more suited to performing the instrumental role of provider/breadwinner.
  ⟹ Women are more naturally suited to remaining in the private/domestic sphere of the home, performing the expressive role of nurturing, caring and providing emotional support.
➤ These biologically based differences are reinforced by the socialisation process, which creates gender differences – the culturally created differences between men and women.
➤ Most sociologists reject the view that the biological differences between men and women are the main reason for the inequalities between them in contemporary societies. They emphasise the role of socialisation from an early age, which encourages men and women to adopt different roles.
➤ Evidence for the cultural, rather than biological, creation of inequalities between men and women is shown by the different and changing roles adopted by men and women in different societies.
➤ Feminists argue gender inequalities are a result of patriarchy. This keeps women in a subordinate position.

Ethnicity as a basis for stratification and differentiation (pages 291–294)

➤ Ethnicity as a basis for differentiation has traditionally been rooted in genetic or biological theories that suggested that humans formed 'racial groups' that were distinct from one another. Within these racial groups, white races were perceived as inherently superior to others.
➤ These theories have been discredited. The theories were developed to justify white domination, and the alleged genetic differences that exist between so-called 'racial groups' are no greater than the range of genetic differences found within each of these groups.
➤ Ethnicity has become a basis for stratification in many countries, with a hierarchy of ethnic groups of some kind, usually – but not exclusively – based on skin colour.
➤ In the UK, membership of a BME group tends, on the whole, to be linked to social exclusion and social disadvantage.
➤ Ethnicity is often linked to personal and institutional racism, where people are discriminated against because of their ethnic origin and/or skin colour.
➤ Dorling suggests that current debates about immigration are more about ethnicity than the number of immigrants – 'It is not the immigration that is of actual concern, it is who the potential immigrants might be.'

Theoretical views about ethnic differences

➤ *Functionalist views*
- ⇒ Different outcomes arise as a result of the meritocratic nature of society. Differences are the result of different socialisation or different educational achievement.
- ⇒ Patterson argued, using the host–immigrant or assimilation model, that BME disadvantages would gradually disappear as the socialisation patterns of BME groups enabled them to become assimilated into the dominant culture, to be merged into a British identity, and to become accepted by the White ethnic majority.

➤ *Marxist views*
- ⇒ The existence of discrimination acts to 'divide and rule' the working class.
- ⇒ BME groups are used as scapegoats to blame for problems that are not their fault.
- ⇒ Disguising that the real source of problems lies in the structure of inequality in capitalist societies, and dividing the working class on ethnic lines, prevent the development of class consciousness among all workers which might threaten the wealth and power of the dominant social class.
- ⇒ BME groups provide a source of cheap labour for the secondary labour market, and a reserve army of labour that can be drawn on in times of economic boom, and easily discarded in times of economic recession.

➤ *Weberian views*
BME groups have a weaker market situation. This means they have poorer educational qualifications or other skills, which, combined with racism, means they face poorer rewards or unemployment when they try to sell their labour in the labour market.

➤ *New Right views*
BME groups are more likely to be part of the underclass, right at the bottom of the social hierarchy. They have cultural features that mean they have only themselves to blame for their disadvantage.

➤ *Postmodernist views*
- ⇒ Globalisation and the influence of consumption are reducing the significance of ethnicity as a source of identity. There are more hybrid identities emerging, mixing different cultural identities.
- ⇒ Ethnic differences are now only a result of choice and no longer imposed by one's birth. However, many criticise this, as factors like unemployment, poverty and racism mean ethnic identities continue to be imposed by others.

Age as a basis for stratification and differentiation (pages 294–297)

➤ Differentiation in the way people are perceived by age and age groups is socially constructed – what is thought of as childhood or old age changes through time and between societies.
➤ In many societies, there are clear 'rites of passage' or rituals marking specific stages in the transition from childhood to adulthood. This contrasts with contemporary Western views of childhood as a long transitional phase between infancy and adulthood.
➤ This transitional period is not a fixed number of years, and changes in society have extended the transitional period to fully independent adult status beyond the 'official' adult age of 18.
➤ Old age, like childhood or the teen years, is also a social construct: people tend to think of the elderly as somehow different, but there is little agreement around the age people become 'old'.
➤ Older people are most likely to vote, and this gives older people disproportionate political power beyond that justified by their numbers in the population.

Theories about age differences

➤ *Functionalists* tend to consider age at the two extremes: childhood and old age.

  ⇒ Childhood is considered in the context of the socialisation of the young and preparation for allocation to appropriate roles in the workforce in a meritocratic society.

  ⇒ Older people are considered in the context of their (alleged) declining ability to work, and their contribution to society therefore (allegedly) diminishes. Retirement makes way for a new, younger workforce to the advantage of the whole society. However, the skills and expertise of the older worker are lost to the economy.

➤ *Feminists* tend to explain the differences between male and female children and elderly men and women in terms of patriarchy.

➤ *Marxists* suggest that capitalism will use the young as a cheap form of labour and dismiss older workers as they are more expensive and less productive. Social class is a significant factor in differentiating between different groups among the elderly.

➤ *Postmodernists* argue that consumption is more important than age in defining social identity.

TOPIC 2

Dimensions of inequality: class, status and power; differences in life chances by social class, gender, ethnicity, age and disability (pages 303–322)

Social class differences in life chances (pages 303–308)

Differences in wealth and income

There are wide inequalities in wealth. In 2010–12 in Great Britain:

➤ The richest 10% of households owned 44% of wealth.

➤ The richest 50% owned 90%, which was nine times greater than that of the poorest half (10%).

The rich have high status because of their wealth, and this status gives them the power to hide their wealth, and enables them to avoid inheritance tax and other taxes which might reduce their assets, so official figures probably underestimate the wealth of the very richest.

There are also wide inequalities in income. In 2012/13 in the UK:

➤ The richest 20% of the population got 44% of all income.

➤ The poorest 20% got only 6% of all income.

Within these groups, women and BME groups will generally own less than white men.

These inequalities are found across the world, and are growing in the UK and in most other countries.

Differences in health

From birth onwards, social class has a marked effect on health chances (the life chances relating to health).

➤ People in social class 5 (unskilled manual), compared to those in social class 1 (higher managerial and professional) have, on average:

  ⇒ Twice the death rate.

  ⇒ About 7 years less life expectancy.

  ⇒ Twice the chance of dying before the age of 5, and of dying before reaching state pension age.

  ⇒ Between two and five times greater risk of dying from accidents of all types.

  ⇒ A 50% higher occurrence of long-standing illness.

➤ Four times as many women die of cervical cancer in social class 5 as in social class 1.

➤ Lung cancer and stomach cancer occur twice as often among men in manual jobs as among men in professional jobs.

➤ For the majority of cancers, there is a five-year gap in the survival rates between the best- and worst-off.

Differences in education

Social class is the strongest predictor of educational achievement in the UK, and the key factor influencing whether a child does well or badly at school. Students from the lower working class compared to middle-class children of the same ability:

➤ Are more likely to start school unable to read.

➤ Are less likely to get places in the best state schools.

➤ Are more likely to be placed in lower streams or sets.

➤ Generally get poorer exam results.

➤ Are more likely to leave school at the minimum leaving age of 16, and more likely to be NEETs (not in employment, education or training).
➤ Are more likely to undertake vocational or training courses at the end of compulsory schooling, rather than the more academic AS and A level courses.
➤ Are less likely to go into higher education.

(You should have studied social class differences in education in the first year of your A level studies, and there is further detailed discussion of this on pages 52–66 in the Volume 1 textbook, and pages 20–21 in Revision Guide 1, covering the first year of the course.)

EXAM TIP:

When you get a question on social class inequalities, don't forget you can draw on explanations from Topic 1. You can also draw on relevant issues you may have studied in your first year in the Education unit, or Culture and Identity, Families and Households, Health, or Work, Poverty and Welfare units, which often refer to a range of social-class inequalities in different contexts.

Gender differences in life chances (pages 308–311)

Differences in health

On some indicators, women appear healthier than men . . .
➤ They are much less likely to die from heart disease and cancer.
➤ Their death rates are much lower, at all ages.
➤ They live, on average, around 4 years longer.

Men's shorter lives are linked to a reluctance to take conditions to doctors for fear of undermining their masculinity, greater risk-taking and working in higher-risk occupations.

On other indicators, women appear to be less healthy than men . . .
Compared to men, women:
➤ Go to the doctor, and are admitted to hospital, more, and have more operations.
➤ Consume more prescription and non-prescription drugs.
➤ Are diagnosed with mental illness about twice as often.
➤ Are off work with reported sickness more often.
➤ Live a greater proportion of their lives in poor health or with a disability.

Reasons for these differences have been linked to:
➤ The medicalisation of pregnancy and childbirth.
➤ Gender socialisation as women are more likely to seek medical assistance than men.
➤ More stress in women's lives due to their dual burden of paid work and domestic labour, and patriarchal relations in the family and society.
➤ Differential diagnosis and labelling of women's and men's conditions by doctors.

Social class inequalities are greater than, and override, gender inequalities in health – e.g. women in higher social classes will generally live longer and healthier lives than women in lower social classes.

(There is more on gender and health inequalities on pages 396–9 in the Volume 1 textbook, and pages 119–20 in Revision Guide 1, covering the first year of the course.)

Differences in education

➤ Since the early 1990s, females have been out-performing males in education. Compared to males, females:
  ⇒ Are more successful in most GCSE and AS and A level subjects.
  ⇒ Are more likely to stay on in sixth form and further education.
  ⇒ Are more likely to apply, and get accepted, for full-time university degree courses, and to get top first-class and upper second-class degrees.

Social class and ethnicity cut across these – e.g. it is generally middle-class, White females who overall perform the most successfully, though middle-class BME females are more likely to go on to higher education.

(You should have studied gender differences in education in the first year of your A level studies, and there is further detailed discussion of this on pages 67–77 in the Volume 1 textbook, and on pages 21–23 in Revision Guide 1, covering the first year of the course.)

Differences in paid and unpaid work

➤ Women as a whole are less likely than men to be in paid employment, in full-time work, or in highly paid occupations.
➤ Women get lower-paid and lower-status work, and are more likely than men to be in part-time and temporary jobs.
➤ The labour market is segregated by gender:
  ⇒ *Vertical segregation* – men tend to be concentrated in higher-level, higher-status jobs than women.
  ⇒ *Horizontal segregation* – women and men do different types of work, e.g. women are concentrated in feminised sectors such as personal service, administration or sales.
➤ Women in full-time work earn about 14% less overall than men in full-time work. This gender pay gap is due to:
  ⇒ Sex discrimination – it's illegal, but still happens.
  ⇒ Women's greater caring responsibilities – e.g. for children, the sick or the elderly. This leads them into more part-time jobs, which generally pay less and have fewer promotion opportunities.
  ⇒ Career breaks for children, interrupting promotion opportunities.
  ⇒ The dual labour market – where women are concentrated in the lower-paid, lower-status, and less secure secondary labour market.
➤ Women, in all social classes and ethnic groups, have the primary responsibility for unpaid work in the home. This limits their access to and advancement in paid work.

The gender divide in the amount of housework and childcare done by men and women tends to differ by social class and ethnicity:
➤ The gap is a bit smaller in higher social classes, as noted by Oakley.
➤ In African Caribbean families, about half are lone parent mothers who work full-time and rely on honorary or natural grandmothers to help with childcare.

➤ In South Asian families, a more extended family network means household chores are shared between generations of women, with full-time work for some female members.
➤ South Asian women are more likely than White British women to experience the dual burden of paid employment and domestic labour.

EXAM TIPS:

If you studied Family and Households in your first year, you can draw on some of the material you studied there for examples of gender differences in the family and society.

Ethnicity and differences in life chances (pages 311–317)

Differences in health
➤ In many respects, the health of BME groups reflects the same social class and gender divisions found in the White British population.
➤ Most BME groups, particularly Black Caribbeans, Pakistanis and Bangladeshis, have poorer health than the White British majority:
  ➠ They have higher adult and child mortality rates.
  ➠ They are more likely to suffer limiting long-term illness.
  ➠ They are more likely to report their health in general as worse than the average.
  ➠ They are more likely to be diagnosed with mental illness and admitted to psychiatric hospitals.

These differences are generally explained by factors such as higher levels of social deprivation and poverty; diet and lifestyle choices; language influencing access to healthcare; and cumulative effects of racism.

(There is more on ethnicity and health inequalities on pages 400–2 in the Volume 1 textbook, and pages 120–121 in Revision Guide 1, covering the first year of the course.)

Differences in education
➤ The highest-achieving are Chinese and Indian Asian pupils.
➤ The lowest-achieving are Black Caribbean, Pakistani, Bangladeshi and Gypsy/Roma and Traveller-of-Irish-Heritage pupils.
➤ Overall, BME groups are more likely to enter higher education than the White British population, though they are less likely to obtain upper-second- or first-class degrees (so-called 'good' degrees).
➤ Black students face higher than average rates of permanent exclusion.

The influence of ethnicity on educational achievement works alongside the influences of social class and gender.
➤ BME students in higher social classes outperform those in lower classes.
➤ Girls outperform boys from the same social class.
➤ White British lower-working-class boys and girls are the lowest-achieving ethnic group.

(You should have studied ethnicity and education in the first year of your A level studies, and there is further detailed discussion of this on pages 78–86 in the Volume 1 textbook, and on pages 23–24 in Revision Guide 1, covering the first year of the course.)

Differences in employment

➤ BME groups, except for Indian Asians and the Chinese, face higher rates of unemployment and part-time employment, and lower average pay than the White British majority.

➤ Pakistani men have the highest rates of self-employment. Platt suggests that this reflects their concentration in poorly paid and low-status taxi and chauffeuring work.

➤ BME women have lower rates of pay than BME men in all ethnic groups.

Age differences in life chances (pages 317–318)

Differences in wealth and poverty

➤ The dependency of the young, and some elderly people, means they have lower status than other groups. Their power, particularly for children, is very limited due to the controls that their parents and/or wider society place upon them.

➤ Not all old people lack status and power, and there are many wealthy elderly who achieve high status through their consumer spending power and political power stemming from networks of social connections.

➤ Being young and being old are both conditions with a higher chance of being in poverty:

➥ Around 13% of those living in poverty in the UK are pensioners, with a higher proportion of women than men. Poverty in old age is more likely for those from an ethnic minority, and even more so if they are disabled or in ill-health.

➥ Around 27% of all children in the UK were living in poverty in 2012–13. The children most vulnerable to poverty are those with disabled parents, from Pakistani and Bangladeshi households, and from marginalised groups like asylum seekers and Gypsies/Travellers.

➥ Hirsch points out that poverty in childhood affects educational achievement, and leaves children facing greater risks of poverty as adults.

Differences in health

➤ Older people, particularly the most socially disadvantaged, tend not to get the same access to healthcare as do younger people, even though they generally have greater need for it.

➤ Age UK suggests that the majority of chronic illnesses affecting older people could be prevented or postponed if more health services and public health initiatives did not exclude older people.

➤ Ageism – stereotyping, prejudice and discrimination – can mean they face a range of disadvantages not encountered by those who are younger.

Disability and differences in life chances (pages 318–322)

Differences in education

➤ Overall, compared to the non-disabled, those with physical or mental disabilities are less qualified, and nearly three times as likely to have no formal qualifications.

➤ At 19 years of age, disabled young people are twice as likely as their non-disabled peers to be NEET (not in any form of education, employment or training).

➤ Disabled young people are now more likely than non-disabled young people to participate in higher education at the age of 19.

Differences in employment and income

Compared to non-disabled people, disabled people:

➤ Are nearly twice as likely to be unemployed.
➤ Are more likely to be working part-time than full-time.
➤ Are more likely to be found in manual than in non-manual jobs.
➤ Are around four times more likely to be economically inactive (not looking for work).
➤ Earn significantly less than those with similar qualifications (which can mean lower pensions in old age).
➤ Are more likely to be dependent on state benefits.
➤ Are more likely to be living in poverty.

In general, gender adds to these inequalities – disabled women experience these inequalities more severely than disabled men.

Social class also links to disability – Longhi found that the disabled are more likely to be found in the lower social classes, and are under-represented in the highest classes.

Differences in health and access to healthcare

➤ Tudor-Hart suggests there is an inverse care law in access to healthcare, medical treatment and equipment – that those whose need is least get the most resources, while those in greatest need get the fewest resources. This is mainly class-based, which means middle-class people are generally more successful in getting effective treatment from the NHS.
➤ Disabled people often get poorer healthcare, as they are seen as a low priority within the NHS, and many healthcare professionals do not have much training in understanding, diagnosing and treating patients with disabilities.

Overall, the differences faced by disabled people, compared to the non-disabled, arise from factors such as:

➤ Overt and direct discrimination – e.g. employers refusing to give them jobs (which is illegal).
➤ Covert discrimination – e.g. establishing rules or physical barriers which make it difficult for disabled people to apply for jobs or access workplaces.
➤ Lack of accessible transport.
➤ Difficulties arising from their impairment in accessing public, commercial and leisure goods and services.
➤ Lack of understanding by the non-disabled of what disabled people can do.
➤ Inadequate welfare benefits, which don't recognise the extra costs that disability brings.
➤ Prejudiced and stereotyped social attitudes.

EXAM TIP:

In questions on differences in life chances in relation to social class, gender, ethnicity, age or disability, include some discussion of how these interact with one another – e.g. how social class and gender influence disability, or how differences related to age are affected by social class and ethnicity. Also draw on your studies in these areas from other parts of your course, and explain differences applying the theories of stratification considered in the first Topic in this chapter.

TOPIC 3

The problems of defining and measuring social class; occupation, gender and social class (pages 323–330)

The Registrar General's (RG) scale (pages 323–324)

This was based on a status-/skill-ranking of occupations into five classes. It was first devised by the Registrar General for use in government statistics in 1901, before being abandoned in the UK in 2000.

Problems of the RG scale

➤ It became inaccurate as certain occupations changed their social status over time. Some occupations became deskilled, and others disappeared altogether.

➤ It classified women, and indeed whole families, by the occupation of the male head of household. Feminists in particular objected to this, and it produced a false picture of households where the woman's job, or that of adult children, was of a higher status or more highly paid than that of the man.

➤ It ignored people who did not work, whether it was because they had enough wealth to live on or because they were unemployed or retired.

➤ It disguised major differences in income and life chances between occupations within the same occupational class – e.g. between highly paid lawyers and junior NHS doctors, who both appear as 'professional'.

National Statistics Socio-economic Classification: NS-SEC (pages 324–325)

This replaced the RG scale and has been used in government and other statistics since 2001. This scale:

➤ Ranks occupations into eight classes, according to income and job-related benefits, job security, promotion prospects and how much authority or control the occupation in question has over other people/employees.

➤ Categorises households according to the highest-earning individual, rather than the assumed male 'head of household' in the RG scale.

➤ Recognises women as a distinct group of wage earners, overcoming the clear sexist bias in the RG scale.

The Hope–Goldthorpe scale (pages 325–326)

This scale ranks occupations into seven classes in terms of their social desirability and status in the labour market, and how much the individual is in control of their own work situation and that of others. It is broadly based on a Weberian perspective. This scale categorised households based on the position of the male head of household.

➤ They exclude: the very wealthy who do not need to work; unpaid workers/volunteers; those never employed and the long-term unemployed.
➤ They tend to be based on the occupation of just the highest earner in a household.
➤ Occupational scales can be very broad and include in the same category people whose interests, status, power and life chances might be very different.
➤ They assume a similarity of tastes and attitudes amongst people in the same occupational group.
➤ Occupational scales tend to be static – but occupational status is constantly changing.

This scale (based on a BBC internet survey) attempted to move beyond simply employment/occupation in defining classes. It ranked seven classes according to their possession of three capitals:
➤ *Economic capital* – people's wealth, earnings, assets and savings.
➤ *Cultural capital* – people's cultural interests and participation in cultural activities.
➤ *Social capital* – people's social networks of influence and support.

Criticisms of the GBCS
➤ The internet survey on which it is based was self-selecting and unrepresentative.
➤ The seven 'classes' are not really social classes, but rankings of people's different lifestyles.
➤ The emphasis on social and cultural capital puts people with the same occupation in different classes.
➤ There is nothing which really binds these 'classes' together into coherent groups of people.
➤ It underplays the traditional Marxist and Weberian concerns with economic position.

➤ *Objective views of class* are those which can be easily measured and classified – e.g. income.
➤ *Subjective views of class* are about how people themselves see their class. Savage found that most people did not attach any particular class label to themselves, but preferred to see themselves as 'just like everybody else'.
➤ Giddens suggests class identification based on occupation is being replaced by identification with people's consumption patterns and lifestyles – a view also held by postmodernists.
➤ A major criticism of this is that objective factors like occupation and income are still significant constraints on the choice of consumption patterns and lifestyle that people can make.

> **EXAM TIP:**
>
> In any question on defining social classes, you can refer to the various ways of defining class raised in this topic, but you can also draw on the functionalist, Marxist, Weberian and postmodernist theories which were referred to in Topic 1.

TOPIC 4
Changes in structures of inequality and the implication of these changes (pages 331–346)

The upper class (pages 331–332)

➤ The upper class is distinguished by its high amounts of wealth and income (capital), and ownership and control of the means of production.
➤ Marxists like Westergaard and Resler argue that the upper class forms a power elite or ruling class which makes the major decisions affecting life in the UK.
➤ The policies of elected governments are influenced by this power elite.
➤ Evidence from the Sutton Trust reveals that political and economic power is maintained across generations by shared family and educational backgrounds forming a supportive 'old boys' network'.
➤ From a New Right perspective, Saunders disputes that such a wealthy ruling elite or ruling class exists. He argues that anyone with a pension is bound to have an interest in the workings of capitalism since their pensions are invested in the stock market: the capitalist class has 'fragmented into millions of tiny pieces' spread across society.
➤ Marxists argue Saunders ignores the role played by financial institutions in controlling these pension funds, and the large incomes and shareholdings of the managers and chief executives of such institutions.

The establishment
➤ Jones suggests this consists of big business, bankers and politicians, media owners, accountancy firms, the arms trade, the lobbying industry and many foreign oligarchs who have found in Britain a safe tax haven for their wealth.
➤ This group is bound together, not by shared family and educational backgrounds, but by shared financial interests and a political ideology based on the free market economy.
➤ The establishment maintains that the only way that the UK can hope to compete in an increasingly competitive and globalised world is by reducing the role of the state, cutting down on welfare provision, and supporting the interests of big business.

The middle class (pages 332–335)

➤ In the past, the distinction between the middle and working class was based on the division between non-manual and manual work. From a Weberian perspective, non-manual workers had a better:
   ⮕ *Market situation* – e.g. shorter hours, more job security, better pay.
   ⮕ *Work situation* – e.g. more autonomy/independence at work, better working conditions.
   ⮕ *Status situation* – e.g. prestige from working in 'the office' close to employers.
➤ The middle class is broad and now divided into at least two distinct groups: the professions and the lower middle class.

The professions
➤ There are two main groups of professionals: *higher professions*, e.g. doctors and lawyers, and *lower professions*, e.g. nurses and teachers.
➤ Functionalists, such as Parsons and Barber, suggest professionals have four features that distinguish them from other groups:
➠ A body of specialised and expert knowledge.
➠ A concern for the interests of the community above self-interest.
➠ A set of rules of behaviour, to which they must conform if they wish to continue working.
➠ High rewards and status, reflecting their expert training.

Criticisms of the functionalist view . . .
➤ Professionals are more concerned with self-interest – they're in it for the money more than serving others.
➤ Weberians, like Parry and Parry, argue professionalism is just a strategy to improve the professionals' market situation and gain higher rewards.
➤ Parry and Parry argue that the lower professions, like teachers and social workers, are not really professionals at all, since they do not have the market control enjoyed by the higher professions.

The lower middle class
The lower middle class consists of routine white-collar workers. Braverman, from a Marxist perspective, argues these jobs have been subject to two related processes:
➤ *Deskilling* – the skills and knowledge once needed to perform the work are no longer needed as fragmentation of tasks, automation and computerisation have simplified the work.
➤ *Proletarianisation* – where the market, work and status benefits associated with office and administrative work have declined to such an extent that these jobs have become more like typical working-class manual jobs. This decline in pay and status was accompanied by growing feminisation of the work – as it lost status, it became defined more as women's work.

The middle class or the middle classes?
➤ Giddens argues that there is one middle class defined by the facts:
➠ It does not own 'property in the means of production' – separating it from the upper class.
➠ It sells mental labour ('brain work') – separating it from the manual labour ('brawn work') of the working class.
➤ Savage et al. argued that the middle class consists of three distinct groups:
➠ Those with property assets, which includes the self-employed and small employers.
➠ Those with organisational assets, who hold important positions in large organisations.
➠ Those with cultural assets deriving mainly from educational qualifications.
➤ Functionalists regard the middle class as divided into a range of groups, with differences in pay and status reflecting the functional importance of different jobs to the economy.
➤ Marxists continue to regard these differences as insignificant in comparison with the fundamental divisions in wealth and power between the proletariat and the bourgeoisie.

The working class (pages 335–337)

The working class is now generally seen as divided into *proletarian traditionalists* and *the new working class*.

Proletarian traditionalists

➤ Lockwood suggested proletarian traditionalists shared the following characteristics:
  ⮕ *Living in close-knit working-class communities*, often based on long-established industries such as mining, docking, iron and steel, and shipbuilding.
  ⮕ *Social solidarity* – shared values, a common culture, and social ties binding them together.
  ⮕ *Workmates who were also neighbours and friends*, who they spend leisure time with.
  ⮕ *Little geographical or social mobility*.
  ⮕ *Solidaristic collectivism* – a sense of loyalty to others in their class.
  ⮕ *Fatalism* – a view that there is little they can do to change their lives or their circumstances.
  ⮕ *Present-time orientation and immediate gratification* – a focus on getting pleasures now, and not worrying too much about the future, or planning for it.
  ⮕ *An 'us' and 'them' view of the world* (workers and the bosses).
➤ This section of the working class has largely disappeared, as the industries on which it was based have declined.
➤ Fulcher and Scott found that some features still remain in many working-class jobs, such as the keen sense of an 'us and them' attitude to employers. MacKenzie et al. found that workers still retain a sense of solidarity with workmates.

The new working class

➤ From the late 1950s onwards, rising living standards in the working class led to a growing belief that affluent manual workers were adopting more middle-class norms, values and lifestyles: the embourgeoisement thesis.
➤ This theory was tested by Goldthorpe and Lockwood who concluded that embourgeoisement was not taking place, but that a new working class was being formed, with the following features:
  ⮕ *An instrumental orientation to work* – work was about making money to get consumer goods, not a source of community solidarity (proletarian traditionalism) or status and future career (middle class).
  ⮕ *Instrumental collectivism* – joining together was purely a means to an end, not an expression of class solidarity (proletarian traditionalists).
  ⮕ *A privatised home-based family lifestyle*, with little involvement with neighbours or the wider community.
  ⮕ *A money model view of society* – income decides your social position. Society was divided only by a hierarchy of income, not by 'us' v. 'them' power differences (proletarian traditionalists) or by status (middle class).

This new working class is now, by far, the largest section of the working class. Traditional Marxists argue there is still only one working class, as they all still share in exploitation by the owners of the means of production in capitalist society.

The underclass/poor (pages 337–339)

There are two main 'versions' of the underclass:
1. *Structural/economic version* – This suggests the underclass consists of disadvantaged groups whose poverty and dependence on state benefits mean they are excluded from taking part in society to the same extent as the rest of society.
2. *Cultural/normative/New Right version* – This suggests the underclass have different attitudes and behaviour – a different culture – from the rest of society, which explains their poverty (e.g. lone parent families, criminality, school exclusion, drug abuse, etc.).

The main criticisms of the New Right version are:
➤ It blames the victims, not the causes.
➤ There is not much evidence, as Shildrick et al. found, that the characteristics the New Right identifies actually exist. Those in the underclass have many of the same hopes and aspirations as everyone else, but lack the same opportunities to realise them.

EXAM TIP:

There are a number of issues covered in this topic which could form the basis of exam questions, and with which you need to be familiar – e.g. is there still a ruling class or power elite? Is there a single middle class or working class, or are these classes divided? What are the arguments for and against proletarianisation and embourgeoisement? Is the underclass a separate class or a part of the working class, and is it created by structural/ economic factors or cultural factors? You should also apply the theories of stratification in Topic 1, including the postmodernist view that consumption and lifestyle have replaced social class as the most significant factor in forming people's social positions and lifestyles.

Globalisation and inequality (pages 340–342)

Globalisation and the transnational capitalist class (TCC)
The neo-Marxist Sklair suggests the transnational capitalist class is made up of four main groups:
1. The owners and controllers of transnational (global) corporations (TNCs).
2. Top officials and politicians, who work to promote the interests of TNCs.
3. Top professionals, who advise and develop proposals for TNCs and free world trade.
4. Consumerist elites of the media, and businesses which trade globally in consumer goods.

The TCC shares a number of common characteristics:
➤ Economic interests that are global, rather than exclusively local or national in origin.
➤ An aim for control in domestic, international and global politics.
➤ Promotion of a global ideology of consumerism.
➤ Employment of accountants and lawyers to minimise the amounts its members pay in tax.
➤ Education in elite universities, usually in the UK or USA.
➤ Luxury lifestyles.

The formation of the TCC is linked to the growth of what Frobel calls the 'new international division of labour'. This is where TNCs design and plan products in the highly developed rich countries, but manufacture and assemble them using cheap labour in poorer developing countries. This creates a global working class exploited by the TCC, and is accompanied by a rapid increase in global inequality.

Globalisation, migration and stratification

➤ Migration between countries occurs because of 'push' and 'pull' factors:
  ⟹ *Push factors* – encourage people to leave their home country.
  ⟹ *Pull factors* – attract people to a new country.
➤ There are two types of migrants:
  ⟹ *Economic migrants,* seeking work and higher living standards.
  ⟹ *Refugees and asylum seekers*, escaping war and persecution.

Migration affects stratification in several ways:

➤ Economic migrants strip the country they leave of trained personnel. This may provide more opportunities for upward social mobility for those who remain, but could slow down economic development and make poverty worse.
➤ Economic migrants may be willing to work for lower pay than the existing population. This may lead to resentments as people see their pay levels being cut by competition from cheaper migrant labour.
➤ Skilled migrant labour may reduce opportunities for upward social mobility among the existing population.
➤ Growing global and national inequalities have led to more undocumented (illegal) migrant workers. Such migrants may be super-exploited for very low wages, and by people-traffickers who smuggle them into the country by various means, and keep them in conditions of semi-slavery.
➤ This swells the underclass, and the growing resentment between different parts of the working class could, as Marxists suggest, prevent working-class solidarity and opposition to the exploitative capitalist class.

EXAM TIP:

You can refer to globalisation issues as an important addition to changes in the class structure of the UK – e.g. is there now a new TCC which has more power and influence than the power elites or ruling classes in individual countries? Is migration arising from globalisation changing the class structures of contemporary societies?

Changes in gender inequality (pages 342–343)

The passing of the Equal Pay Act (1970) and the Sex Discrimination Act (1975) led to some improvements to the position of women in society. For example:

➤ Girls are now doing far better than boys throughout the entire education system.
➤ Women are now better represented in many of the professions.
➤ More women are represented on the boards of directors and as chief executives in larger companies, and are working in more senior managerial and executive roles in business and local government.

Continuing inequalities

Women still face a 'glass ceiling' – an invisible barrier of discrimination which makes it difficult for them to reach the same top levels in their chosen careers as similarly qualified men.

Women overall, compared to men:

➤ Are less likely to be in paid employment, in full-time work, or in highly paid occupations.
➤ Get lower-paid, lower-skilled, lower-status and less secure work and have fewer promotion opportunities.
➤ Earn about 14% less overall in full-time work.
➤ Are more likely to encounter sex discrimination.
➤ Are much more likely to have the primary responsibility for unpaid work in the home.
➤ Have less control over household finances.

Changes in ethnic inequality (pages 344–345)

Overt racism – direct discrimination on the grounds of ethnicity – has been made illegal through a series of Race Relations Acts during the 1960s and 1970s, which are now part of the Equality Act of 2010. The position of BME groups has improved substantially since the 1950s–1970s, but a number of inequalities remain. BME groups overall (but there are differences between them) compared to the White British majority face:

➤ Higher rates of unemployment.
➤ Lower pay.
➤ More insecure employment.
➤ Lower levels of educational achievement.
➤ Higher risks of poverty.
➤ More overcrowded and poorer-quality housing.
➤ Higher risks of homelessness.
➤ Higher risks of being stopped and searched by the police.
➤ Higher risks of being victims of personal crime.

EXAM TIP:

Draw on the theories and explanations given in Topics 1 and 2 to explain continuing gender and ethnic inequalities. You can also draw on your studies in other areas you may have covered during your course for examples and explanations – e.g. Family and Households; Education; Health; Work, Poverty and Welfare; or Crime and Deviance, etc.

TOPIC 5

The nature, extent and significance of patterns of social mobility (pages 347–359)

Key terms and concepts (pages 347–348)

➤ *Social mobility* is the movement of people either up or down from one social class to another.
➤ *Open systems of stratification* are those where social mobility is possible, and individuals have some chance of changing social position based on their achievements.
➤ *Closed systems* are those where social mobility isn't possible, and social positions are based on ascribed characteristics that can't be changed.
➤ There are two main types of social mobility:
  ⟼ *Intragenerational* – an individual moves during their working life.
  ⟼ *Intergenerational* – an individual moves compared to the social class of their parents.
➤ *Perfect social mobility* occurs in meritocratic societies where individuals move up or down between their class of birth and the class they end up in, based purely on their own efforts, skills and abilities.
➤ *Absolute mobility* is the total number of people moving up and down the class structure within a given time period.
➤ *Relative mobility* is the number of movements adjusted to take into account the changes there have been in the occupational structure of society, and whether all social classes are able to benefit equally from these.

Studying social mobility is useful . . . (pages 347–348)

➤ It uncovers the extent to which an individual's life chances are determined by the circumstances into which he or she is born.
➤ It uncovers the extent to which society is open and allows people to move freely from class to class.
➤ High rates of social mobility are likely to limit the development of class solidarity and of a shared class culture, as the composition of classes is constantly changing. Low rates of social mobility are likely to lead to higher levels of class consciousness.
➤ It is important to understand what effect mobility has on those who are mobile.
➤ The extent of social mobility can create resentment and dissatisfaction.

Measuring social mobility (page 349)

➤ Studies of social mobility have been based on employment/occupation, as this is easily measurable. But there are some problems with this:
  ⟼ How are those who don't have a job classified?
  ⟼ Women were traditionally assigned a class based on the occupation of their partner.
➤ These dilemmas have led to three main positions on how to measure social mobility:

1. Goldthorpe suggests counting the occupation of the person in the family with the most direct link to the labour market (typically the person employed and earning the most).
2. Heath and Britten suggest taking the occupational position of both the adult male and the adult female to give a class position for the whole family.
3. Stanworth suggests that the family is left out altogether, and that individuals should be the unit of stratification.

Influences on social mobility (pages 349–351)

Changes in the economy
Economic growth can create more jobs, and better-paid ones, which can ensure more absolute social mobility, as most people become better-off than their parents.

Changes in education
➤ In the UK, free and compulsory education opened up more fluidity in the workforce as more people were educated and able to move from one social class to another, and into higher-status occupations, particularly non-manual jobs.
➤ The improvement in girls' education in the UK gave greater opportunities for women to enter the higher professions in larger numbers.

Globalisation
National governments have less control over their national economies. Transnational corporations will often move manufacturing jobs from countries like the UK, with high wage costs, to developing countries with low wage costs. This can result in the loss of jobs. This changes the occupational structure, and the chances of upward mobility for some groups.

Migration
More skilled immigrant labour moving to the UK from less economically developed countries, who are prepared to work for lower pay than the native population, has the potential to reduce opportunities for upward social mobility among the existing population. However, labour shortages in skilled manual and higher-level non-manual work, and the effects of an ageing population, mean such migrant labour will be essential for British society for the foreseeable future.

Studies of social mobility (pages 351–355)

The Glass Study
This covered intergenerational mobility in the 1930s and 1940s, and compared the occupations of men over 21 with that of their fathers. It found:
➤ There was a fairly high rate of short-range mobility: most movement was to a class adjacent to that of the father. Long-range mobility from top to bottom or bottom to top was very rare.
➤ There was very little mobility into or out of either the middle or working class.
➤ Those in the top social classes closed ranks to those from lower down the hierarchy and recruited the offspring of others like themselves.
➤ Overall, there were very limited and unequal chances of individuals achieving upward mobility.

Criticisms of the Glass Study
➤ The sample used was unrepresentative, and failed to reflect the growing number employed in white-collar occupations.
➤ Many of the fathers had been working, or perhaps not working, through the period of very high unemployment in the 1930s depression, which may have distorted their real occupational level.
➤ It was a snapshot in time, and the men interviewed in 1949 may have achieved higher positions (intragenerational mobility) as the economy expanded in the 1950s.
➤ It ignored women.

The Oxford Mobility Study (OMS) (also referred to as the *Nuffield* or *Goldthorpe Study*)
This covered intergenerational mobility in the 1950s – early 1970s. It found:
➤ Higher rates of long-range upward mobility than Glass.
➤ High rates of absolute upward mobility (the total number moving).
➤ Relative mobility (the chances of those from different backgrounds achieving higher class positions) remained very unequal.

Criticisms of the OMS
➤ Like Glass's study, it ignored women.
➤ It did not explore the extent of social closure/self-recruitment in the top elite positions.

The Essex Study
This covered both intergenerational and intragenerational mobility in the 1980s, and considered both male and female mobility. It confirmed many of the findings of the OMS:
➤ Absolute mobility was improving due to the expansion of white-collar jobs, but slowing down, and it was less for women than men.
➤ Relative mobility was largely unchanged: the class of origin had a strong effect on the opportunities for upward mobility.
➤ Only about two-thirds of men, and less than half of women, born into the working class who achieved intergenerational upward mobility when beginning their adult careers stayed in that class: they experienced intragenerational downward mobility during their working lives.

Other social mobility findings
➤ *Educational inequality* – The Sutton Trust found that pupils from disadvantaged homes (on free school meals) underachieve in education, and many lack the qualifications to enable upward social mobility.
➤ *Opportunity hoarding and the glass floor* – McKnight found high-attaining disadvantaged children have less chance of obtaining high earnings by the age of 42 than lower-attaining children from more advantaged middle-class backgrounds. McKnight suggested a 'glass floor' (an invisible base-line below which more advantaged groups will prevent their children from falling) was created by upper-middle-class parents using their social and cultural capital to protect their offspring's class position (opportunity hoarding).
➤ This would suggest we do not live in a meritocratic society.

Social mobility and women (page 356)

Women, compared to equivalent men:
➤ Are more likely to be downwardly mobile and less likely to be upwardly mobile.
➤ Are less likely to reach the top two classes, for those born in lower classes.
➤ Are as likely to face downward mobility as upward mobility.
➤ Have generally lower absolute mobility rates.

Social mobility and Black and Minority Ethnic (BME) groups (page 356)

➤ BME groups in Britain are experiencing more absolute upward mobility.
➤ BUT they face poorer chances of achieving upward mobility compared to their White British peers (relative mobility).
➤ Black men and women are particularly likely to experience downward mobility during periods of recession.
➤ Most BME groups have improved their levels of educational attainment, but these have not been reflected in their employment patterns.
➤ First-generation BME immigrants have lower rates of upward mobility than their British-born children and the rest of British society.
➤ First-generation middle-class BME immigrants are more likely to suffer downward mobility than upward.
➤ BME women are, overall, more likely to remain in the same social class throughout their lives, or to experience downward mobility.

Summary – the bottom line

Absolute mobility
➤ From the 1950s to the present, there have been high rates of intergenerational and intragenerational mobility.
➤ Around three-quarters of people have changed their social class compared to their parents, with the rest staying in the same class.
➤ Roughly half of those moving went up, and half moved down.
➤ BUT, for most, mobility is short-range – a bit up or a bit down: few move from the bottom to the top.
➤ In recent years, rates of upward mobility have been decreasing, as a result of the declining growth of higher-class positions, and the effects of economic recession.

Relative mobility
➤ Relative mobility increased from the 1970s onwards, but still remains starkly unequal:
  ➠ The chances of upward mobility into the higher middle class for those born into the working class remain very low.
  ➠ The chances of downward mobility for those born into the middle class remain very low.

➤ There is still a high degree of social closure and self-recruitment in the elite groups.
➤ The chances of social mobility, as with life chances in general, are still largely determined by a person's social class of birth, sex/gender, and ethnicity.

EXAM TIPS:

➤ To gain marks for knowledge and understanding, you need to know your mobility studies and what their findings show about the extent of social mobility, the problems/difficulties of studying social mobility, and the key terms and concepts – e.g. intergenerational and intragenerational, absolute and relative mobility.
➤ Watch out for time periods mentioned in questions or an Item, and stick with research and findings linked to that period – e.g. 'the past 30 years' or 'the past 50 years'. You won't get many marks for evidence outside the timescales specified, unless you're using them to show trends affecting social mobility within the time period.
➤ Watch out for 'hidden' questions where you can refer to social mobility – e.g. questions about whether or not Britain is a meritocracy, or the functionalist theory of stratification.
➤ Gain marks for application by using examples and referring to theories – e.g. feminist, functionalist or Marxist theories.
➤ Gain marks for analysis and evaluation by locating the evidence/importance/ significance/implications of social mobility in different perspectives – e.g. does the evidence on social mobility back up the functionalist/New Right theory of stratification of a meritocratic society based on equal opportunities for all? What does it show about feminist theories of patriarchy? Weberian theories of class and life chances? What implications does it have for Marxist theories of working-class solidarity and the development of class consciousness, or the social closure of the ruling class? Is the promise of social mobility, given most is just short-range, just a myth spread by the dominant ideology to maintain false class consciousness that society is fair? Examiners will LOVE this, as long as you keep it clearly focused on, and relevant to, the particular question being asked.

GENERAL EXAM TIP:

Remember that two out of the three exam questions on Stratification and Differentiation involve an Item to refer to. You *must* refer to that Item to achieve top-band marks. For 10-mark ('Applying material from Item O, analyse two') questions, you must refer *only* to ideas or issues that are raised in the Item. For 20-mark ('Applying material from Item P and your knowledge, evaluate') questions, you must refer to the Item and your knowledge gained elsewhere in your studies of Stratification and Differentiation. Remember the Item is there to help and guide you, so use it.

By the time you go into the exam, you should know all the material listed on page 360 and the key terms listed on page 361 of the textbook. Knowing the key terms and using them correctly will help you gain marks for knowledge and understanding. You can check their meaning on-the-go by going to the online glossary by following the link at www.politybooks.com/browne. Put it on your phone for ready reference.

6
THEORY AND METHODS

TOPIC 1
Consensus, conflict, structural and social action theories (pages 367–395)

Consensus and conflict theories (page 369)

➤ *Consensus theory* – Society is primarily harmonious. Social order is maintained through a widespread agreement between people on the important goals, values and norms of society – a value consensus. It is primarily associated with functionalist theory, which has its origins in the work of Durkheim.
➤ *Conflict theory* – Society is primarily conflict-ridden and unstable, as individuals and groups struggle with one another, pursuing competing interests. It is associated with Marxist, Weberian and feminist theories.
  ⟶ *Marxists* see societies divided by conflict and exploitation between bourgeoisie and proletariat.
  ⟶ *Feminists* see societies divided by patriarchy, with men in positions of power and dominance over women.
  ⟶ *Weberians* see conflicts in society arising between:
    ➤ *Social classes* – pursuing economic interests.
    ➤ *Status groups* – pursuing social prestige and respect.
    ➤ *Parties* – groups pursuing power to influence policies in their interests.

Structuralism (pages 369–370)

➤ The behaviour, values and identities of individuals are formed by external social forces.
➤ Sociology should study the overall structure of society, the social institutions which make up this structure, and the relationships between these social institutions (a macro, or large-scale, approach).
➤ Positivism is the main methodological approach, using quantitative research methods to measure the social forces acting on individuals to control their behaviour.
➤ The individual states of mind and meanings of individuals are seen as a reflection of these external forces, and so are not seen as worth studying in their own right.

Functionalism (consensus structuralism) (pages 370–375)

➤ Society is a system or a structure of interconnected parts which fit together to form an integrated whole. Institutions such as the family, religion and education are analysed in relation to the contribution they make to the maintenance of this system.

➤ Societies have functional prerequisites – basic system needs that must be met if societies are to survive.
➤ Parsons suggests society works a bit like the human body, with all body parts (social institutions) interconnected to maintain the needs of the human body (society) as a whole.
➤ To understand the workings and importance of one part, it is necessary to discover its function in maintaining the whole.
➤ All social phenomena have some function in society.

Functional prerequisites: Parsons's G.A.I.L. model

Parsons suggests that all societies, to survive in a healthy state, have to resolve instrumental and expressive problems by meeting four functional prerequisites or system needs, each of which is carried out by a separate sub-system:

Problems to resolve	Functional prerequisite	Sub-system
Instrumental problems (providing material needs for survival)	**G**oal attainment (means of setting collective goals and priorities)	Political
	Adaptation (adapting to the environment to provide material necessities)	Economic
Expressive problems (maintaining efficient cooperation and a sense of social solidarity)	**I**ntegration (coordinating all parts of the system through socialisation)	Cultural/community organisations
	Latency (minimising social tensions and interpersonal conflicts)	Family and kinship

The establishment and maintenance of social order: value consensus and social integration

➤ Durkheim suggested that people are basically selfish and pursue their own ends; society would soon collapse into chaos and disorder unless they learned to cooperate by sharing some common goals and values.
➤ Durkheim saw social order being maintained by the collective conscience (or value consensus) – a set of shared beliefs and values.
➤ Parsons saw the agencies of socialisation, like the family and the education system, playing a central role in building value consensus and integrating individuals into society.
➤ Socialisation is reinforced by social control.

Social change and social evolution

➤ Functionalists suggest social change is a slow process of social evolution, and occurs when new functions emerge or society needs to adapt.
➤ If change is too rapid, anomie may occur – a sense of moral confusion and uncertainty over social norms.

Evaluation of functionalism
✓ It is a reasonably successful attempt to produce a general theory of the workings of society.
✓ It recognises the importance of social structure in constraining individual behaviour, and how the major social institutions, like the family, education and the economy, often have links between them.
✓ It provides an explanation for social order and stability, and why most people generally conform to the rules of social life.
✗ It is too deterministic – it sees individuals as simply passive products of the social system.
✗ It is a metanarrative or grand theory that tries to explain everything from a single perspective.
✗ It does not explain social change very effectively, especially periods of very rapid social change.
✗ It paints a rosy picture of society, and over-emphasises the beneficial functions of social institutions. It has no sense of inequalities in life chances and power and their effects.
✗ It takes for granted there is a value consensus in society which will provide social stability. But value consensus in itself does not provide stability – it depends on the values.
✗ Conflict theorists argue that the value consensus assumed by functionalists just consists of the ideas of the dominant social class imposed on the rest of society through institutions like the education system, religion and the media.
✗ It tends to be very conservative, supporting the status quo.

Functionalism and the New Right
'New Right' describes a political ideology that stresses:
➤ Individual freedom.
➤ Self-help and self-reliance.
➤ A reduction of the power and spending of the state.
➤ The free market and free competition.
➤ The importance of traditional institutions and values.

New Right ideology shares much in common with functionalist theories of society:
➤ The importance of socialisation into shared core values for the maintenance of social stability.
➤ The importance of traditional institutions in building shared values, such as conventional marriage and family life, and traditional education.
➤ The maintenance of social order requires strong social control, such as cracking down hard on criminals and deviants.

EXAM TIPS:

➤ In questions on functionalism and/or the New Right, you should draw both on the criticisms of functionalism, and on other areas you have studied, to show application and evaluation skills – e.g. functionalist and/or New Right perspectives on Education, Families and Households, Beliefs in Society, Stratification and Differentiation, Crime and Deviance, etc.
➤ You can also draw on Marxist, feminist, postmodernist and social action theories to criticise functionalist theory.

Classical Marxism (conflict structuralism) (pages 375–379)

The social structure is divided into two main parts:

1. *The economic base, or infrastructure*, which is the driving force in society and underpins and determines everything else in society. This consists of:
   ⮕ *The means of production*.
   ⮕ *The relations of production* – the relations between those involved in production.
2. *The superstructure* – society's social institutions, such as the family, education, the media, religion and the political system, and beliefs and values (ideology), which are determined (or influenced) by the economic base.

In class societies, the means of production are privately owned. Society is divided into two fundamental social classes:

➤ The *bourgeoisie or capitalists* – a small, wealthy and powerful class of owners.
➤ The *proletariat or working class* – a much larger, poorer class of non-owners who sell their labour to the owners for wages in order to live.

The relationship between these two classes is exploitative because the workers produce more than is needed for employers to pay their wages – this 'extra' produced by workers is what Marx called 'surplus value', and provides profit for the employer.

Exploitation of workers by capitalists generated an inevitable class conflict and a class struggle for power.

➤ *The owning class was a ruling class and the dominant ideology is ruling-class ideology* – All the major institutions in the superstructure, e.g. the media, religion, the education system, the legal system, etc., spread this ruling-class ideology. This enables the ruling class to maintain ideological control over the working class.
➤ *False consciousness* – Ideological control means workers have a false consciousness, seeing their position as normal and accepting it rather than rebelling against the bourgeoisie.
➤ *Social change, class consciousness, revolution and communism* – Growing inequality between the classes would lead the working classes to develop an awareness of their exploitation, overthrow the ruling class, and form a classless, communist society.

Evaluation of classical Marxism

Strengths
✓ It recognises the importance of the economy and how economic change can influence a wide range of other social institutions.
✓ It recognises the importance of society's social structure, and links this to the ideas, consciousness and behaviour of individuals and groups.
✓ Its focus on private ownership provides an explanation for the extreme and increasing social inequalities in wealth, income and power that persist in contemporary societies.
✓ It explains the source of many conflicts and upheavals that periodically surface, many of which are rooted in social class inequalities.
✓ There is still evidence of capitalist exploitation on a global scale.
✓ There is widespread evidence that those from wealthy backgrounds occupy all the top elite positions in the superstructure.
✓ Media research shows a clear bias in the media that favours the dominant ruling-class ideology.

Weaknesses

- ✗ Marx's predictions of communist revolution have not come true and almost everyone in Western societies has far higher living standards than ever before.
- ✗ The collapse of the so-called 'communist' regimes in Russia and Eastern Europe casts some doubt on the viability of Marx's ideas.
- ✗ Globalisation has spread Western capitalist consumer culture throughout the world, making capitalism stronger than ever before.
- ✗ It over-emphasises the extent of conflict in society.
- ✗ Its two-class model of inequality is inadequate, missing out the middle class.
- ✗ It pays little attention to other sources of inequality such as ethnicity, age and gender.
- ✗ It gives too much importance to the economy, and doesn't allow for the possibility that the institutions of the superstructure may independently influence behaviour and cause social change.
- ✗ Institutions in the superstructure do not always spread the dominant ideology.
- ✗ It doesn't allow for free will and individual choice.
- ✗ Postmodernists argue that the main social divisions in contemporary societies are now around media-driven individual choices in consumption patterns and lifestyle.

Neo-Marxism (pages 379–381)

Humanistic neo-Marxism: Gramsci's concept of hegemony

- ➤ Institutions and ideology in the superstructure have relative autonomy from the economy, rather than being directly determined by it.
- ➤ The ruling class maintains its power mainly through its hegemony – ideological dominance and moral leadership of society, which persuades the rest of society to see its rule as legitimate and consent to it.
- ➤ Gramsci's neo-Marxism leans more towards a social action approach to society, with its emphasis more on the importance of people's ideas and meanings in bringing about revolutionary change, and less on the structuralist economic determinism of classical Marxism.

Structuralist neo-Marxism

Althusser argued that the structure of capitalist society consists of three levels: the economic level, the political level (including the *repressive state apparatus*) and the ideological level (the *ideological state apparatuses*). The political and ideological levels have relative autonomy from the economic base.

Althusser does not share Gramsci's view that people have free will and choice. Althusser retains the structuralist emphasis of classical Marxism: social structures are the key influences on people's ideas.

Evaluation of neo-Marxism

- ✓ It retains many of the strengths of classical Marxism.
- ✓ It has tried to overcome the economic determinism of classical Marxism, in which everything is explained by the operation of the economic base.
- ✓ The concept of hegemony (Gramsci) recognises the importance of people's ideas and actions.
- ✓ Althusser's concept of relative autonomy suggests that institutions in the superstructure can impact on the economy, and not simply the other way round.
- ✗ It underplays the importance of the economy in shaping social reality.
- ✗ It still has many of the weaknesses of classical Marxism.

EXAM TIPS:

➤ In questions on Marxist theory, you should refer to both classical and neo-Marxist theories.
➤ You can show application and evaluation skills by drawing on both the criticisms of Marxist theory, and examples of Marxist theories applied in other areas you have studied – e.g. Education, Families and Households, Beliefs in Society, Stratification and Differentiation, Crime and Deviance, etc.
➤ You can also draw on functionalist, feminist, postmodernist and social action theories to evaluate Marxist theory.

Social action or interpretivist theories (pages 381–382)

Social action approaches have the following features:
➤ Society and social structures/institutions are socially constructed creations of individuals, not something separate from and above them.
➤ An emphasis on the free will and choice of individuals, and the beliefs, meanings, feelings and interpretations they give to situations.
➤ A micro (small-scale) approach, which focuses on the study of individuals or small groups, rather than the overall structure of society.
➤ Interpretivism is the main methodological approach, using qualitative research methods, to study, uncover and interpret the meanings and definitions individuals give to their behaviour.

Symbolic interactionism (pages 382–384)

Symbolic interactionism is associated with Mead and Blumer, and has the following features:
➤ People interact in terms of symbols – objects, words (language), expressions or gestures to which individuals have attached meanings.
➤ These meanings develop and can change during the course of interaction between individuals.
➤ Individuals can only develop a conception of themselves by understanding how others see them.
➤ People are constantly forming and negotiating roles, and choosing how they interact with others.
➤ This process of negotiated interaction was called by Cooley the 'looking-glass self'.

The symbolic interactionist approach has been applied in two theories:
1. *Labelling theory* – This suggests that individuals and situations are labelled in particular ways, which can have consequences for them, e.g. in the Education topic, teacher attitudes, streaming and labelling can influence educational achievement and lead to self-fulfilling prophecies; in the Health topic, the consequences which flow for those labelled as mentally ill; in the Crime and Deviance topic, how police racist stereotypes affect the behaviour and attitudes of people in black communities.
2. *Goffman's dramaturgical theory and impression management* – Goffman compared the process of interaction to the idea of people being like actors on a stage. People act out performances to create an impression of themselves to try to convince others of the identities they wish to assert.

Ethnomethodology (page 385)

Ethnomethodology is associated with the work of Garfinkel, and has the following features:

➤ It rejects the view that society has any kind of social structure or social order outside of individuals' consciousness.

➤ Social order only appears to exist because members of society create it using their own common-sense assumptions and because other people share these assumptions.

➤ Social reality is simply a social construction.

➤ The task of sociologists is to discover how individuals make sense of the social world, and to uncover their taken-for-granted assumptions that enable them to impose some sense of order in their daily lives.

Evaluation of social action theory (page 386)

Strengths

✓ It shows that people are active and creative, and make sense of the world either through interaction with others (symbolic interactionism) or by drawing on their own common-sense understandings (ethnomethodology).

✓ It recognises that people actively create meanings and interpretations which influence the way they act. They are not simply puppets moulded by the social system.

✓ The micro approach and the use of qualitative methods mean research findings often have high levels of validity.

Weaknesses

✗ It doesn't pay sufficient attention to how social structures constrain behaviour and choice.

✗ It only describes people's motivations. It doesn't explain where people get their meanings and goals from.

✗ It underestimates or ignores the distribution of power. Not everyone has the same chance of getting their definition or classification of others to 'stick'.

✗ Postmodernists suggest that action theory is a metanarrative that claims to provide a full explanation of social life. Action theory is just one of many competing points of view.

✗ The micro approach and the use of qualitative methods mean research findings may lack reliability and representativeness.

Integrated approaches – combining structure and action (pages 386–389)

➤ Social structures provide the framework of rules which make interactions between individuals possible.
➤ These structures depend on people supporting and conforming to them, and people can make choices within those structures and change them.

Weber's sociology
➤ Weber argued it was necessary to develop empathetic understanding of the meanings people give to their behaviour by trying to see the world through their eyes: *Verstehen*.
➤ People can act to change structures, but the structures of inequality influence people's ideas and life chances, and limit the choices available to them.

Giddens's theory of structuration
➤ There's a duality of structure: structure and action depend on one another – it's a two-way process, or two sides of the same coin.
➤ Structures exist as long as people continue to take action to support them.
➤ Change occurs through reflexivity – people are constantly reflecting on the things they do and how they do them as they live their daily lives.
➤ Social structures, while constraining human action, also enable human action to take place in an orderly way, and people constantly reproduce these structures by their actions in supporting them. At the same time, people can also act to change those structures.

Evaluation of integrated approaches
✗ *Structuralists* argue that integrated approaches overstate the capacity of individuals to change society's social structures, and underestimate the constraints on individual choices of action.
✗ *Action theorists* argue that integrated approaches understate the capacity of individuals to change society, and overestimate the constraints of the social structure on individual choices of action.
✓ This probably means integrated approaches have got it about right. To develop a full understanding of social life, it is necessary to combine both structural and action theoretical approaches, macro and micro approaches, and positivist quantitative and interpretivist qualitative research methods.

EXAM TIPS:

If you get a question on structuralist or social action approaches to studying society:
➤ Show *knowledge and understanding* by referring to the general features of the approaches, and illustrate them using particular theories – e.g. for structuralism, refer to examples drawn from functionalism and Marxism; for social action approaches, refer to symbolic interactionism and ethnomethodology.
➤ Show *application* by using examples from other areas you've studied – e.g. for structuralism, use material factors explaining educational underachievement; for action approaches, refer to labelling and the self-fulfilling prophecy.
➤ For *evaluation*, use action theory to evaluate structuralism; use structuralism to evaluate action theory; and use integrated approaches as a conclusion for either.

Feminist theories (pages 389–394)

➤ There are inequalities in power and status between men and women, with women dominated by men and subordinate to them in most areas of social life.

➤ These inequalities generate differences of interest and conflict between men and women. Feminist theories are therefore conflict theories.

➤ Gender roles and inequalities are primarily socially constructed, and not based on innate (inborn) biological differences between men and women.

➤ Patriarchy is the main cause of gender inequality. Walby argues women are kept in a subordinate position through six structures:

1. *The household* – in which women have the primary responsibility for domestic labour and child-care, limiting their access to and advancement in paid work.
2. *Paid work* – women get lower-paid and lower-status work, and are more likely than men to be in part-time and temporary jobs.
3. *The state* – whose policies are primarily in the interests of men.
4. *Sexuality* – where different standards are expected from women and men.
5. *Male violence*.
6. *Cultural institutions* – which reinforce patriarchy and patriarchal ideology.

Liberal feminism

➤ Liberal feminists, like Oakley, suggest women's inequality arises primarily from society's culture and values.

➤ These generate a lack of equal opportunities for women, and keep women in a subordinate position to men.

➤ Equality for women can be achieved through a gradual process of reform.

Evaluation of liberal feminism

✓ Liberal feminist research has produced much evidence demonstrating that gender differences are socially constructed.

✓ It has had important effects on social policy, with the passing of anti-discrimination laws like the Equal Pay Act (1970), the Sex Discrimination Act (1975) and the Equality Act (2010).

✗ It merely deals with reducing the effects of women's subordination, rather than challenging the fundamental causes.

Radical feminism

➤ Patriarchy is the most fundamental form of inequality, with the world divided into two 'sex classes' of women and men.

➤ Men dominate women in all areas, are the key instruments of women's oppression, and all men benefit.

➤ All women, whatever their social class or ethnicity, have shared interests in challenging men.

➤ Patriarchal power inequalities are found in all public (outside the home) and private (family and personal relationships) spheres of life.

➤ Radical feminists propose the complete destruction of patriarchy. Equality between the sexes can only occur when the family is abolished, childbirth is carried out independently of men, and women begin to live their lives separately and apart from men.

Criticisms of radical feminism

➤ It assumes all women share common interests, but ignores inequalities between women.
➤ It doesn't recognise that gradual reforms have improved women's opportunities and weakened patriarchy.
➤ Living totally separately from men is a personal lifestyle choice, a means of escaping patriarchy rather than challenging it, and unlikely to appeal to all women.
➤ Not all men are engaged in the domination of women, and working-class or black women may find they have more in common with men in the same social class or ethnic group than they have with women outside these groups.

Marxist feminism

➤ Gender inequality arises primarily from the nature of capitalist society, not from an independent system of patriarchy.
➤ Capitalism intensifies patriarchal inequalities in the following ways:
  ➠ In the family, women are used as free labour in the form of unpaid domestic labour and child-care, which reproduces the next generation of workers, including ideological conditioning, at no cost to the capitalist.
  ➠ Women and children act as a brake on revolutionary ideas – men cannot afford to strike to improve their working conditions because their families would suffer while the strike lasted.
  ➠ Women's expressive role in the family is to absorb men's anger at their exploitation at work and this helps to keep capitalism stable.
  ➠ Women are used as a cheap labour force, and as a reserve army of labour, which can be sacked and returned to the home during periods of economic recession, and re-employed during periods of prosperity.
  ➠ It is working-class and other disadvantaged women who suffer the worst effects of these, and should be the focus of feminist action for change. Equality of women with men will only come about through revolutionary change which challenges both capitalism and patriarchy.

Criticisms of Marxist feminism

➤ It underplays the fact that patriarchy has existed in all known societies, not just capitalist societies.
➤ It is men, not just capitalism, who benefit from women's subordination.

Dual systems feminism

➤ Blends Marxist and radical feminist theories. Walby is the main theorist.
➤ Capitalism and patriarchy are two (dual) separate systems that interact with and reinforce one another in the form of 'patriarchal capitalism'.
➤ Lasting solutions to women's inequality lie in removing the twin structures of patriarchy and capitalism in both the private sphere of the family and the public spheres.
➤ Dual systems feminism has been criticised for its primarily theoretical approach, and for not offering many solutions to the problems of women's subordination that have not been already considered by other feminist theories.

Intersectional feminism*

- ➤ The subordination of women and women's experiences takes diverse forms in different contexts and among different social groups.
- ➤ In postmodern societies, there has been a weakening of structures like gender, social class and ethnicity as sources of identity. This is reflected in a diversity of meanings attached to being a woman in contemporary Western societies.
- ➤ The strength of intersectional feminism is that it recognises diversity in the experience of women's subordination, and that it is necessary to explore patriarchy and women's subordination in this increasingly complex and fragmented context.
- ➤ Liberal and radical feminists are critical because, by emphasising the differences between women, intersectional feminism deflects attention away from those problems shared by all women.

> **EXAM TIPS:**
>
> - ➤ Patriarchy is a key concept in feminist approaches – you should refer to it to gain marks for knowledge and application.
> - ➤ In answering questions on feminist theories, you can show application and evaluation skills by drawing on both the different varieties of feminism, and examples of feminist theories applied in other areas you have studied – e.g. feminist approaches to the family, education, health, religion, crime and deviance etc.

*In previous printings of this book, this was incorrectly referred to as 'Difference feminism'.

TOPIC 2

The concepts of modernity and postmodernity in relation to sociological theory (pages 396–403)

Modernism has three key features:

➤ Rational thought and scientific theories replace tradition, religion, magic and superstition as means of understanding the world.

➤ The belief that rational thought, science and technology would lead to the discovery of objective truths, and would enable human progress and improvement.

➤ Sociological theory and research could provide explanations of the social world in order to improve it.

Postmodernism has the following key features:

➤ A loss of faith in the superiority of rational thought and science as a means to progress and improvement of the world.

➤ 'An incredulity towards metanarratives' (big theories) and the 'myth of truth' (Lyotard). Objective truth does not exist. All knowledge of any kind is now equally valid. Rational thought and scientific theories are replaced by doubt and uncertainty.

➤ Society is changing rapidly and social structures like the family and social class are breaking down.

➤ Lyotard suggests postmodern societies are characterised by growing individualism. People form their identities without structural constraints, and through their individual lifestyle choices and the consumer goods they buy. Baudrillard called this 'the end of the social'.

Evaluation of postmodernism (pages 401–403)

Strengths

✓ It has highlighted some important cultural and social changes – e.g. in the media, culture, identity and consumerism.

✓ It recognises that identities are more fluid, changeable, and based on consumption and greater choice, and cannot be seen as a simple response to structural factors.

✓ It provides insight into most contemporary issues – e.g. increasing risk and uncertainty, globalisation, and the growing power of the media.

✓ In challenging sociological metanarratives, it has encouraged sociologists to reflect more on their assumptions, how they set about their research, and the meaning of some contemporary social changes.

Criticisms

- ✗ *Late modernity – not postmodernity.* Giddens says that we are now living in a new stage of modernity – late modernity or high modernity – not in a new era of postmodernity. People still plan rationally to change and improve their lives and the wider world.
- ✗ *Risk society and reflexive modernity – not postmodernity.* Beck, like Giddens, argues there's a new stage of modernity – 'reflexive modernity' in the 'risk society'. Science still has the capacity to make things better and control or reduce the new risks it has created, and reflexivity involves rationality, planning, progress and hope of improving society.
- ✗ *What is called 'postmodernity' is little other than the latest developments within modernity.*
- ✗ *It over-emphasises the influence of the media,* and tends to assume people are passive, and easily duped and manipulated by them.
- ✗ *It exaggerates the scale of social change.* Cultural tastes are still strongly influenced by class, gender and ethnicity. National cultures and identities, and national governments, are still strong.
- ✗ *It is too voluntaristic* in that it assumes that all individuals are free to act as they wish and can pick 'n' mix and change identities at will. It ignores significant influences from structural factors like differences in power, and the existence of widespread social inequality and poverty.
- ✗ *Postmodernism is itself a metanarrative* (an overarching attempt to describe the world and society).

EXAM TIPS:

- ➤ Make sure you know the differences between modernism and postmodernism, and why most sociological theories are modernist.
- ➤ Evaluate postmodernism by reference to structural and social action theories – e.g. by showing that structural factors and the power of social institutions, or social interaction, or the combination of structure and action (structuration) are still important constraints on people's behaviour – people may not have the free pick 'n' mix choices postmodernists suggest.
- ➤ Gain marks for application by drawing on examples of postmodernist approaches in other topic areas – e.g. in family and household diversity, in the fragmentation of beliefs, in culture and identity, in the media topic, etc.

TOPIC 3

The nature of science and the extent to which sociology can be regarded as scientific (pages 404–415)

The scientific method (pages 404–405)

Popper suggests that science involves the hypothetico-deductive method. This involves:
1. *Hypothesis formation*.
2. *Falsification* – Testing hypotheses against the evidence to try to prove them wrong.
3. *Empirical evidence*.
4. *Replication* – Test results should be capable of being verified by other researchers who can repeat (or replicate) the research.
5. *The accumulation of evidence*.
6. *The possibility of precise predictions*.
7. *Theory formation*.
8. *Scrutiny* – A scientific theory will stand only until some new evidence comes along to show the existing theory is false.

Science also involves objectivity and value-freedom by scientists . . .
➤ Open-mindedness – A willingness to consider all possibilities and evidence.
➤ Keeping personal prejudices, opinions and values out of the research process.
➤ Being prepared to submit research findings for checking and criticising by others.

Positivism (pages 405–406)

➤ Society is made up of what Durkheim called 'social facts' which exist outside individuals.
➤ Human behaviour is a response to observable social facts, and can be explained in terms of cause-and-effect relationships.
➤ Social facts should be treated as things, like objects in the natural world, and studied by direct observation and the use of quantitative, statistical methods of data collection.
➤ Sociology can be – and should be – an objective, value-free science if it follows similar scientific approaches to those used in the natural sciences.

➤ *The problem of prediction* – Human behaviour cannot be predicted with certainty.
➤ *Artificiality* – Sociology wants to study society in its normal state, not in the artificial conditions of a laboratory experiment.
➤ *Ethical issues* – Human beings might well object to being boiled, weighed, wired, prodded with sticks, interrogated or observed in laboratories.
➤ *The Hawthorne effect* – People may change their behaviour when being studied, making findings invalid.
➤ *Validity* – People may distort and conceal the truth, refuse to answer questions, raising the problem of obtaining valid evidence.
➤ *Empirical observation* – Not all social phenomena are observable or quantifiable, such as the meanings and motives people have for their behaviour.

Interpretivism

➤ To understand and explain human society, it is necessary to discover and interpret the meanings people give to situations, e.g. by Weber's *Verstehen*.
➤ Meanings are not social facts, but social constructions that do not exist independently of people's definitions.
➤ Sociologists cannot hope to explain anything without moving from quantitative, empirical data towards a more qualitative understanding of peoples' own subjective views of the world.

Realist view

➤ *Not all phenomena are observable* – Bhaskar adopts a realist view of science. This suggests that events in both the social and natural worlds can be caused by underlying structures and processes that can't be empirically observed, but we can discover them by their effects.
➤ *Prediction is not a precise process* – Much natural scientific research, like most sociological research, takes place in open systems where not all variables can be controlled, and scientific prediction is often difficult and imprecise.
➤ *Both positivists and interpretivists are using scientific approaches* – Positivists are focusing on the observable, and interpretivists on the unobservable, but both are engaged in 'doing science' as much as any natural scientist.

Social constructionist approach

➤ *Science is socially constructed* by the actions and interpretations of scientists themselves.
➤ *Kuhn argues scientists work within paradigms* – frameworks of taken-for-granted scientific laws, concepts, theories, methods and assumptions. These influence how they approach research.
➤ *Scientists don't always do what they claim to do* – Kaplan suggests that the research process is much more haphazard, unsystematic and ad hoc than the ideal of good scientific practice suggests.
➤ *Scientists cheat.*
➤ *Lack of scrutiny* – there is little prestige or career progress to be gained by replicating (repeating) other scientists' work to check their findings, so scientific research is not really scrutinised as carefully as it should be.
➤ *Science is also influenced by a wide range of social factors that undermine its objectivity and value-freedom*:
⇒ The values and beliefs, and career aspirations, of researchers will influence whether they think issues are worth studying or not.
⇒ Scientists (like sociologists) face a constant struggle to get money to fund their research and this may determine which research is carried out.
⇒ The pressure to publish findings (for career progression) may mean that data are misrepresented, or that exhaustive experiments to attempt to falsify a hypothesis are not carried out.

Postmodernism, sociology and science (pages 413–414)

➤ *Science is simply a metanarrative claiming a monopoly of the truth*, alongside similar social theories.
➤ *There is a loss of faith in the modernist view* that rational thinking and the application of scientific methods can control and improve the world.
➤ *No sociological research provides a factual description of social life*, and such research is a social construction created by sociological researchers.
➤ *There is no longer anything called 'society' or 'a social structure'*, and there is only a mass of individuals making separate choices about their lifestyles.
➤ *Objectivity and value-freedom are myths*, created by scientists (and positivist sociologists) to try to claim their views are superior to others, when all are just social constructions.

The bottom line (pages 414–415)

1. *Positivists argue sociology can and should be a science* – This can be achieved by studying social facts following the detached, objective, empirical and quantitative methods making up the scientific approach found in the natural sciences.

2. *Interpretivists argue sociology cannot be a science*, because of the different nature of the social world, the unpredictability of human behaviour, and the need to explore people's subjective states of mind and the meanings they give to their actions.

3. *Realists argue that both positivists and interpretivists have an incorrect understanding of what science is* – Science deals with both observable empirical data and hidden unobservable underlying structures, and in open systems.

4. *Social constructionists, and postmodernists, suggest that what counts as science is a social construction*. There is no objective science or scientific method 'out there' which is somehow independent of the beliefs and activities of scientists themselves or the society of which they are a part.

5. Sociologists can justly claim their work is no less objective or scientific than natural science as long as they *strive* to achieve the following five objectives.
   ⇒ *Value-freedom* – keeping their personal beliefs and prejudices out of the research process itself.
   ⇒ *Objectivity* – approaching topics and evidence with an open mind, in a detached and fair-minded way.
   ⇒ *Use of systematic research methods to collect evidence.*
   ⇒ *Analysing and evaluating data and drawing conclusions on the basis of evidence*, rather than personal opinion or hearsay.
   ⇒ *Making findings available to other researchers*, for inspection, criticism, debate and re-evaluation or replication.

EXAM TIPS:

➤ Questions on sociology and science usually revolve around whether the use of the scientific method is appropriate for use in sociology, or whether sociology can be or should be a science. To answer these well, you need to have a good grasp of what science is, and of the competing views of positivists and interpretivists.

➤ Evaluate by examining the realist, social constructionist and postmodernist views of science.

➤ Conclude by questioning whether science is really what positivists and interpretivists think it is, whether scientists always do what they claim to do, and maybe draw on the five points concluding this topic to suggest sociology can strive to be at least as scientific as the natural sciences.

➤ As always, stay focused on what the question is actually asking, and adapt material to fit the precise wording of the question.

TOPIC 4

The relationship between theory and methods (pages 416–423)

Positivism, interpretivism and research methods (pages 416–420)

Positivists and interpretivists have conflicting views about the nature of society, and this means they employ different research methods to gain knowledge about society. You should know the research methods and their strengths and weaknesses from your first-year studies, summarised in the following table.

Positivism	Interpretivism
View of society	
Society is an objective reality, made up of social structures/social facts independent of individuals, which mould their behaviour.	Society is a social construction of meanings and interpretations shared by a social group and actively created by their social action.
Theoretical perspective	
Structural theories, e.g. functionalism and Marxism: macro approaches.	Social action or interpretivist theories, e.g. symbolic interactionism and ethnomethodology: micro approaches.
Methodological approach	
Positivist or scientific approaches, using quantitative methods.	Interpretivist approaches, using *Verstehen* and qualitative data.
Research methods used to collect data	
➤ Statistics. ➤ Experimental method. ➤ Comparative method. ➤ Large-scale representative sample surveys. ➤ Structured questionnaires. ➤ Structured interviews. ➤ Non-participant observation.	➤ Personal accounts and documents. ➤ Uncontrolled experiments. ➤ Unstructured questionnaires. ➤ Unstructured interviews, focus groups and group interviews. ➤ Small-scale case studies. ➤ Participant observation.

Evaluation of positivism and interpretivism

Positivist criticisms of interpretivism	Interpretivist criticisms of positivism
Interpretivist methods do not allow for falsification and are not objective and scientific.	Positivist methods impose researcher's framework. Scientific methods inappropriate for study of society.
Interpretivist qualitative research methods lack reliability.	Positivist quantitative research methods lack validity.
Close involvement with those they are studying can lead to invalid results due to the Hawthorne effect and interviewer bias. Findings are highly subjective and depend on the researcher's own interpretations. Small scale of research means not representative, and so is of limited use.	The detachment of the researcher means they do not develop the empathy and closeness necessary to really understand the meanings that people hold. Statistics and data are social constructions. Large-scale surveys and quantitative data lack sufficient depth and detail.

Feminist methodology (pages 420–422)

Positivism
Feminist researchers have generally been critical of much quantitative positivist research in the past because:
- It ignored and excluded women and issues of concern to women.
- Findings from research on men were generalised to women.
- Its methods are 'malestream' in that they involve unequal power relationships – the researcher takes control. They also make a virtue of having as little involvement as possible with those being researched. Oakley argued that such approaches contradicted the aims of feminist research, which are concerned with encouraging women to open up and describe and share their experiences.

Feminism and interpretivism
Feminist researchers generally prefer interpretivist methods to research the lives of women because:
- *Verstehen* provides more valid, in-depth accounts of women's lives.
- Such methods enable feminist theory to emerge from the research itself (inductive approach/ grounded theory), rather than being imposed by the theoretical framework of the researcher.

Evaluation
- Feminists don't completely dismiss positivist research methods. Westmarland suggests that positivist large-scale surveys and official statistics may be useful to discover the scale of problems.
- Westmarland argues that different feminist issues need different research methods.
- Kelly et al. argue that 'what makes feminist research feminist is less the method used, and more how it is used and what it is used for' – that is, a clear commitment to improving the lives of women.

Is theory all that affects methods? (pages 422–423)

You should be aware of the following PET issues from your first-year studies. Figure 2 summarises these.
> Practical issues, e.g. funding, time available, characteristics of researcher, etc.
> Ethical issues, e.g. harmful consequences, informed consent, etc.
> Theoretical issues, which influence research methods and the choice of topic.

The real world of practical research will often involve . . .
> *Methodological pluralism* – The use of a variety of methods.
> *Triangulation* – The use of a variety of methods to check that the results obtained by a particular method are valid and reliable.

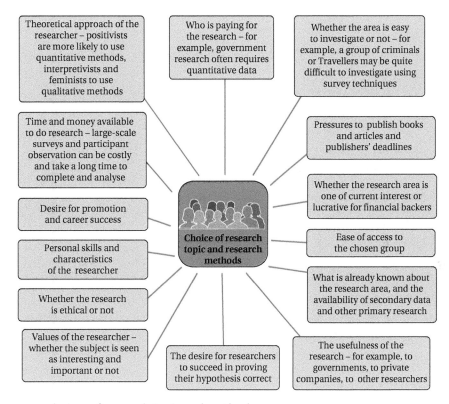

Figure 2 *Influences on choices of research topic and method*

EXAM TIPS:

> You need a good grasp of how the different theoretical perspectives of positivists and interpretivists mean they favour using different research methods.
> Evaluate one perspective by referring to the other – e.g. the strengths of positivism are often the weaknesses of interpretivism; the strengths of interpretivism are often the weaknesses of positivism. Draw also on feminist criticisms of positivist research methods.
> In any question on theory and methods, remember the PET (**P**ractical, **E**thical and **T**heoretical) formula. If the question picks on one, evaluate by showing the other two are important as well.

TOPIC 5
Debates about subjectivity, objectivity and value-freedom (pages 425–431)

Subjectivity, objectivity and values in sociology

➤ Subjectivity suggests sociologists are part of the society they are studying, and their own values and beliefs will affect the research in some way.
➤ Objectivity suggests researchers approach topics with a totally open mind and with complete detachment, separation and distance from those being researched.

Values in sociology
There are four main competing positions regarding the extent to which values influence sociological research:
1. Sociology should be, and can be, value-free.
2. Sociology cannot be value-free.
3. Sociology should not be value-free, even if it were possible.
4. The subjectivity/objectivity and values debate is meaningless and pointless.

Sociology should be, and can be, value-free (page 426)

This is the position taken by positivists.
➤ Sociology *should be* value-free so that it can be properly regarded as a science.
➤ Value-freedom would enable sociology to provide impartial, objective facts that can be used to influence social policy and improve the world.
➤ Sociology *can be* value-free if it uses similar methods to those used in the natural sciences.
➤ Since the collection of facts could be wholly separated from the subjective views and values of researchers, sociology could become an unbiased, objective, value-free science of society.

Sociology cannot be value-free (pages 427–428)

➤ A researcher's academic training, the paradigm or perspective they have learnt for collecting, interpreting and evaluating evidence, and their assumptions about society and their beliefs about what are important or unimportant areas to study are all sources of values.
➤ Sociological research does not uncover facts that 'speak for themselves'. 'Facts' have to be interpreted.
➤ The personal values and political views of the researcher influence the selection of the subjects studied.

➤ Gouldner argues that the idea of value-freedom:
  ➠ Serves the career interests of sociologists who will take funding from anyone and sell their research to the highest bidders.
  ➠ Enables sociologists to avoid taking any moral responsibility for the uses or consequences of their research.
  ➠ Allows sociologists to avoid having to take a stand and criticise society in the light of their findings.
  ➠ Supports the powerful in an unequal society by the pretence of being neutral.
➤ Gouldner argues sociologists should not even try to be value-free, but that there should be in sociology a clear value-commitment to improving an unequal society.
➤ Becker argues no knowledge is value-free, and all knowledge must favour somebody, and therefore we have to decide whose side we are on.
➤ This value-committed position has been taken by many feminists and Marxists.

This is the position adopted by postmodernists. They argue:
➤ There is no objective truth, and all forms of knowledge are social constructions.
➤ The assertion of the importance of value-free knowledge is simply an attempt by some groups to establish their interpretation as the only true or valid approach to studying society.

There are three ways that we can accept the existence of values in sociology, and still produce valid and/or reliable data:
1. Researchers' values in choosing a topic are unavoidable and should be made clear from the outset, but values and personal prejudices should never be allowed to enter the research process itself.
2. Values and personal prejudices should be considered when examining the ethics of research.
3. Findings should be open to inspection, criticism, debate and testing by other researchers, to check for any distortion and manipulation of results as a result of researchers' values, even if unintended.

EXAM TIPS:

➤ Questions on values typically take the form of 'can be', 'should be', 'can't be' . . . value-free. You should range across the four areas of debate mentioned in this topic, using the different positions to evaluate the specific one mentioned in the question – e.g. if it says 'sociology can be, and should be, value-free', outline the positivist position, and then criticise it using the three other views.

➤ Don't be afraid of challenging whatever view the question proposes, but explain it first, and then give good reasons for rejecting it.

➤ You can pick up marks for application by giving examples of where values intervene in research in other areas of your course – e.g. in Marxist, feminist or functionalist views of the family or religion.

TOPIC 6
The relationship between sociology and social policy (pages 432–441)

The contribution of sociology to social policy (pages 432–434)

Giddens and others suggest seven ways that sociology and sociological research can contribute to social policy-making:

1. *Providing an awareness of cultural differences* – Seeing society from different perspectives, and developing an awareness of the needs and problems of others.
2. *Providing self-awareness and understanding* – Providing evidence that enables and empowers individuals and groups to change their lives.
3. *Changing assumptions* – McNeill suggests social research can indirectly influence social policy by being absorbed into the taken-for-granted common-sense assumptions involved in society's dominant culture.
4. *Providing a theoretical framework for social policies adopted by governments.*
5. *Providing practical professional knowledge and research to support evidence-based social policy-making.*
6. *Identifying social problems, their causes and solutions.*
7. *Evaluating policies* – Research can evaluate existing policies, to see whether they achieved what they set out to, if they are working as intended, or they have any unintended consequences, and whether they need changing or scrapping.

Influences on social policy-making (pages 434–437)

➤ *Cost* – Governments may not be able to afford to implement social policies, or choose to make financial savings which can actually generate social problems.
➤ *Globalisation* – Governments have to take into account wider global issues, such as commitments under international law or membership of the European Union.
➤ *Political ideologies* – Governments may choose to ignore research evidence, or only selectively use – or misuse and distort – such evidence to implement policies which are political priorities driven by their ideologies or moral preferences.
➤ *Electoral popularity* – Policies that are unpopular with the public (or the media which influence it) stand less chance of being adopted.
➤ *Inequalities in power* – In an unequal society, the final decisions on what are defined as social problems and which social policies should be adopted fall to those who have the most power.

Sociological theories/perspectives and social policy (page 438)

➤ *Positivists* see their research as providing objective value-free data on which governments can form policies.
➤ *Functionalist/New Right perspectives* see the aim of social policy as reducing the involvement of the state in people's lives, encouraging self-help, and increasing social conformity.
➤ *Feminist perspectives* see their research as providing evidence to implement social policies that undermine patriarchy, promote equal opportunities and remove discrimination against women.
➤ *Conflict theorists* of all kinds emphasise research that promotes social policies that reduce social inequality and poverty, and the social conflict that arises from them.

Should sociologists be involved in social policy research? (pages 438–441)

YES

➤ *It is the only responsible thing to do* – The founders of sociology, like Comte, Durkheim and Marx, said the point of studying society was to improve it. This is the view taken by, for example:
  ⟹ *Positivists* – the researcher's role is to provide objective, value-free data uncovering the causes of social problems and the means of solving them.
  ⟹ *Many feminist sociologists*, particularly liberal feminists, who see their research into the inequalities facing women as a means of formulating policy recommendations and changing laws and policies to improve the position of women.
  ⟹ *Poverty and health researchers* who study issues with a view to making recommendations to government for social policies to make improvements.
➤ *It is necessary to access funding* – The largest sources of funding are government and other public bodies which commission research for social policy development.
➤ *It is necessary to ensure that social policy takes proper account of empirical sociological research* (Marsland).
➤ *It is necessary to get involved to reduce the risks of social policy becoming even more vulnerable to manipulation by powerful groups.*

NO

➤ *The funders of research can constrain what studies are undertaken and the methods used.*
➤ *There are potential ethical difficulties.*
➤ *Problems of objectivity in research* – There is a risk that policy-making becomes the driving force of sociology, with sociology being reduced to an extension of the political arm of government and serving its needs.
➤ *Unreasonable compromises* – Sociologists may have no control over the use to which their research is put.
➤ *Postmodernists suggest sociology should not be involved in social policy research* because, as Bauman and May argue:
  ⟹ It provides only interpretations of the world, rather than objective evidence on which social policy should be based.

⮕ Any successful use of sociological evidence in influencing social policy would simply be imposing sociologists' view of reality on others.

⮕ It would be contributing to the management of society, and enhancing the power of those who are already in control of society.

⮕ Sociology's role should be to contribute to social understanding and tolerance by enabling people to understand more about themselves and others.

EXAM TIPS:

➤ Questions on the relationship between sociology and social policy are usually fairly straightforward, and focus on the areas identified in this topic (contribution of sociology/other influences/different perspectives/whether sociologists should or should not be involved).

➤ Gain marks for application by giving examples of particular social policies or research drawn from other topics you've studied – e.g. policies on the family, education, poverty or crime.

➤ Evaluate the contribution of sociology by referring to the other influences on social policy, and the arguments of those who say sociologists shouldn't be involved.

➤ The postmodernist view as a critical conclusion might – in the right question – please examiners.

GENERAL EXAM TIPS:

➤ Theory and Methods questions appear on Paper 1 (1 x 10 marks, 'Outline and explain two . . .') and Paper 3 (1 x 10 marks, 'Outline and explain two . . .', + 1 x 20 marks with Item, 'Applying material from Item [C] and your knowledge, evaluate . . .' .

➤ On the Paper 3 20-mark question, you *must* refer to the Item to achieve top-band marks, and use it to give you clues to your answer if your mind goes blank.

➤ At A level, you are expected to have a good grasp of theory and methods, and you should refer to theoretical and methodological issues not only in answering specific Theory and Methods questions, but also, where appropriate, in answers on all topic areas.

By the time you go into the exam, you should know all the material listed on pages 442–443 of the textbook. You should also know the key terms listed on page 443. Knowing the key terms and using them correctly will help you gain marks for knowledge and understanding. You can check their meaning on-the-go by going to the online glossary by following the link at www.politybooks.com/browne. Put it on your phone for ready reference.

7
CRIME AND DEVIANCE

TOPIC 1
Crime, deviance, social order and social control (pages 446–472)

The social construction of crime and deviance (pages 447–449)

The social construction of crime
➤ Newburn suggests that crime is a label attached to behaviour which is prohibited by the state, and has some legal penalty against it.
➤ Crime is socially constructed – an act only becomes a crime when the label of 'crime' is applied to it.
➤ Crime covers a very wide range of behaviour, so it is extremely difficult to develop explanations that account for the vast diversity of acts that are labelled as criminal.

The social construction of deviance
➤ Like crime (itself a form of deviance), deviance is a social construction. Plummer distinguishes between societal and situational deviance:
   ⇒ *Societal deviance* – acts that most members of a society regard as deviant because they share similar ideas about approved and unapproved behaviour.
   ⇒ *Situational deviance* – acts where whether or not they are seen as deviant depends on the context or location in which they take place.
➤ These two conceptions suggest that what is regarded as deviant may:
   ⇒ *Vary between different societies, cultures, contexts and locations.*
   ⇒ *Vary between groups within the same society.*
   ⇒ *Change over time.*

Functionalist and subcultural theories (pages 450–454)

➤ Functionalism sees crime and deviance arising from the structure of society.
➤ Durkheim argued that some crime is inevitable, because not everyone is equally committed to the shared values and moral beliefs of society.
➤ Durkheim saw some deviance and crime as performing necessary and beneficial functions:
   ⇒ *Strengthening collective values* – punishing criminals reasserts the boundaries between acceptable and unacceptable behaviour.
   ⇒ *Enabling social change* – deviance is necessary to allow new ideas to develop.
   ⇒ *Acting as a 'safety valve'* – to ease stresses and frustrations in society.
   ⇒ *Acting as a warning device that society is not working properly.*

Strain theory and anomie
➤ Merton suggests that social order is based on a consensus around social goals.
➤ In an unequal society, not all individuals have the same opportunities of realising these goals by approved means.
➤ This means they face a strain or tension between goals they aspire to and the legitimate opportunities for achieving them. This leads to anomie. Most people conform and achieve goals by approved means. Merton argues those facing strain show four different 'modes of adaptation': innovation, ritualism, retreatism and rebellion.

Evaluation of Merton's strain theory
✓ It provides an explanation for different forms of deviance.
✗ It takes for granted a consensus around means and goals.
✗ It focuses on individual responses, and doesn't recognise the social pattern of crime.
✗ It doesn't explain why most people who face strain do not turn to crime or deviance.
✗ It exaggerates working-class crime.
✗ It only explains crime involving material goals, and doesn't explain violent crime or crimes that bring no obvious material or financial benefit.

Subcultural theories (pages 452–454)
➤ Explain deviance in terms of how groups, rather than just individuals, respond to the strain facing them in achieving social goals.
➤ Focus on male working-class juvenile delinquents, who constitute the largest group who are labelled criminals and deviants.

Status frustration
➤ Albert Cohen argues that working-class male youth accept mainstream goals, but cultural and material deprivation block legitimate means of achieving them, leading to status frustration.
➤ They react by forming a subculture that reverses mainstream values and replaces them with delinquent values. This gives working-class youth a chance to achieve status in their peer group.

Evaluation
✓ Cohen's theory explains working-class delinquency as a group response rather than an individual response.
✗ It wrongly assumes that delinquents originally accept the mainstream goals against which they react.

Cloward and Ohlin
Not all working-class youth have the same chances of accessing illegitimate opportunities. This leads to three types of delinquent subculture:
➤ *Criminal subcultures* – Found in more stable working-class areas. Adult criminals provide training and career opportunities for aspiring young criminals to achieve material goals by illegitimate means.
➤ *Conflict subcultures* – Found in socially disorganised areas. Young people respond by achieving status through violence, gang culture and opportunist street crimes.
➤ *Retreatist subcultures* – Those who fail not only in mainstream society but also in the criminal and conflict subcultures. They retreat into drug addiction and alcoholism.

Evaluation

✓ Cloward and Ohlin give insights into why working-class delinquency takes different forms in different social circumstances.

✗ They exaggerate the differences between the three types of subculture.

Miller

➤ Miller argues it is over-conformity to lower-working-class male subculture, rather than the rejection of dominant values, that explains working-class delinquency.

➤ This subculture revolves around focal concerns that carry the risk of law-breaking, but become exaggerated among young delinquents searching for peer-group status.

Criticisms of functionalist-based explanations of crime and deviance

➤ They assume there is some initial value consensus, from which people deviate in some way.

➤ They only explain working-class crime, and not white-collar and corporate crime.

➤ They rely on the pattern of crime shown in official crime statistics.

➤ The idea of a delinquent subculture implies that working-class youth are committed to delinquent values, but most working-class youth don't engage in deviant/criminal acts.

➤ Matza stresses that delinquents hold many of the values of mainstream society – they aren't seriously committed to delinquent values and most abandon delinquency as they grow older.

> **EXAM TIP:**
>
> In any question on functionalist or subcultural theories of crime and deviance, try to apply the theories to contemporary examples – e.g. blocked opportunities due to underachievement in education; gang and knife culture among some young people; or the 2011 riots in England. Evaluate the theories using other theories – e.g. Marxist and labelling theories.

Control theory (pages 454–456)

➤ Hirschi suggests that most people would commit crime if they had the chance. What stops them from doing so is the strength of their social bonds with other people.

➤ There are four social bonds that, if weakened or broken, will encourage people to turn to crime:

⮕ *Commitment* to conventional activities.

⮕ *Attachment* to those around them.

⮕ *Beliefs*, such as moral beliefs.

⮕ *Involvement* with sports teams, school activities, community and religious groups, etc.

Evaluation of control theory

✓ It recognises the importance of social integration in encouraging people to avoid crime.

✗ It assumes that those who commit crime and deviance have broken away from the bonds tying them into mainstream values, but Merton's theory and Matza's work suggest that criminals are committed to those values.

- ✘ It doesn't explain why some have weaker bonds than others, or why all those with weaker bonds don't turn to crime.
- ✘ It doesn't explain the variety of forms of deviance and crime.
- ✘ It doesn't recognise that it is possible to be deviant and have tight social bonds.

Traditional Marxist theories (pages 456–457)

- ➤ Capitalist society is criminogenic: crime is an in-built feature of capitalist societies that emphasise economic self-interest, greed, personal gain and consumerism. Crime is a rational response to the competitiveness and inequality of life in capitalist societies.
- ➤ Relative poverty means some are excluded from participation in the consumer society, encouraging crimes like theft, or vandalism arising from hostility caused by frustration at social exclusion.
- ➤ Laws are instruments to protect ruling-class interests.
- ➤ Box argues that what is defined as serious crime is ideologically constructed – usually that committed by the working class, rather than corporate, white-collar or state crimes.
- ➤ Official statistics suggesting crime is mainly a working-class phenomenon are largely due to the selective enforcement of the law.
- ➤ Snider suggests the biggest, most costly and most damaging crimes of all are those committed by the ruling class.
- ➤ Individuals, not the system of inequality, are blamed for crime. This diverts the working class's attention away from their exploitation and directs it towards other members of their own class.

Neo-Marxist theories (pages 457–458)

- ➤ Many facing poor economic circumstances do not commit crime, and so choosing crime is a voluntary act.
- ➤ Neo-Marxist theories view working-class crimes like theft, burglary and vandalism as meaningful and symbolic political acts of resistance to ruling-class oppression.
- ➤ The neo-Marxist approach is generally associated with the New Criminology. This suggests that to understand crime and deviance fully, it is necessary to draw on both structural (Marxist) and interactionist (labelling) approaches, involving an exploration of six dimensions:
  - ⇒ The wider social origins of the deviant act.
  - ⇒ The immediate origins of the deviant act.
  - ⇒ The meaning of the act to the deviant.
  - ⇒ The immediate origins of the societal reaction.
  - ⇒ The wider origins of the societal reaction.
  - ⇒ The effects of societal reaction on the deviant's further action.

✓ They highlight the importance of inequalities in power and wealth, and the conflicts these create.
✓ They emphasise the biggest crimes are white-collar, corporate and state crimes, not working-class crimes.
✗ They over-emphasise property crime – they say little about offences like rape, domestic violence, child abuse and murder.
✗ They over-emphasise class inequality, and neglect other inequalities.
✗ Feminists regard them as malestream, for focusing primarily on male criminality.
✗ Traditional Marxist theories ignore the fact that most working-class people, even the poorest, do not commit crime.
✗ It is difficult to interpret all laws as reflecting ruling-class interests.
✗ They romanticise crime, viewing criminals as fighting political oppression, when the main victims of their crimes are mainly other working-class people.
✗ They don't suggest practical policies to prevent crime and protect victims, who are overwhelmingly working-class.

EXAM TIPS:

➤ In questions on Marxist theories of crime, refer to both traditional Marxist and neo-Marxist theories. You should also consider white-collar and corporate crime.
➤ Watch out for broader questions on crime which might involve Marxist and a wider range of theories, including functionalist and labelling theories – e.g. questions about inequality, power or social class and crime.
➤ Gain marks for application by referring to research and contemporary examples.
➤ Evaluate by referring to other theories – e.g. functionalism, labelling theory and Left Realism, as well as criticisms of Marxist approaches themselves.

Interactionist theories: labelling theory (pages 459–463)

➤ Many people involve themselves in some deviant or illegal behaviour, so it is hard to sustain a distinction between deviants and non-deviants.
➤ Official crime statistics are social constructions, showing only an unrepresentative group of offenders who have been caught and publicly labelled as criminal.
➤ Becker suggests there is no act that is in itself deviant – deviance is a social construction, and only exists when someone defines an act or person as deviant.
➤ Moral entrepreneurs are those who have the power to create their own definitions of deviance and impose them on society.
➤ Agencies of social control, like the police, have and use considerable discretion and selective judgement in deciding how to deal with illegal or deviant behaviour. Becker suggests that police responses to deviant behaviour are influenced by stereotypes.

➤ Lemert distinguishes between primary deviance (deviant acts before the person is publicly labelled) and secondary deviance (deviance that follows after public labelling). Primary deviance has few social consequences, because no one knows about it. Being caught and publicly labelled as deviant may have major consequences for the individual as the label becomes a master status that overrides all others.

➤ This can lead to a self-fulfilling prophecy and what Becker called 'a deviant career' – as people can't shake off the label. Labelling theorists therefore see societal reaction, and labelling people as deviant, as producing more deviance than they prevent (deviancy amplification).

Evaluation of labelling theory

Strengths
✓ It challenges the idea that deviants are different from 'normal' people.
✓ It shows the importance of the reactions of others in defining and creating deviance.
✓ It reveals the importance of stereotyping in understanding deviance.
✓ It reveals the way official crime statistics are a product of bias in law enforcement.
✓ It reveals the importance of those with power in defining acts and people as deviant.
✓ It shows how labelling can lead to a self-fulfilling prophecy and to deviant careers.

Weaknesses
✗ It tends to move the blame for deviance away from the deviant and on to those who label other people as 'deviant'.
✗ It assumes an act isn't deviant until it is labelled as such.
✗ It doesn't explain the causes of deviant behaviour which precede the labelling process (primary deviance), or where stereotypes come from in the first place.
✗ It is too deterministic and doesn't allow for the possibility that some people choose deviance, or that labelling doesn't always lead to a self-fulfilling prophecy and more deviance.
✗ It ignores the importance of wider structural factors in creating deviance, and assumes it is all down to societal reaction.
✗ It has little to say about the victims of crime.
✗ It has no real policy solutions to crime.

> **EXAM TIP:**
>
> In questions asking you to assess the contribution of labelling theory to explanations of crime and deviance, emphasise the social construction of crime and crime statistics, and concepts like moral entrepreneurs, primary and secondary deviance, selective law enforcement, deviant careers and deviancy amplification. Refer to how the label of 'deviant' is applied differently according to class (white-collar and corporate criminals versus working-class offenders), gender (men more than women) and ethnicity (black more than white). Include in your evaluation reference to other theories – e.g. structural explanations by Marxists and functionalists – to show it's not all down to labelling.

Feminist theories of crime and deviance (pages 463–464)

Feminists have criticised much sociological theory and research on crime and deviance:

➤ It was malestream – gender issues and female offending were largely forgotten or ignored.
➤ There was little attempt to explain female offending or other forms of female deviance.
➤ Female victimisation was ignored.

Feminist criminology has grown to focus on the following issues:

➤ Female offending and the experiences of women in the Criminal Justice System (CJS).
➤ Female victimisation, particularly from male physical and sexual violence.
➤ The gender gap in offending.
➤ The importance of gender identity in the understanding and labelling of crime and deviance.

> **EXAM TIP:**
>
> Refer to feminist theory as a standing criticism/evaluation of theories of crime which tend to focus on men – e.g. subcultural and Marxist theories.

Realist theories of crime (pages 464–465)

Realist theories differ from other theories of crime and deviance in that they:

➤ Disregard abstract theoretical structural explanations (Marxism and functionalism) or explanations that see crime as simply a social construction (labelling theory).
➤ Focus on the real-world impact of crime on victims and local communities, and the development of practical policies to reduce crime.

> Note: Left and Right Realist policies for crime reduction are covered in Topic 4 (see pages 189–190).

Left Realism (pages 465–468)

Left Realists use three concepts to explain why working-class people turn to crime . . .

➤ *Relative deprivation* – A sense of feeling deprived relative to others they compare themselves with, generating discontent and resentment.
➤ *Marginalisation* – Social inequality generating political, economic and social exclusion from mainstream society.
➤ *Subculture* – Working-class deviant subcultures emerge as group solutions to the problems of status frustration arising from relative deprivation and marginalisation.

Late modernity and the bulimic society

Young has emphasised how features of society in late modernity have intensified the sense of relative deprivation among young people:

➤ Constant exposure in a media-saturated society to a consumer culture from which the poorest are excluded. This creates a 'bulimic society' in which people gorge themselves on media images of expensive consumer lifestyles, but are then forced by economic circumstances to vomit out their raised expectations.

➤ Growing individualism.

➤ The weakening of informal controls.

➤ Growing economic inequality.

The frustration this causes finds outlets in all kinds of thrill-seeking and risk-taking behaviour that Lyng called 'edgework', which can lead to crime and violence.

The square of crime

Lea and Young suggest it is necessary to examine the interrelationships between four elements of 'the square of crime':

➤ *Social structural factors and formal control by the state.*

➤ *The public and informal social control* – how local people react to crime.

➤ *The role of victims.*

➤ *The offenders* – why do they choose to offend?

Evaluation of Left Realism

Strengths

✓ It draws on a range of theories, producing a fuller explanation for crime than any one theory.

✓ It does not glamorise crime as Marxist writers do, and takes the importance of tackling crime and the fear of crime seriously.

✓ It recognises that ordinary crime typically affects deprived communities the most.

✓ It sees the importance of community solutions to crime (see page 189).

Limitations

✗ It neglects other responses to relative deprivation and marginalisation apart from crime, such as Merton's retreatism and ritualism.

✗ It neglects gender as a significant issue.

✗ It doesn't pay much attention to white-collar and corporate crime.

✗ It doesn't really explain why most deprived working-class youth don't turn to crime.

Right Realism (pages 468–469)

➤ *Value consensus underpins society and the law* – Criminals breach this consensus, threaten social order, and spread fear in communities.
➤ *People are naturally selfish and self-seeking*, and will take shortcuts to achieve rewards by committing crime if they can.
➤ *Inadequate socialisation and lack of community controls underlie crime and anti-social behaviour* – This view is found among New Right theorists.
➤ *Rational choice and opportunity theory* – Cornish and Clarke say people are rational and take opportunities to commit crime only after weighing up the costs and benefits and deciding whether it's worth taking the risk.
➤ *Crime will always exist* – The most that can be achieved is to reduce the impact of crime on victims.

Evaluation of Right Realism

✓ It addresses the immediate causes of crime, and provides policies for reducing the opportunities for crime (see pages 189–90).
✓ It recognises the importance of community control and community responses to crime in affecting crime levels.
✗ It doesn't address the wider structural causes of crime as other theories do.
✗ It doesn't pay any attention to white-collar and corporate crime, and other 'hidden crimes' like domestic violence and child abuse.
✗ It suggests that offenders act rationally, but some crimes are impulsive or irrational, and do not bring any obvious gain – e.g. vandalism or violence.

EXAM TIPS:

➤ Right Realism might appear in questions as the New Right – treat them as the same, but for the New Right add emphasis to New Right ideas of the underclass and crime.
➤ There are two main types of question on Realist theories of crime. First, those that ask about the contribution of Realist (in general)/Left Realist/Right Realist theories to understanding crime. Second, those that ask about their policies for reducing crime. In either case, you should evaluate the theories or policies in relation to other theories of crime.
➤ If the question asks about Realism in general, refer to both Left and Right Realism drawing out the similarities and differences between them. If it asks about Right (or Left) Realism, evaluate using Left (or Right) Realism and other theories or policies.
➤ Always include policies that follow from the theories when evaluating their contribution to the understanding of crime and deviance.
➤ Refer to examples and research to gain marks for application (as you should in *any* exam question).

Postmodernist theories of crime (pages 469–471)

➤ There is no consensus about what constitutes conformity and deviance.
➤ The law, and what is defined as 'crime', reflect an outdated metanarrative expressing a particular view among those with power.
➤ Henry and Milovanovic suggest that crime should be reconceptualised as people using power to show disrespect for, and causing harm of some sort to, others, whether or not it is illegal.
➤ Postmodern societies are characterised by a range of features which increasingly undermine people's integration into society and respect for others, and free them from the constraints arising from social norms:
  ➠ Growing individualism.
  ➠ A diversity of values.
  ➠ Consumerism – growing importance of owning goods as a source of identity.
  ➠ Rapid change causing anomie.
  ➠ Insecurity, uncertainty and risk.
  ➠ Weakening or disintegrating social structures.
  ➠ Growing social fragmentation.
➤ The individualism of identity in postmodern society means that the social causes of crime are undiscoverable, as they lie in the individual, not in society.

Evaluation of the postmodernist approach
✔ It recognises that there are other dimensions to the causes of crime beyond the more structural theories which have dominated in the sociology of crime and deviance.
✔ It offers explanations for non-utilitarian crime, which brings no material benefit.
✔ It provides a fuller picture of crime than that traditionally provided, as the transgressive conception of crime as 'harm' encompasses a range of behaviour that has been largely neglected in the law and in sociological theories.
✘ It doesn't explain why most people don't use their power to harm others.
✘ It fails to recognise that inability to participate in consumer society can lead to resentment.
✘ It fails to recognise that many people still have strong conceptions of right and wrong.
✘ The features of postmodern societies it identifies can't explain the decrease in crime since the 1990s.
✘ Lea argues that postmodernist theories are not contributing anything new, and that labelling theory and Marxist theories concluded long ago that crime was simply socially constructed by those with power.

TOPIC 2

The social distribution of crime and deviance by ethnicity, gender, and social class (pages 473–500)

Crime statistics (pages 473–480)

The sources of crime statistics
➤ Police recorded crime (PRC) – Offences either detected by or reported to the police, and recorded by them.
➤ Victim surveys of people who have been victims of crime. The largest of these is the annual Crime Survey for England and Wales (CSEW).
➤ Self-report studies – Anonymous questionnaires in which people are asked to own up to committing crimes, whether or not they have been discovered.
➤ Court and prison records, and records on police cautions, which reveal some of the characteristics of offenders who have been caught.

The social construction of crime statistics
➤ *Reliability* – There may be inconsistencies in the way crimes are classified and the police have some discretion in how they classify offences.
➤ *Validity* – They are not a complete picture, as there's a 'dark figure' of undiscovered, unrecorded and unreported crime.

Unreported crime
The CSEW suggests around 60% of the crimes it covers are never reported to the police. Reasons include:
➤ It was too trivial, involved no loss, or the police couldn't do anything.
➤ It was a private matter which people dealt with themselves.
➤ It was inconvenient to report.
➤ It was the victim's own fault or the offender was not responsible for their actions.
➤ Fear of reprisals for reporting it.
➤ Embarrassment at the offence.
➤ Dislike or fear of, or previous bad experiences with, the police and courts.

Reported but unrecorded crime
The police may decide not to record an offence that has been reported to or observed by them because:
➤ They regard the matter as too trivial to waste their time on.
➤ It has already been satisfactorily resolved, or the victim does not wish to proceed with the complaint.
➤ They may regard the person complaining as too unreliable to take his or her account of the incident seriously.
➤ They may interpret the law in such a way that what is reported is not regarded as an offence.

Changes in reporting, and counting and recording crime

➤ *Media reports may exaggerate and distort events and make problems seem worse than they are,* which may make people more likely to report such crimes.
➤ *Changing police attitudes, priorities and policies* – which can influence areas, groups or offences they target.
➤ *Changing norms and public attitudes* may encourage more offences to be reported, even though more offences may not necessarily have been committed.
➤ *Community policing and higher policing levels* may lead to more crimes being detected and reported.
➤ *Changing counting rules.*
➤ *More sophisticated police training, communications and equipment* can lead to increasing detection of crime.
➤ *Changes in the law* can lead to more things becoming illegal, so more recorded crime.
➤ *People have more consumer goods to lose today,* and insurance claims for theft or criminal damage require the offences to be reported to the police.

Attempts to overcome the limitations of official statistics

Victim surveys
Victim surveys provide insights into the victims of crime. They have the following limitations:
➤ People may exaggerate, or lie.
➤ People may forget when and whether they were victimised.
➤ People may not realise they have been the victims of a crime.
➤ Victims may feel embarrassment or guilt at admitting to being a victim.
➤ Consensual or victimless crimes, where both parties agree to commit an offence and both have something to lose, are not likely to be reported.

Self-report studies
These ask people to 'own up' to their offending. They have some limitations:
➤ Validity – Offenders may exaggerate the number and type of crimes they've committed to impress researchers, or understate or lie about more serious offences.
➤ They may ignore respondents' own definitions of crime.
➤ They rely on memory.
➤ Lack of representativeness – Those who live more chaotic lifestyles, like many young offenders, are the least likely to participate in such surveys.

The use of crime statistics by sociologists
Sociologists from different theoretical perspectives have responded to the ambiguity and uncertainty in the official statistics in the following ways:

Functionalism, New Right, Right Realism	Broadly accept statistics as accurate and representative of most crime. Useful for establishing patterns and trends.
Interactionism/labelling theory	Statistics are social constructions, and useful only to reveal the stereotypes, labelling and assumptions of the Criminal Justice System (CJS) and the public.
Marxism/neo-Marxism	Statistics provide a biased view of crime – they under-represent white-collar and corporate crime.
Feminism	Statistics under-represent the extent of female crime, and crimes by men against women.
Left Realism	Statistics are broadly correct, though they under-represent white-collar and corporate crime.

Trends in crime

Official statistics show the following trends in crime:

➤ From the 1930s to the early 1950s, there was a gradual rise.
➤ From the 1950s to the early 1980s, there was a steeper rise.
➤ From the 1980s to the mid-1990s, there was a rapid increase.
➤ From the mid-1990s to 2016, there was a gradual annual decline – though some offences have been increasing.

EXAM TIP:

You should remember the limitations of crime statistics for most questions, and refer to them when evaluating theories and patterns of crime – e.g. if the statistics lack reliability and validity, how can the theories based on them be adequate? The social construction of statistics is a good example to use when discussing labelling theory and the construction of crime and deviance – e.g. showing police stereotypes etc.

Ethnicity and crime (pages 480–487)

Official statistics suggest what appear to be higher levels of criminality among some Black and Minority Ethnic (BME) groups. Compared to white people, BME people are over-represented at all stages in the Criminal Justice System (CJS).

Explanations of the links between ethnicity and offending

Neo-Marxists

➤ Deny there is greater criminality among BME people than whites: it is a myth created by negative stereotyping and labelling by the police and the media.
➤ Gilroy argued BME crime is a form of political resistance to inequality, the racism in white culture, and police racism, harassment and oppression.
➤ Stuart Hall argued black youth have been used as scapegoats on which to blame social problems which have their origins in the wider social system.

Evaluation of neo-Marxist explanations
- ✓ They offer an explanation for BME crime.
- ✗ Gilroy seems to be imposing his own interpretation of the meaning of black crime when he describes it as a political act against oppressors.
- ✗ Lea and Young point out that most crimes are reported by the public, not uncovered by the police, so it is hard to explain BME crime purely in terms of police racism.

Left Realism
Accepts that BME crime, for some offences, is higher than that committed by whites because of:
- ➤ *Marginalisation* – Some BME groups are marginalised and lack power, and so legitimate opportunities to achieve mainstream goals are blocked.
- ➤ *Relative deprivation* – Many BME people are deprived.
- ➤ *Subcultures* arise from marginalisation and relative deprivation.

Poverty, social exclusion and the search for identity
- ➤ Bowling and Phillips suggest higher levels of robbery by black people are linked to higher levels of poverty and social exclusion amplified by racism.
- ➤ Crime can provide peer-group status and a sense of a powerful black identity otherwise denied.
- ➤ Pakistanis and Bangladeshis suffer worse poverty, but have lower crime rates because Asian communities offer a clearer cultural identity, and stronger controls limiting the opportunities and desire to establish status through crime.

Labelling, stereotyping and racism in the criminal justice system (CJS)
- ➤ Labelling theorists and Marxists argue that statistics suggesting BME people are more likely to be offenders than whites are evidence of racist police stereotyping and of selective law enforcement rather than more criminality.
- ➤ Phillips and Bowling suggest evidence of indirect or direct racial discrimination in the CJS is shown in the following ways:
  - ⟹ Institutional racism.
  - ⟹ Mistrust of the police by BME suspects makes them less likely than white offenders to cooperate with police officers, making them ineligible for reduced sentences.
  - ⟹ BME groups are more likely than white offenders to fit the stereotype of those thought most likely to jump bail, so they are more commonly remanded in custody.
  - ⟹ BME people, especially youth, are targeted for heavier policing, and stop and search, as they fit police stereotypes of 'troublemakers'.
  - ⟹ The police arrest and charge some BME suspects without sufficient evidence: charges are more likely to be dropped before reaching court, and those that do reach court have a lower conviction rate than those involving white offenders.
  - ⟹ Discrimination in sentencing – Black people face a greater likelihood both of being given a prison sentence and of receiving longer sentences.
  - ⟹ The cumulative effects of social exclusion and racism mean BME groups make up twice the proportion of prisoners compared to their proportion in the general population, and black people are over-represented by four times.

Gender and crime (pages 487–493)

In England and Wales, men account for around three-quarters of all persons convicted of any offence, and 95% of prisoners. Men are more likely to be repeat offenders and in general they commit more serious offences.

Why do females appear to commit less crime than men?
➤ Women commit less detectable offences so appear less in official statistics.
➤ Sex-role theory, generally associated with functionalism and the New Right, argues:
  ➠ Women are socialised to be less competitive and aggressive, and more averse to the risk-taking involved in crime.
  ➠ The dual burdens of housework/family management and paid employment give them fewer opportunities to commit crime.

Labelling, control theory and rational choice and opportunity
Carlen argues women are encouraged to conform by the class deal and the gender deal:
➤ *The class deal* refers to the material rewards that arise from working in paid employment.
➤ *The gender deal* refers to the rewards and status that arise from fulfilling their roles in the family and home.
➤ If opportunities of achieving these rewards are blocked, some women may make a rational decision to choose crime.

Heidensohn suggests that women face greater pressures to conform:
➤ Tighter social controls reducing their opportunities to deviate.
➤ A greater risk of stigma or shame if they get involved in crime and deviance.
➤ The double jeopardy of being condemned for committing a crime and losing their 'respectable' reputation through labelling by men as 'unfeminine'.

Heidensohn suggests that there is a patriarchal ideology of different spheres:
➤ *The public sphere*, which is dominated by men and where most crime takes place, restricts women's opportunities to deviate.
➤ *The private sphere* of the home, where women face patriarchal control through being allocated domestic responsibilities, so they have less opportunity for crime.

The chivalry thesis
Pollak first proposed the chivalry thesis, which suggests that women are treated more leniently than men by the CJS and less likely to be labelled as criminal.

Evidence for the chivalry thesis
➤ Female first offenders are about half as likely to be given a sentence of immediate imprisonment as their male counterparts.
➤ Women are less likely to be remanded in custody.
➤ Women are more likely to receive suspended or community sentences rather than imprisonment.
➤ Women receive, on average, shorter prison sentences.
➤ Female offenders are more likely to benefit from more informal approaches to their offences by the police, particularly for minor offences.

Evidence against the chivalry thesis
➤ Women's less severe treatment by the CJS is mainly due to the fact that they commit less serious offences than men.
➤ Women have more 'mitigating factors' which reduce the length of prison sentences; men generally have more 'aggravating factors', leading to their longer sentences.
➤ Heidensohn suggests that women are on trial both for the crime they commit and for deviating from stereotypes of femininity ('double jeopardy').
➤ In rape cases, women often have to prove their respectability and conformity before their evidence is even taken seriously by juries and judges.

Growing female criminality
The main explanation for this is Adler's 'liberation thesis'. This suggests:
➤ Women now have more independence, and are becoming more successful than men in both education and the labour market. This opens up more opportunities for crime.
➤ The traditional forms of control on women are weakening, particularly among younger women.
➤ There is much more of a masculinised 'ladette' culture.

Evidence against the liberation thesis
➤ Heidensohn and Silvestri suggest that the reported increase in girls' violence is only due to the police and the CJS acting more formally in arresting, prosecuting and labelling and criminalising girls' bad behaviour, rather than their behaviour becoming more criminal.
➤ The main offences women commit still tend to be much less serious than those committed by men.

Why do males commit more crime than women?
Many of the explanations above can be reversed to explain why men commit more crime than women and have more opportunities to do so.

The masculinity thesis
➤ Male crime is related to masculine gender identity, Connell's 'hegemonic masculinity': toughness, aggression, competitiveness, risk-taking, etc.
➤ Messerschmidt suggests that when legitimate means of achieving masculine identity are blocked or missing, men seek out alternative means, such as crime.

Evaluation of the masculinity thesis
- ✓ It provides a plausible explanation for why men might commit more crime than women.
- ✗ It doesn't explain why only some men who don't have access to legitimate means of asserting masculinity turn to crime.
- ✗ Not all male crime can be interpreted as an expression of masculinity.

Labelling, control theory and rational choice and opportunity
- ➤ Labelling theorists suggest that police assumptions and stereotypes are the opposite of those discussed above in relation to women: the police are more likely to see men as potential offenders, to label their behaviour as criminal, to press charges against them.
- ➤ Men dominate the public sphere where most crime is committed, and they face fewer constraints than women, such as responsibility for housework and childcare.
- ➤ Men have less to lose in terms of reputation if they are labelled as criminal.
- ➤ Men have more independence and opportunities to commit crime than women.

EXAM TIPS:

- ➤ Questions on gender and crime could be wrapped up in various ways – e.g. the chivalry thesis, why men commit more crime than women, why women commit less crime than men, gender and crime in general, or the masculinity thesis, etc. Make sure you apply your answer to the specific issue asked about in the question, and evaluate by referring to other explanations.
- ➤ Don't forget to apply your theories – e.g. labelling, control theory, feminist theories, rational choice and opportunity theories, etc.
- ➤ Remember, you can use issues in gender and crime as examples in theory essays – e.g. feminist theory, labelling theory, Right Realism, control theory, etc.

Social class and crime (pages 493–499)

The working class and crime
- ➤ Official statistics show that it is predominantly working-class young males, both black and white, who are the main offenders.
- ➤ Part of the explanation is that the working class commit more public, detectable property offences – the 'crimes of the streets'.
- ➤ The theories of crime covered in Topic 1 provide a range of explanations for this pattern.

Evaluation of explanations for working-class crime
Many evaluative points concerning the explanations for working-class crime have been made in Topic 1, but there are two major criticisms which you should bear in mind:
- ➤ The explanations don't give any reason why only some of those in the same circumstances in the poorest sections of the working class turn to crime (and most don't).
- ➤ Offences committed by members of other social classes may be undetected and unrecorded, or dealt with outside the criminal law. The suggestion that most criminals are working-class may therefore be exaggerated.

EXAM TIPS:

➤ In any question on crime and social class, raise the general point that the statistics suggesting offenders are mainly working-class may be invalid/exaggerated. Crime appears in all social classes, but many offences committed by the middle class, in the form of white-collar and corporate crimes, remain undetected, or are dealt with outside the formal CJS, so they never appear in official statistics.

➤ Reversing the explanations for the circumstances creating working-class crime can also account for the supposedly lower crime rates in the middle class, as they don't experience those conditions.

The middle class and crime

➤ *White-collar crime* is that committed by middle-class individuals who abuse their work positions for personal gain.

➤ *Corporate crime* refers to offences committed by large companies, or individuals acting on behalf of those companies, which directly benefit the company rather than individuals.

➤ White-collar and corporate crimes are under-represented in crime statistics because:

➥ They are hidden from view, covered up, and hard to detect.

➥ They are often without personal victims who might report an offence.

➥ They may benefit both the parties concerned, so both will conceal an offence.

➥ They are complex and hard to investigate.

➥ Any victim is often unaware that a crime has been committed.

➥ Even if detected, they are often not prosecuted and dealt with as criminal acts.

➥ Even if reported and prosecuted, offenders have a better chance of either being found not guilty, or receiving lenient sentences. Offenders are affluent, well educated and outwardly respectable, so benefit from not fitting the stereotype of the 'typical criminal'.

Explanations for white-collar and corporate crime

Strain theory and relative deprivation

➤ Middle-class offenders may still have a sense of relative deprivation, and want even more than they can achieve by legitimate means, so they innovate by turning to crime.

➤ Corporate crimes are also forms of innovation, as businesses break laws to achieve the approved goal of profits which may otherwise be unachievable by legitimate means.

Control theory

➤ Individuals who carry out corporate crimes to benefit companies are driven by socialisation into, and conformity to, self-seeking, aggressive management cultures.

➤ Sutherland's theory of differential association suggests that if people associate with others who commonly support illegal activities, then they are more likely to commit crime.

Marxist explanations

➤ Marxists like Box, and Slapper and Tombs, argue that corporate crime is driven by the need to maintain profits in competitive criminogenic capitalism.

➤ Selective law enforcement means these 'crimes of the powerful' often go unpunished.

Labelling theory

➤ Nelken suggests these offences are more likely to escape labelling as 'criminal' because they are often similar to normal business practices.

➤ Nelken points out that powerful individuals or corporations develop techniques of neutralisation in order to redefine their crimes as non-criminal mistakes or errors.

➤ Avoidance of the attachment of the 'criminal' label can encourage further crimes by reducing the risks associated with offending.

Rational choice and opportunity theories

All the explanations above combine to suggest opportunities to commit offences are readily available, and the benefits of committing white-collar and corporate crimes outweigh the risks, making offending a rational choice.

The seduction of crime and edgework

As postmodernists like Katz and Lyng suggest, thrill-seeking and risk-taking may in themselves be motivations for crime.

Evaluation of white-collar and corporate crime

✓ Studying it contributes to an understanding of the social construction of crime statistics.

✓ It draws attention to the crimes of the powerful.

✗ The explanations fail to give reasons why not all individuals or corporations turn to crime to resolve their problems, or are prepared to take the risks in doing so.

✗ Marxists fail to explain why, in non-capitalist countries or in public organisations, corporate crimes and corruption are still found.

EXAM TIPS:

➤ White-collar crime and corporate crime are different types of offence, but they are often confusingly merged together in textbooks and exam questions. If a question asks about middle-class crime in general, draw the distinction between the two types of crime and then write about both. If it asks about white-collar crime, define it first, and then focus on individual benefit, so the examiner knows you're using the correct interpretation of white-collar crime, but also make reference to corporate crime, as these are also committed by middle-class individuals, but on behalf of the company.

➤ Questions on crime and social class could appear in a variety of forms – e.g. focusing on working-class crime, or white-collar and corporate crime, or the links between patterns of crime and social class, or a particular theory linked to social class, e.g. the contribution of Marxist or labelling theories to understanding the links between crime and social class, or variants of these. Make sure you focus on the specific issue raised in the question, and evaluate by touching on a range of alternative views.

➤ Be sure to apply theories in your explanations, rather than just listing reasons; refer to research; and apply any contemporary examples you've picked up from the media.

➤ Remember, you can use white-collar and corporate crimes as examples in theory questions – e.g. to illustrate labelling theory and selective law enforcement.

TOPIC 3

Globalisation and crime in contemporary society; the media and crime; green crime; human rights and state crimes (pages 501–523)

Globalisation and crime (pages 501–506)

Karofi and Mwanza, and Castells, argue globalisation has led to new opportunities for crime and new types of crime, such as the illegal trade in weapons, nuclear materials, body parts and drugs; human-trafficking; child sex tourism; cybercrime; international terrorism; money-laundering, etc.

Transnational organised crime
➤ Castells argues that globalisation has created transnational networks of organised crime, which operate in many countries.
➤ Glenny uses the term 'McMafia' to describe the way transnational organised crime mirrors the activities of legal transnational corporations like McDonald's.
➤ Hobbs and Dunnighan suggest that global criminal networks work within local contexts. Hobbs coined the term 'glocal' to describe this interconnectivity between the local and the global.

How globalisation has affected crime
1. *Disorganised capitalism* is how Lash and Urry refer to the way globalisation has been accompanied by less state regulation over business and finance.
   ⇒ Taylor argues this gives more opportunities for corporations and the wealthy to commit crimes.
   ⇒ This has been accompanied by a reduction in state provision, blocking legitimate opportunities for achieving consumerist lifestyles.
2. *Widening inequality* – The most disadvantaged in both developed and developing countries are exposed to ever more risks and insecurity in their lives. This feeds crime.
3. *Supply and demand* – Demand for drugs, sex workers, body parts and cheap labour in affluent countries is supplied by the poor of developing countries.
4. *More opportunities for crime* taking advantage of the speed, convenience and anonymity of the internet.
5. *Cultural globalisation* has spread a similar ideology of consumerism across the globe. Young points out many people have little chance of adopting this lifestyle, encouraging crime.
6. *Growing individualisation* puts personal gain above community benefit.
7. *Global risk society* – Beck argues people become more fearful of global risks, exaggerated by the media, and this can fuel hate crimes towards scapegoats.

Evaluation of crime and globalisation
✓ Its study focuses attention on some of the newest, most dramatic and serious forms of crime.
✓ The rate of globalisation-linked crime is rising.
✓ Globalisation of crime has been accompanied by more global law enforcement.
✗ It is a difficult and potentially dangerous area for sociologists to investigate.
✗ The impact of globalisation on crime is exaggerated – it has affected some countries more than others, but most crime is fairly routine, low-level offending unaffected by globalisation.

EXAM TIP:

It's always useful to include, in answers on globalisation and crime, a definition of globalisation. Questions are likely to focus on some variant of how globalisation has affected crime in general, or the amount of crime, and/or the new types of crime it has created, and/or new means of committing crime. Make sure you read the question and Item carefully so your answer is adapted to fit the particular issues raised. You can always refer to the other ways globalisation has affected crime in your evaluation.

Green or environmental crime (pages 506–511)

➤ The term 'green crime' (also called 'environmental crime') is used to describe actions that break laws protecting the environment. Problems with this are:
  ⮕ The same harmful environmental action may be defined as illegal in some countries but not in others.
  ⮕ Laws change over time.
  ⮕ Many actions that harm the environment may be regarded as breaches of health and safety regulations rather than as criminal offences.
➤ To overcome this problem of legal/illegal, green criminology considers green crime to be any human action that causes environmental harm, whether it is illegal or not.
➤ The main causes of green crime include the deliberate breaking or avoidance of rules that seek to prevent environmental damage, and negligence.

Globalisation and green crime
➤ *Global risk society* – Environmental harm in one country can have consequences in many others. Environmental crime is not just the concern of one country.
➤ *Transnational corporations* move manufacturing operations and hazardous waste disposal from developed countries to the Global South, where pollution and health and safety controls are weaker, and enforcement action is less effective.

Who commits green crimes?
Brian Wolf identifies four groups:
  1. *Individuals* – e.g. littering, fly tipping.
  2. *Private business organisations* – e.g. toxic emissions, dumping of waste.
  3. *States and governments* – e.g. military nuclear waste, the lasting damage caused by wars.
  4. *Organised crime* – organised global criminal networks, attracted by the low-risk and high-profit nature of these types of crime.

The victims of green crimes

➤ Potter suggests the least powerful are the most likely victims of green crimes in all countries. 'Environmental racism' means those suffering the worst effects of environmental damage are of different ethnicity from those causing the damage, with the latter, most often, being white.

➤ White shows that people living in the developing world face far greater risks of exposure to environmental air, water and land pollution than those in the developed world.

Explaining green crimes

➤ White argues green crime arises because transnational corporations and nation-states hold an anthropocentric view of the world, which gives priority to human well-being achieved through economic growth. The environment is only a secondary consideration.

➤ Brian Wolf suggests that green crime is motivated by many of the same factors as ordinary crime, as suggested by rational choice, strain, control and Marxist theories.

➤ Marxists suggest that the most serious green crimes are examples of what Pearce called 'the crimes of the powerful' – corporate crimes arising from criminogenic capitalism, in which maximising profits overrides any concern for the environment.

Problems of researching green crimes

➤ Different laws in different countries – official statistics may not be comparable.

➤ Different definitions of what counts as a green crime.

➤ Difficulties in measurement – easy to conceal them.

➤ Case studies have limited use in explaining and making generalisations about the causes of green crime.

Evaluation of green criminology

✓ It addresses the growing threats of environmental harm.

✓ It locates green crime within the context of globalisation.

✓ It puts green crime within a wider framework of sociological theories of crime.

✗ There is a lack of clarity and agreement about what environmental crime actually is – this exposes green criminology to risks of influence by the value judgements and subjective interpretations of researchers.

EXAM TIP:

In any question on green crime, it is worth mentioning the lack of clarity/ambiguity about what green crime is, and the transgressive approach adopted by green criminology.
Link green crime to globalisation and corporate crime, and state crime (deliberate environmental harm as a human rights abuse).

Human rights and state crimes (pages 511–515)

Problems with defining state crimes

➤ The state defines what a crime is. It therefore has the power to avoid defining its own acts as criminal.

➤ Even when states commit acts that are clearly illegal under international law, they have the power to disguise, decriminalise and justify these offences.

➤ Green and Ward suggest that state crimes should be considered as state organisational deviance involving the violation of human rights.

➤ Human rights are those that suggest that everyone, because of their common humanity, is entitled to the same fair and just treatment, wherever they might be in the world.

➤ The human rights dimension puts the study of state crime within a wider transgressive context of social harm rather than simply law-breaking.

Explaining state crimes

Integrated theory

This suggests state crime arises from similar circumstances to those of conventional street crimes. It involves integrating three factors, and how these interact to generate state crimes:

➤ The motivations of offenders.

➤ Opportunities to commit crimes.

➤ Failures of control (whether intentional or unintentional).

The crimes of obedience model

Developed by Kelman and Hamilton, this emphasises three features:

1. *Authorisation* – Individuals know they are acting in accordance with official policy, and with explicit state authority and support.

2. *Dehumanisation* – The group being abused is marginalised and excluded, and portrayed as a sub-human species to whom normal rules of civilised behaviour do not apply.

3. *Routinisation* – Organising the abusive actions so they become part of a regular routine that can be performed in a detached way (de Swann's 'enclaves of barbarism').

Techniques of neutralisation

Stan Cohen applies Sykes and Matza's concept of techniques of neutralisation to explain how states:

➤ Deny that their actions were abuses.

➤ Re-label them as something else.

➤ Excuse them as regrettable but justifiable.

➤ Appeal to higher loyalties and ideals.

Problems of researching state crimes

➤ It is difficult to discover the true extent of state crime because governments adopt strategies either to deny or to justify their actions, or reclassify them as something else.

➤ State power and secrecy mean there are no official statistics or victim surveys to show the extent of such crime.

➤ Researchers are often reliant on secondary data that tend to focus on state crimes in developing countries, rather than those committed by Western democracies.
➤ In dictatorships, researchers additionally risk imprisonment, torture and death as enemies of the state.

Evaluation of state crime
✓ This focuses attention on the crimes of the powerful, and shows that crime is not simply a working-class phenomenon.
✗ It is not always easy to know what a state crime is, and there is a subjective element involved in deciding whether the action of states is criminal or not.
✗ Its study tends to be ethnocentric – assuming state crimes happen in developing countries rather than in Western democracies.

The media and crime (pages 515–523)

Agenda-setting and news values
➤ Media reporting of crime, rather than personal experience, provides most people's only knowledge about the extent and type of crime in society. These impressions are influenced by:
   ➠ *Agenda-setting* – the media's power to select the issues they choose to include in or leave out of their reports.
   ➠ *News values* – the criteria by which journalists and editors decide whether a story is exciting, interesting, and one that media audiences want to know about.
➤ The media seek out newsworthy stories of crime and exploit the possibilities for a 'good story' by exaggerating some crimes out of all proportion to their actual occurrence in society.
➤ Greer and Reiner suggest it is news values that explain why all mainstream media tend to dramatise and sensationalise the extent of violent and sexual crime.

The backwards law
➤ Surette suggests the media construct images of crime and justice which are an opposite or backwards version of reality.
➤ Left Realists suggest media reporting disguises the reality that both offenders and victims are mainly from the working class and the poor.
➤ Marxists suggest the media conceal the significance of white-collar and corporate crimes.

The hyperreality of crime
The backwards law, combined with agenda-setting and news values, means the media:
➤ Socially construct a distorted view of crime and the Criminal Justice System (CJS).
➤ Exaggerate the risks of becoming a victim of crime.
➤ Unnecessarily increase the public's fear of crime.

This illustrates Baudrillard's postmodernist idea of hyperreality – the media do not reflect reality but actively create it through representations which have little connection with the real world.

Moral entrepreneurs, deviancy amplification, folk devils and moral panics

➤ The media act as moral entrepreneurs in that they have the power to define deviance and to label behaviour or groups of which they disapprove as deviant.

➤ The media can portray these groups, through stereotyping, as problems, and demonise them as folk devils who pose a threat to society.

➤ The media, through negative labelling and false or exaggerated reporting, can sometimes generate a moral panic – a wave of public concern about some alleged threat to society.

➤ This can lead to widespread demands for a crackdown on the group by the police and the CJS, and sometimes changes in the law to criminalise deviant activities.

➤ Media reporting and public reaction can create a self-fulfilling prophecy and lead to deviancy amplification, as deviants play up to their media stereotype.

Evaluation of moral panics

✓ They show the media's power to define what is normal and what is deviant.

✓ They show how the media can amplify deviancy.

✗ McRobbie and Thornton suggest that the concept of moral panics is now outdated. There is more diversity in beliefs about what is or isn't deviant behaviour.

✗ Most events that might generate a moral panic now have such short shelf-lives in sustaining audience interest that they are unlikely to be newsworthy for long enough to become a moral panic.

✗ Pluralists and postmodernists argue citizen journalism and social media have made people more sceptical of mainstream media interpretations.

✗ Steve Hall rejects the concept of moral panics. The media might sensationalise crime and cause public concern, but they also exaggerate the CJS's ability to solve crimes and punish criminals. This increases the public's faith in the existing political and administrative system and creates complacency – the opposite of panic.

Do the media cause crime?

➤ *Labelling, moral entrepreneurship and deviancy amplification* suggest that media reporting can create and/or make crime and deviance worse.

➤ *Motives for crime* – The media's promotion of consumerist culture creates crime by intensifying feelings of relative deprivation; images of crime and violence encourage people to commit crime by imitating what they pick up from the media; repeated viewing of violence through the media makes it appear more normal.

➤ *Knowledge and learning of criminal techniques.*

➤ *New means of committing crimes* – e.g. the internet enables cybercrimes.

➤ *Weakening social controls over crime*:

    ➥ External controls (fears of police action and arrest) are undermined by stories/reports mocking the police and the CJS as corrupt, ineffective and inefficient.

    ➥ Internal controls (self-control and conscience) are undermined by stories/reports/images which present crime as glamorous and exciting.

➤ *Providing targets for crime* – Media hardware and software provide new targets for property crime, such as smartphones, TVs, computers, etc.

EXAM TIPS:

➤ There are a lot of theories and concepts in the media and crime – e.g. labelling theory, control theory, agenda-setting, news values, hyperreality, relative deprivation, moral entrepreneurship, deviancy amplification, folk devils, moral panics, self-fulfilling prophecy, etc. Use and apply them (correctly) to gain marks for knowledge and understanding and for application.

➤ There are a number of possibilities for 'media and crime' questions: general ones like the relationship between the media and crime, and ones that focus on specific aspects – e.g. moral panics and deviancy amplification; media representations/distortions of crime; whether the media cause crime. Be sure to focus on the specific issues raised in the question. If the question is a general one, you'll need to be selective in which issues you give most prominence to, but try at least to mention the majority of them. Moral panic is a key concept, so make sure you're well prepared on that, and criticisms of it.

➤ If the question is linked to an Item, make sure you refer to the Item if you want to get into the top band, and take clues from the Item about which issues to focus on.

➤ Crime and deviance stories are always in the media – so apply contemporary examples to show examiners how well informed you are and that you can apply your sociology to everyday events and, of course, to gain marks for application.

TOPIC 4

Crime control, surveillance, prevention and punishment, victims, and the role of the criminal justice system and other agencies (pages 524–546)

The criminal justice system (CJS) (pages 524–525)

➤ The CJS refers to all the different agencies and organisations involved in crime control and prevention, and identifying, controlling and punishing known offenders.
➤ The CJS establishment is dominated by older, middle-class people, and, in crown courts, senior judges are predominantly white and male, drawn from elite social backgrounds.
➤ The CJS has four aims:
   1. Deterrence.
   2. Public protection.
   3. Retribution (retributive justice).
   4. Rehabilitation (rehabilitative justice).

Changing approaches to criminal justice

➤ Since the 1970s, there has been a growing emphasis on retributive justice, rather than rehabilitation, shown by a huge increase in imprisonment.
➤ Since the 1980s, crime reduction strategies have been changing to give higher priority to crime prevention in the future, rather than simply to punishing offenders after the event.
➤ There has been a growing recognition that the CJS should be more concerned with protecting the rights and needs of victims of crime.

The culture of control: from Left Realism to Right Realism

➤ Garland sees the changes in criminal justice reflected in sociological theory:
   ➟ *A shift from* Left Realist-style theories focusing on the causes of crime rooted in social injustice and inequality.
   ➟ *A shift to* Right Realist-style approaches, focusing on the consequences of crime, and the need for more social control, and reducing the opportunities to commit crime, and the harm and fears that crime produces.
➤ Garland argues there is now a 'culture of control', concerned with more retribution/punishment and controlling, preventing and reducing the risks of people becoming victims of crime.

Restorative justice

Rising uncertainty about the effectiveness of imprisonment on reducing crime has led to:
➤ More use of community sentences, rather than imprisonment, for less serious offences.
➤ More use of restorative justice – where offenders meet their victims to make offenders face up to the consequences of their actions and help repair the harm done to victims.

The role of punishment in crime control and prevention (pages 526–530)

Newburn suggests five main reasons for punishing criminals:
1. To discourage re-offending (rehabilitation) or to deter others from offending (deterrence).
2. To force them to make amends to victims (restorative justice).
3. To protect society from those who are dangerous (incapacitation).
4. To reinforce social values and bonds (the functionalist view).
5. To punish them simply because they deserve it (retribution).

The changing form of punishments
Forms of punishment vary between societies and have changed over time.
➤ **FROM** public spectacles of cruel brutality and the infliction of bodily pain, suffering, mutilation and death on criminals (though these are still found in some countries today).
➤ **TO** the less brutal, more regulated private forms of punishment found in most contemporary Western societies.

From sovereign power to disciplinary power
Foucault (postmodernist) links the decline in public forms of brutal physical punishment and the infliction of pain to changing structures of power in society.
➤ **FROM** *sovereign power* – a way of asserting the monarch's power over citizens.
➤ **TO** *disciplinary power* – criminals are controlled and disciplined by constant surveillance, encouraging criminals' self-discipline or self-control.

Sociological approaches to punishment

Functionalist approaches
➤ Punishment provides an opportunity to express society's disapproval and anger at violation of the collective conscience.
➤ It reasserts and strengthens collective values and the boundaries between right and wrong.
➤ It reinforces social regulation and social control, and deters others from offending.
➤ It contributes to building social order and social cohesion for the benefit of all.

These approaches have been criticised because:
➤ It assumes that the law reflects a value consensus.
➤ Punishments like imprisonment may actually threaten, rather than assist in re-establishing, social order – e.g. prisons can act as 'universities of crime' creating crime rather than rehabilitating offenders, and, through labelling, prevent their eventual reintegration into society.

Marxist approaches
➤ Law and punishment are part of the repressive state apparatus (Althusser), concerned with reinforcing ruling-class power in unequal class societies (Rusche and Kirchheimer).
➤ The law is selectively enforced, and punishment is directed against the most disadvantaged in society.
➤ The crimes of the powerful either escape punishment altogether or are treated leniently.

These approaches have been criticised because:

➤ It is difficult to see all punishments as linked simply to the interests of the dominant class.

➤ Some would argue that the working class fill the prisons because they commit some of the most harmful offences, and, as Left Realists point out, their victims are most commonly other disadvantaged people.

Weberian approaches

➤ Punishment is based on legal–rational authority – impersonal rules and regulations based on legislation decided by governments, and administered by bureaucracies.

➤ The length, form and location of punishments are tightly regulated by rules and regulations, and there is little scope for the arbitrary punishment of offenders.

This approach has been criticised because individual law enforcement officers have considerable discretion in interpreting rules and regulations.

Does imprisonment prevent crime?

Right Realists see imprisonment as a key way of deterring people from offending. However, high levels of imprisonment have little impact on reducing the crime rate. Reasons include:

➤ Spending time in prison may make pre-existing problems worse.

➤ Interactionist sociologists like Goffman suggest prisons have their own subcultures, which provide training grounds for criminals, and confirm the 'criminal' label.

➤ The label of 'ex-con' becomes a stigmatised master status (Becker) which makes it difficult for released prisoners to re-enter conforming mainstream society successfully.

➤ Punishment through imprisonment becomes a self-fulfilling prophecy. Prisons act as institutions for the manufacture of crime rather than the rehabilitation of criminals.

Surveillance and crime control and prevention (pages 530–532)

➤ Monitoring through round-the-clock surveillance technologies is now a key means of controlling crime and disorder.

➤ Foucault argues contemporary society has been transformed into a surveillance or disciplinary society.

➤ Foucault sees surveillance as a form of disciplinary power: the fear and uncertainty of whether they are being watched encourage people to practise self-discipline.

➤ Lyon argues that surveillance has become so pervasive and such a routine and inescapable part of everyday life that it now makes sense to talk of 'surveillance societies' in which those with power can exercise total social control.

Evaluation of the surveillance society

✓ Foucault's analysis shows how surveillance can be used by the state to control the behaviour of citizens, promote conformity and prevent crime and disorder.

✓ Surveillance can be useful for reducing crime and social disorder and improving people's sense of safety in communities where crime is a real problem.

✓ Surveillance also appears to be of growing assistance in the fight against terrorism and the threats it might pose to public safety.

✗ Surveillance is now so pervasive that it is likely that people have ceased to be aware of it.

✗ The grounds of reducing crime and disorder are just convenient excuses employed by the state for using surveillance to increase its power and undermine civil liberties.

Left Realism and crime control and prevention (pages 532–534)

- ➤ Left Realists recognise that both the offenders and the victims of the crimes that worry people most are found in the more disadvantaged communities.
- ➤ Preventing crime means being tough on the causes of crime – tackling the material and cultural circumstances that are the risk factors for crime.
- ➤ Preventing crime involves social and community policies, such as:
  - ⟹ *Building community cohesion and strong communities*.
  - ⟹ *Multi-agency working*, where a variety of agencies work together with local people to tackle crime, rather than just relying on the police and the CJS.
  - ⟹ *More democratic and community control of policing*, so it becomes more responsive to local needs, concerns and priorities.
  - ⟹ *Tackling social deprivation and the other risk factors for crime*.
  - ⟹ *Intensive parenting and early-years childcare support* – early intervention to help get children at greatest risk of offending off to a better start in life.
  - ⟹ *Restorative justice* to make young offenders recognise the harm they have caused by having to face their victims.

Criticisms of Left Realist approaches

- ➤ They are 'soft' on crime, as they focus too much on the social causes of crime, and downplay the role of the offender in choosing to commit crime.
- ➤ The explanations and policies are inadequate, as the majority of those living in deprived communities and sharing similar risk factors do not turn to crime.
- ➤ They deflect attention away from more practical crime prevention measures, like the tighter social control and situational crime prevention advocated by Right Realists.
- ➤ They (like Right Realists) ignore white-collar and corporate crimes.
- ➤ Neighbourhood/community policing might be seen as an extension of control and surveillance by the state over the whole population.

Right Realism and crime control and prevention (pages 534–537)

Right Realists:
- ➤ Have a focus on individuals and the specific location of crime rather than on wider social issues.
- ➤ Reject broad social and structural theories of crime as unproven and impractical.
- ➤ Emphasise that individuals choose crime and must be persuaded not to do so, by reducing the opportunities for crime and increasing the chances of being caught and punished.

These approaches are underpinned by three interlinked theories:
- ➤ Wilson and Kelling's *'broken windows' thesis* that petty crimes will eventually grow into bigger, more serious crimes. It is necessary:
  - ⟹ To keep environments in good physical condition.
  - ⟹ To adopt zero-tolerance policing to crack down on all anti-social behaviour.

➤ Felson and Clarke suggest that a crime occurs as part of *everyday routines*, when there is a suitable target for the potential offender, no 'capable guardian' to protect the target, and a potential offender present, who then makes a rational choice whether or not to commit the crime.
➤ Cornish and Clarke argue that:
   ⇒ When potential offenders see an *opportunity* for crime, they act *rationally* and weigh up the benefits and costs/risks before choosing whether or not to commit an offence.
   ⇒ To deter potential offenders, it is necessary to reduce the opportunities for crime and increase the costs/risks of offending.

There are two Right Realist policies flowing from these three theories.

Situational crime prevention (SCP)
Situational Crime Prevention (SCP) aims to prevent crime in particular locations by making crime more risky and a less attractive choice.

Increased social control
Measures to achieve this include:
➤ Making parents take more responsibility for the socialisation and supervision of their children.
➤ Schemes like Neighbourhood Watch, to build community controls over crime.
➤ Zero-tolerance policing (ZTP) – cracking down on ALL crime and anti-social behaviour.
➤ Supervision of offenders – e.g. through electronic tagging and curfew orders.
➤ Fast-track punishment of offenders, with more imprisonment and harsher sentences.

Criticisms of Right Realist approaches
➤ SCP doesn't consider the wider social causes of crime, and social and community policies for crime prevention.
➤ SCP doesn't pay sufficient attention to catching criminals or to punishments to deter offenders.
➤ SCP simply displaces crime to other areas.
➤ ZTP involves a wasteful over-emphasis on minor and trivial offences, and diverts police resources away from more serious ones.
➤ Labelling theorists argue that ZTP risks criminalising people for very minor offences, which may have long-term negative consequences for their lives and careers.
➤ They ignore white-collar and corporate crimes.
➤ Not all offenders act rationally, so SCP and ZTP are not necessarily going to prevent them offending.

EXAM TIP:

In questions on Realist approaches to crime prevention, refer to both the theories and the practical measures that flow from them. Evaluate Right Realist policies by contrasting them with Left Realism, and vice versa.

Feminism and the control and prevention of crime (pages 537–538)

- ➤ Feminist approaches involve three main issues:
    - ⮕ Drawing attention to the nature of the offenders and crimes that particularly affect women.
    - ⮕ Trying to get a male-dominated and patriarchal CJS to respond more seriously and appropriately to crimes against women.
    - ⮕ Exposing the extent of male crimes against women.
- ➤ *Liberal feminists* emphasise policies that:
    - ⮕ Encourage more women to report crimes against them.
    - ⮕ Boost the confidence of women and reduce their fears of crime.
    - ⮕ Reduce women's offending, most of which is related to poverty, debt and drug abuse.
- ➤ *Marxist feminists* focus on how inequality and hardship affect working-class women the most, which drives women to commit 'female' crimes such as prostitution and shoplifting. Tackling female crime therefore means tackling social inequality.
- ➤ *Radical feminists* focus on patriarchy, which lies behind both much female victimisation and women's offending. They emphasise policies like opening more rape crisis centres and women's refuges so women can escape male violence.

Postmodernism and the control and prevention of crime (pages 538–540)

Postmodernists argue:
- ➤ The law is a metanarrative that expresses a particular view, among those with power.
- ➤ The centrally managed formal processes of the CJS do not reflect the diversity of contemporary societies.
- ➤ Offenders have a range of complex individual motivations for causing harm, so the social causes of crime are undiscoverable.

Postmodernist policies for reducing crime and harm involve:
- ➤ A need for the CJS and the police to recognise, and become more sensitive to and tolerant of, a diversity of identities and lifestyle choices.
- ➤ More informal localised arrangements, responsive to the needs of particular communities and groups, for preventing and controlling harms caused by crime and disorder.
- ➤ Growing surveillance, restrictions and control of entry to reduce the risks of harm in certain areas, such as shopping malls, and housing complexes in gated communities.
- ➤ More individualised justice, reflecting the particular problems of the individual offender.

Evaluation of the postmodernist approach
- ✓ It draws attention to the diversity of identities and lifestyle choices in postmodern societies, and to the possibility that a centralised CJS may not meet all needs.
- ✓ It can explain developments like extensive surveillance, more private security, localised policing, and control of entry to some private 'public' areas like shopping malls.
- ✗ It doesn't recognise the importance or impact of social inequality.
- ✗ It doesn't recognise that decentralised policing and more informal arrangements for crime control are likely to benefit the middle-class groups.

- ✗ It doesn't really consider the implications, for people's civil liberties and human rights, of the growing use of customised private 'policing' and surveillance.
- ✗ There may be a fairer, more equal distribution of justice for all through a centrally managed, publicly run and accountable CJS.

> **EXAM TIP:**
>
> In questions on crime prevention strategies, refer to the range of policies adopted and their limitations, but link them to theories about the constraints that encourage conformity and prevent deviance – e.g. Right Realism/control theory/broken windows/rational choice and opportunity/SCP and ZTP. Don't forget you can also refer to punishment as a strategy for crime reduction (deterrence, restorative justice, rehabilitation, etc.).

The victims of crime (pages 540–545)

- ➤ Victimology has been a growing focus in academic research, and the success of the CJS is now judged by the extent to which it meets the needs of victims.
- ➤ The greater focus on victims is to encourage them to have more confidence in the CJS, so they are more willing to report crime and give evidence.

The social construction of victimisation
- ➤ There are many unreported and unrecorded victims who never come to the attention of the CJS.
- ➤ Victims may not realise they have been victimised.
- ➤ Victims may refuse to accept they have been victimised.
- ➤ Victims may reject the label of 'victim' as it may show them to be weak or foolish.
- ➤ Some are denied the status of victim because others regard them as responsible for their own victimisation.
- ➤ The state, via the police or CJS, has the power to refuse or attach the label of victim and provide victim status.

The effects of victimisation
Hoyle suggests the effects of victimisation may include:
- ➤ *Psychological effects.*
- ➤ *Greater fear of crime.*
- ➤ *Restrictions over movement* – e.g. women victims fearing to go out at night or forced to avoid certain areas for fear of patriarchally based violence.
- ➤ *Fear of repeat victimisation.*
- ➤ *Wider effects beyond the victims* – e.g. whole neighbourhoods or groups of people can be put in fear as a result of hate crimes against BME groups or gays.
- ➤ *Secondary (or double) victimisation* as a result of the original or primary victimisation – e.g. rape trials, where the female victims rather than the male suspects seem to be on trial.

The pattern of victimisation

Gender
➤ Males are most at risk of non-sexual violence outside the home.
➤ Women are most at risk of sexual violence outside the home, and of both physical and sexual violence inside the home – domestic violence.
➤ Physical and sexual crimes against women are the least likely to be reported to the police, recorded in official statistics, or to result in convictions.
➤ Many female victims of domestic violence suffer repeat victimisation.

Age
➤ Adults aged 16–24 face the highest risk of being victims of personal crimes.
➤ Young men (aged 16–24) have about twice the risk of young women of being victims of violent crime.
➤ Older people (65+) are the least likely to be victims of violent crime.

Ethnicity
➤ BME groups face the highest risks of being victims of personal crimes and homicide.
➤ BME groups are up to fourteen times more likely to be victims of racially motivated hate crimes than white people.
➤ Honour crimes and forced marriages are exclusively linked to BME groups, and women are overwhelmingly the victims.

Social class
The highest rates of victimisation are found:
➤ Among the 'hard pressed' – the unemployed, the long-term sick, low-income families and those living in rented accommodation.
➤ In areas of high physical disorder, with widespread vandalism, graffiti, etc. (think: broken windows thesis).
➤ In areas with high levels of deprivation.

Explaining victimisation

Positivist victimology
➤ Victim proneness – Characteristics of individuals or groups that make them more vulnerable to victimisation.
➤ Victim precipitation – Victims are actively involved in, or to blame for, their victimisation.

Positivist victimology is criticised for:
➤ Victim-blaming.
➤ Downplaying the contribution to victimisation of the police and the CJS.
➤ Focusing too much on the characteristics of individual victims, and not paying enough attention to the wider structural factors.
➤ Failing to recognise that there are situations where people may wholly unwittingly become victims or are not aware of their victimisation.

Radical (or critical) victimology

➤ Radical victimology is associated with conflict theories such as Marxism and feminism.

➤ It focuses on how wider social structural issues and circumstances produce victimisation:

⏵ Social deprivation.

⏵ Patriarchy.

⏵ Racism in the police and CJS.

➤ The main criticism of radical victimology is that it ignores the issues of victim precipitation and proneness that positivist victimology identifies.

EXAM TIP:

Watch out for questions which link victimisation with other issues – e.g. explanations of ethnic differences in both offending *and* victimisation. You should treat both parts of such questions equally, and try to link the two halves – e.g. higher levels of deprivation and younger age profiles among BME groups make them more likely to be both offenders and victims.

GENERAL EXAM TIP:

Remember that two out of the three exam questions on Crime and Deviance involve an Item to refer to. You *must* refer to that Item to achieve top-band marks. For the 10-mark ('Applying material from Item A, analyse two') question, you must refer *only* to ideas or issues that are raised in the Item. For the 20-mark ('Applying material from Item B and your knowledge, evaluate') question, you must refer to the Item *and* your knowledge gained elsewhere in your studies of Crime and Deviance or in other topics. Remember the Item is there to help and guide you, so use it.

By the time you go into the exam, you should know all the material listed on page 547 of the textbook. You should also know the key terms listed on page 548. Knowing these key terms and using them correctly will help you gain marks for knowledge and understanding. You can check their meaning on-the-go by going to the online glossary by following the link at www.politybooks.com/browne. Put it on your phone for ready reference.

INDEX

A

Adler, 175
age
  media representations of, 89–90
  and religion, 31–2
  and stratification and differentiation, 112–13, 118
agenda-setting, 78, 86, 88, 183
aid, 59–60
Althusser, 13, 18, 107, 138, 187
anomie, 26, 135, 161, 169
anti-Malthusians, 65, 73

B

backwards law, 183
Bagdikian, 77, 85
Barnes, 96
Barnett and Seymour, 79, 85, 104
Baudrillard, 25, 82, 145, 183
Bauman, 16, 26, 37
Bauman and May, 158–9
Beck, 146, 179
Becker, 87, 155, 164, 165, 188
beliefs, 13–16
Bellah, 35, 36
Berger, 19–20, 26
black feminism, 109
bottom billion, 43
Box, 163, 177
Bretton Woods institutions, 57–8
broken windows thesis, 189
Bruce, 15, 23, 25, 28, 30, 32, 34, 35, 36, 37, 39
bulimic society, 167

C

Castells, 179
chivalry thesis, 175
Church of England, 32, 35, 36
churches, 23
churnalism, 86, 87, 103
citizen journalism, 78, 79, 85, 88, 103
civil religions, 18, 32
civil society, 57
clash of civilisations, 21, 39
classical/traditional Marxism, 107, 137–8
Cloward and Ohlin, 161–2
Cohen, Albert, 161
Cohen, Stan, 87, 182
collective conscience, 135, 187

colonialism (and neo-colonialism), 46, 64, 69, 73
Comte, 15, 34, 158
Connell, 93, 175
consensus and conflict theories, 134
consumerism, 16, 52, 53, 65, 81, 110, 163, 167, 169, 179, 184
control theory, 162–3, 174, 176, 177
Cornish and Clarke, 168, 190
corporate crime, 177–8, 181
crime and deviance
  control theory, 162–3, 174, 176, 177
  crime control and prevention, 186–92
  crime statistics, 170–2
  criminal justice system, 173, 175, 186, 191, 192
  and ethnicity, 172–4, 193
  feminist theories, 166, 174–5
  functionalist theories, 160–2, 187
  and gender, 166, 174–6, 193
  and globalisation, 179–80
  Left and Right Realism, 166–8, 189–90
  Marxist/neo-Marxist theories, 163–4, 187–8
  and the media, 179, 183–5
  postmodernist theories, 169, 191–2
  realist theories, 166 *see also* Left and Right Realism *above*
  and social class, 176–8
  subcultural theories, 161–2
  and victimisation, 192–4
criminal justice system, 173, 175, 186, 191, 192
criminogenic capitalism, 163, 177, 181
cults, 23–6
cultural capital, 121, 130
cultural convergence, 102
cultural defence, 19, 30, 36, 37, 39
cultural effects model, 99–100, 101
cultural globalisation, 52, 53, 179
cultural homogenisation, 52, 81
cultural imperialism, 39, 52, 53, 69, 81, 104
cultural optimists, 103
cultural pessimists, 104
cultural transition, 30, 36
culture wars, 39

Curran, 79, 85, 104
Curran and Seaton, 103

D

Davie, 28, 32, 35, 36
Davis and Moore, 106
debt crisis, 60–1
demographic change (and development), 72–3
denominations, 23
dependency theory, 46–8, 53, 55, 60, 61, 64, 65, 66, 69, 71–2, 73
deskilling, 123
deterritorialisation, 39
deviancy amplification, 87, 165, 184
differentiation, 105, 110–13
disability
  and life chances, 118–19
  media representations of, 96–7
disciplinary power, 187, 188
disenchantment, 15, 20, 26, 32, 34
Disneyisation, 35
dominant ideology, 13, 78, 81, 88, 99, 107, 137
dominant ideology / hegemonic approach (to media), 78
dual systems feminism, 143
Durkheim, 17–18, 135, 147, 160

E

economic capital, 121
economic development, 41
economic globalisation, 50, 53
edgework, 167, 178
education
  in developing countries, 69–70
  and stratification and differentiation, 114–15, 116, 117, 118
embourgeoisement, 124
employment
  in developing countries, 68–9
  and stratification and differentiation, 116–17, 118, 119
encoding/decoding, 99–100
environment, 49, 65–6
environmental (green) crime, 180–1
EOI (export-oriented industrialisation), 62
epidemiological transition, 71
establishment, 122

ethnicity
  and crime, 172–4, 193
  media representations of, 91–2
  and religion, 30–1
  and stratification and differentiation, 111–12, 117–18, 127, 131
ethnomethodology, 140
existential security theory, 38–9
export processing zones (EPZs), 54

F
Fair Trade, 61
false consciousness, 137
falsification, 14, 147
Felson and Clarke, 190
feminism
  and crime and deviance, 166, 174–5
  and crime control and prevention, 191
  and religion, 28–9
  and research methods, 152
  theories, 108–9, 142–4
Flew, 81
folk devils, 90, 184
formal sector (of the economy), 68
Foucault, 187, 188
Frank, 46, 53
free trade, 45, 50, 54, 58, 61
functionalism, 134–6
  and crime and deviance, 160–2, 187
  and religion, 17–18, 19
  theory of stratification, 106
fundamentalism, 21, 37, 39

G
G.A.I.L. model, 135
Galtung and Ruge, 87
Garfinkel, 140
Garland, 186
gatekeeping, 78, 86, 88
Gauntlett, 89, 94
gender
  and crime, 166, 174–6, 193
  and development, 74–5
  inequality, 70, 108–9, 115–17, 126–7, 142–4
  media representations of, 93–5
  and religion, 28–9
  and stratification and differentiation, 108–9, 111, 115–17, 126–7, 131, 142–4
Giddens, 121, 123, 141, 146, 157
Glasgow Media Group (GMG), 78, 84, 86, 87, 89, 90, 91, 92, 93, 96
glass ceiling, 93, 127
  (stained) glass ceiling, 29
Glenny, 179

global development
  and aid, 59–60
  and the debt crisis, 60–1
  and demographic change, 72–3
  and education, 69–70
  and employment, 68–9
  and the environment, 49, 65–6
  and gender, 74–5
  and globalisation, 50–3
  and health, 71–2
  and industrialisation, 62–3
  and international governmental organisations (IGOs), 57–8
  and international non-governmental organisations (INGOs), 56–7
  measuring development, 41–3
  terminology, 43
  theories of development, 44–9
  and trade, 61
  and transnational corporations (TNCs), 54–6, 68
  and urbanisation, 64
  and war and conflict, 66–7
global popular culture, 81–2
global village, 80, 81, 103
globalisation, 50, 57, 74
  and crime, 179–80
  cultural globalisation, 52, 53, 179
  economic globalisation, 50, 53
  and employment, 69
  and migration, 126
  political globalisation, 51
  and popular culture, 80–3
  and religion, 39
  theories of, 52–3
  and the transnational capitalist class, 53, 125–6
Goffman, 139, 188
Gouldner, 155
Gramsci, 18, 21, 78, 138
Great British Class Survey (GBCS), 121
green (environmental) crime, 180–1
Green and Ward, 182

H
Hall, Steve, 184
Hall, Stuart, 91, 99, 172
Hayter, 60
health
  in developing countries, 71–2
  inequalities in, 114, 115–16, 117, 118, 119
Heelas, 25, 26, 31, 36
hegemony, 18, 21, 78, 138
Heidensohn, 174–5
Henry and Milovanovic, 169
Herberg, 35, 38

Herman and Chomsky, 88
high culture, 80
Hirschi, 162
Hobbs, 179
homosexuality, 95–6
Hoselitz, 44
human rights, 182
Huntington, 21, 39
hybrid culture, 52
hyperreality, 82, 183
hypodermic syringe model, 98–9
hypothetico-deductive method, 147

I
ideological state apparatuses, 13, 18, 107, 138
ideology, 13
  dominant, 13, 78, 81, 88, 99, 107, 137
  patriarchal, 13, 93, 94, 174
  pluralist, 13
  political, 13, 136
  and postmodernism, 16
  and religion, 16, 18, 20
IGOs (international governmental organisations), 57–8
IMF (International Monetary Fund), 57–8
import substitution industrialisation (ISI), 62
impression management, 139
imprisonment/prisons, 175, 186–8
industrialisation, 62–3
informal sector (of the economy), 68
infotainment, 80, 81, 85
INGOs (international non-governmental organisations), 56–7
innovation (and crime and deviance), 161, 177
institutional racism, 111, 173
interactionist theories, 139–40, 164–5
interpretivism, 100, 139, 148, 150
  and religion, 19–20
  and research methods, 151–2
intersectional feminism, 144
inverse care law, 119
ISI (import substitution industrialisation), 62

J
Jones, 90, 91, 122

K
Kaplan, 66, 73, 149
Katz and Lazarsfeld, 99
Kelman and Hamilton, 182
Klapper, 100
Kuhn, 149

L

labelling theory, 139, 164–5, 173
Lash and Urry, 179
late modernity, 146, 167
Lawler, 91
Lea and Young, 167, 173
LEDCs (Less Economically Developed Countries), 43
Left Realism, 166–7, 189
Lemert, 165
lesbian, gay, bisexual or transgender (LGBT) sexuality, 95–6
liberal feminism, 109, 142
liberation thesis, 175
life chances, 107, 114–19
Livingstone, 80
Lynch, 31, 32
Lyng, 167, 178
Lyon, 35, 188
Lyotard, 16, 26, 145

M

Maduro, 19, 21
male gaze, 20, 29, 93
Malinowski, 17, 19
Malthus, 73
manipulative/instrumental approach (to media), 77–8
Marcuse, 80
marginalisation, 30, 166, 173
Marsland, 158
Marxism
    classical/traditional Marxism, 107, 137–8
    and crime and deviance, 163–4, 187–8
    neo-Marxism, 138–9
    and religion, 18–19, 21
    theory of stratification, 107
Marxist feminism, 108–9, 143
masculinity thesis, 175–6
mass culture, 80
Matza, 162
McCombs, 86
McDonaldisation, 50
McGrew, 51, 52–3
McLuhan, 80, 103
McMafia, 179
McNair, 103
McNeill, 157
McQuail and Lull, 100
McRobbie, 87, 94, 184
MEDCs (More Economically Developed Countries), 43
media
    and audiences, 98–101
    content of, 77–9
    and crime, 179, 183–5
    media gaze, 89, 90, 93, 95, 96
    media imperialism, 81, 104
    media news, 84–8
    new media, 76, 102–4
    news values, 87, 90, 183
    ownership, 77–9
    postmodernist view, 80, 82
    representations, 89–97
    social construction of the news, 84–8
    traditional and new, 76, 103
    and violence, 101
Merton, 161
Messerschmidt, 175
metanarratives, 16, 145, 146, 149
methodological pluralism, 153
middle class, 91, 122–3, 177–8
migration, 52, 69, 126, 129
Miller, 162
Mirza, 30, 109
modern world system (MWS), 47–8
modernisation theory, 44–5, 55, 61, 64, 65, 66, 69, 71, 73
modernism/modernity, 15, 145–6
moral entrepreneurs, 164, 184
moral panics, 87, 184
Morley, 99–100
Mulvey, 93

N

Nelken, 178
neo-colonialism (and colonialism), 46, 64, 69, 73
neoliberalism, 45, 52, 54, 55, 59, 61, 65
neo-Malthusians, 65, 66, 73
neo-Marxism, 138–9
neophiliacs, 78, 103
New Age, 25–6, 35
new media, 76, 102–4
new religious movements (NRMs), 24, 25–6, 35
New Right, 112, 122, 125, 136, 158, 168
Newburn, 11, 160, 187
news, 84–8
news values, 87, 90, 183
NGOs (non-governmental organisations), 56
Niebuhr, 26
norm-setting (and the media), 86
Norris and Inglehart, 38–9

O

Oakley, 109, 116, 142, 152
objective and subjective views of class, 121
objectivity, 14, 147, 149, 154
occupation / occupational scales, 120–1
Official Development Assistance (ODA), 59
old boys' network, 122

P

Pakulski and Waters, 110
paradigms, 149
Parry and Parry, 123
Parsons, 17, 19, 28, 111, 123, 135
patriarchy, 20, 28, 108–9, 142–4
    patriarchal ideology, 13, 93, 94, 174
    people-centred development, 49
Phillips and Bowling, 173
Philo, 100
pick 'n' mix religion, 16, 25, 34, 39
Plummer, 160
pluralism, 13, 34, 38, 78–9, 81–2, 88
political globalisation, 51
political ideology, 13, 136
Pollak, 175
polysemic, 98, 100
Popper, 14, 15, 147
popular culture, 80–3
positivism, 134, 147, 148, 150, 154, 158
    and research methods, 151–2
postmodernism, 145–6, 155, 158–9
    and crime and deviance, 169, 191–2
    and ideology, religion and science, 16, 149
    and the media, 80, 82
    and stratification, 110
primary deviance, 165
prisons/imprisonment, 175, 186–8
professions, 122–3
proletarianisation, 123
Protestant ethic, 20
punishment (and crime control and prevention), 187–8

R

radical feminism, 108, 142–3
radicals, 53, 61
rational choice and opportunity theories, 168, 178, 190
realist view (of science), 148, 150
rebellion (and crime and deviance), 161
reception analysis, 99–100
reflexive modernity, 146
relative deprivation, 166–7, 173, 177
religion
    and age, 31–2
    as a conservative force, 17–20, 21–2
    definitions of, 14
    and ethnicity, 30–1
    feminist view, 28–9
    functionalist perspective, 17–18, 19

religion (*cont.*)
  and gender, 28–9
  and globalisation, 39
  and ideology, 16, 18, 20
  interpretivist view, 19–20
  Marxist perspectives, 18–19, 21
  and postmodernism, 16
  religious organisations, 23–7
  religious pluralism, 21, 23, 34, 35, 38
  and science, 15
  secularisation, 33–9
  and social change, 20–1
  and social class, 32
religious market theory, 38
repressive state apparatus, 107, 138,
  187
resacralisation, 35, 36
research methods, 151–3
restorative justice, 186, 187, 189
retreatism (and crime and deviance), 161
Right Realism, 168, 189–90
risk society, 146, 179, 180
ritualism (and crime and deviance), 161
Ritzer, 50
Rostow, 44
ruling-class ideology, 18, 78, 137

S
sacred canopy, 19–20
SAPs (structural adjustment
  programmes), 57–8, 60, 64
Saunders, 122
science
  and postmodernism, 16, 149
  and religion, 15
  scientific methods, 13–14, 15, 147–50
  and sociology, 147–50
secondary deviance, 165
sects, 23–4, 25–7
secularisation, 33–9
selective filtering, 100
self-fulfilling prophecy, 165, 184, 188
self-report studies, 170, 171
sexuality (media representations), 95–6
Shildrick, 91, 125
simulacra, 82
situational crime prevention (SCP), 190
situational deviance, 160
Sklair, 53, 81, 125
Slapper and Tombs, 177
Snider, 163
social action theories, 139–40
social capital, 121
social class
  and crime, 176–8
  and life chances, 114–15
  media representations of, 90–1

and religion, 32
and stratification and differentiation,
  107, 111, 114–15, 120–1, 122–6,
  128–30
theories, 106–7, 110, 137
social construction
  of crime and deviance, 160
  of crime statistics, 170–1
  of gender, 93
  of the news, 84–8
  of science, 149–50
  and study of society, 140, 148–9, 151
  of victimisation, 192
social development, 41, 42
social mobility, 105, 128–32
social policy (and sociology), 157–9
societal deviance, 161
sociology
  and science, 147–50
  and social policy, 157–9
  and value-freedom, 147, 150, 154–6
sovereign power, 187
square of crime, 167
stages of economic growth, 44
Stark and Bainbridge, 19, 23, 25, 38
state crimes, 182–3
status frustration, 26, 28, 161, 166
stereotypes
  and the media, 89–97
  and policing, 172, 173, 176
strain theory, 161
stratification and differentiation
  bases for, 110–13
  changes in structures of inequality,
    122–7
  defining and measuring social class,
    120–1
  differences in life chances, 107,
    114–19
  dimensions of inequality, 114–19
  and disability, 118–19
  and ethnicity, 111–12, 117–18, 127,
    131
  feminist theories, 108–9
  functionalist theory, 106–19
  and gender, 108–9, 111, 115–17,
    126–7, 131, 142–4
  Marxist theory, 107
  and migration, 126, 129
  postmodernist approaches, 110
  and social class, 107, 111, 114–15,
    120–1, 122–6, 128–30
  social mobility, 105, 128–32
  Weberian theory, 107
Strinati, 80, 82
structural adjustment programmes
  (SAPs), 57–8, 60, 64

structuralism, 134–8, 141
structuration, 141
subcultural theories (of crime and
  deviance), 161–2
subjectivity, 154, 155
Surette, 183
surveillance (and crime control and
  prevention), 188
sustainable development, 49, 65
Sykes and Matza, 182
symbolic annihilation, 89, 93, 96
symbolic interactionism, 139

T
tabloidisation, 85
Taylor, 179
techniques of neutralisation, 178, 182
technological convergence, 102
theodicies of disprivilege, 19, 25, 32
Thornton, 87, 184
tourism, 63
trade, 61
  slave trade, 46, 110
traditional media, 76, 103
transformationalists, 53
transnational capitalist class (TCC), 53,
  125–6
transnational corporations (TNCs), 54–6,
  68, 125
triangulation, 153
Tuchman, 89, 93
Tumin, 106
two-step flow model, 99

U
underclass, 125
universe of meaning, 19–20
upper class, 91, 122
urbanisation, 64
uses and gratifications model, 100–1

V
validity, 33, 104, 140, 148, 152, 170,
  171
value consensus, 134, 135, 136, 162,
  168, 187
value-freedom (and sociology), 147,
  150, 154–6
Verstehen, 141, 148, 151, 152
victim surveys, 170, 171
victimisation, 192–4
violence (and the media), 101

W
Walby, 108, 142, 143
Wallerstein, 47, 51, 53
war and conflict, 66–7

Weber, 15, 20, 25, 26, 34, 107, 134, 141
Westergaard and Resler, 122
White, 181
white-collar crime, 177–8
Wilkinson and Pickett, 105, 106
Wilson, Bryan, 27, 33

Wilson and Kelling, 189
Wolf, Brian, 180, 181
Wolf, Naomi, 93
working class, 91, 124, 176
World Bank, 58
world systems theory, 47–8
WTO (World Trade Organization), 58

Y
Young, 167, 179

Z
zero tolerance policing (ZTP), 189, 190